Exile Space

☙ ❧

Also by Esther Pasztory

Aliens and Fakes: Popular Theories About the Origins of Ancient Americans

Conversations with Quetzalcoatl and Other Stories

Jean-Frederic Waldeck: Artist of Exotic Mexico

Inka Cubism: Reflections on Andean Art

Remove Trouble from Your Heart

Thinking with Things: Toward a New Vision of Art

West by Nonwest: Anniversary Conference on Pre-Columbian Art

Daughter of the Pyramids: Colonial Tales

Pre-Columbian Art

Teotihuacán: An Experiment in Living

Aztec Art

Berrin and Pasztory, Teotihuacán: Art from the City of the Gods

Middle Classic Mesoamerica: AD 400-700

The Murals of Tepantitla, Teotihuacán

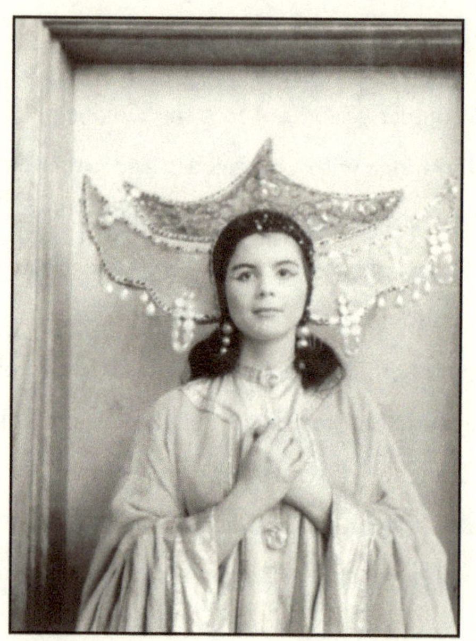

Author in the school play, *Marco Millions*.

EXILE SPACE

Encountering Ancient and Modern America in Memoir with Essay and Fiction

Esther Pasztory

Polar Bear & Company
An imprint of the
Solon Center for Research and Publishing
Solon & Rockland, Maine

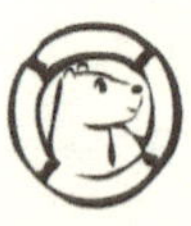
Polar Bear & Company™
Solon Center for Research and Publishing
20 Main Street, Rockland, ME 04841
207.643.2795, polarbearandco.org, soloncenter.org

ISBN: 978-1-882190-82-9
First print edition, first printing September 2018
Library of Congress Control Number: 2018957719

Cover design by Polar Bear & Company. Cover image of hand holding a paintbrush emerging from a supernatural maw, from an engraved bone found in the tomb of Ruler A in Temple I at Tikal, Guatemala, Maya, c. 700 AD, *Thinking with Things* by Esther Pasztory, drawing by Janice Robertson, page 189. Cover image based on detail of a Wari (Andean) tunic fragment, c. 1000 AD, showing the abstraction of a figure with two outstretched hands holding staffs, *Pre-Columbian Art* by Esther Pasztory, plate 93. All other photos are from author's collection, including on page 161 by Adam Pasztory.

Frontispiece from author's collection of Esther Miskolczy at age sixteen (1959) portraying the Chinese princess Kököchin in Eugene O'Neill's play *Marco Millions* at the Cambridge School of Weston, Massachusetts.

Manufactured on durable, acid-free paper in more than one country.

Contents

I

Multiple Horizons
Tales from the Life of a Refugee

II

Stone Age Civilization in the New World

III

Foreword

Memoir in a Sense of Place

I did not know about Esther's background when she introduced herself to me in a musty Columbia University classroom in the mid 1960s. We were both new doctoral students, enrolled in the school's program in what was then known as "primitive art history." Esther's English was impeccable, and she dressed like any other female graduate student, so I had no idea she had not been born in America and had not spent the first thirteen years of her life here.

I did learn shortly afterward that Esther had been born in Hungary, that she had come to the US as a refugee in the mid '50s, and that her then-husband was Hungarian. Although we became good friends, for a long time that was all I knew, beyond my occasional enjoyment of her excellent chicken *paprikash*. Here and there, a few other hints of her Hungarian roots emerged. This book shows me that the Esther I thought I knew at Columbia—and with whom I have remained friends through the four and a half decades since we received our doctorates—was only part of the whole person she really is. Her memoir brings forth, in terse, highly enjoyable, often humorous prose, an even deeper insight connected to her sense of place. A side of her that I had not, until I read the manuscript, fully realized existed.

This is a tale of profound rupture in the life of a thirteen-year-old Hungarian girl who, once she had arrived in the US after a traumatic nocturnal escape from the Soviets and had assimilated, would henceforth always be searching for a place where she could comfortably fit in. Where she could be herself. Where the different components of her life could be reconciled and peacefully alternate or coexist. In the US, she notes in her memoir, she had to figure out not only *where* she now found herself, but also *who* she now was. It has been a search impelled by a great curiosity and love of adventure that she seems, at least to some degree, to have been born with. Her favorite childhood book in Budapest was about a fairy princess who left home for life in an underground paradise, never to return. Esther clearly didn't mind the ending.

She did eventually return to Budapest, as an adult, but after a time decided she could not stay. Like the title of Thomas Wolfe's novel, "you can't go home again." When she returned to the States, she rearranged all the furniture and artwork in her apartment, so as to integrate—that is, mix—all of her Hungarian belongings with those that were American and pre-Columbian. She did this, in her words, "to match my new sense of self."

In later years, when she and her husband Richard left New York for Deer Isle, Maine, Esther found herself the subject of their neighbors' distrust. Whereas her husband was a native of Deer Isle, Esther was regarded as a person "from away." Echoing her experience in New York, she again felt an outsider, an interloper, a person without a long history in the area. The pair eventually moved on.

The theme of going and coming, leaving and returning, weaves its way throughout Esther's memoir, emphasized by her essay, "Stone Age Civilization in the New World," helping to explain her choice of a career in pre-Columbian art history, as well as her unique understanding of both the Mexican past and her new home in the US. In *The Maya Vase*, Esther spins a tale of a young female archaeology student who time travels into the Maya past and a comfortable life at Tikal, only to easily return later, at will, to her life in New Jersey. Similarly, while living and teaching in New York, Esther would change into a ballroom gown or a fur coat to attend strictly Hungarian dances and parties, then change back into clothes more suitable for a normal American mother and academic when she got home. During her first marriage and when raising her son, she spoke English at school and Hungarian in their apartment. Switching personas, to a degree, when it made sense.

Esther's work—her insights into pre-Columbian art and in the field itself, as well as her fictional writings and recollections—are ultimately about place. There is Budapest, then boarding school in Massachusetts, followed by New York and its favored haunts, vacations in more rural places, Mexico, Paris, Deer Isle, and so on. In particular, Esther relates many of her past experiences to places that afforded peace and quiet. She writes of the importance of frequent visits with her mother and sister to the Frick museum to escape the heat and humidity of the New York summers. The museum was peaceful and cool; it "freshened the body and reinforced the spirit." At Lake Owassa, where she could mingle with other Hungarians during some summers, she could relax in a place where "we could be ourselves." The Sistine Chapel was too noisy; Teotihuacán, in contrast, was not as well known and therefore allowed her to be by herself, as though she were "the first person to come upon it." Teotihuacán became the focus of her research for many years. Mexico, she suggests, was a substitute for Hungary, each perceived as "a great backward country with fantastic antiquities and art." Her summer home in Dingmans Ferry, which Esther describes in exquisite detail, afforded total privacy. Milford, Pennsylvania, once a small and quaint rural town, was "minimal" and "compact."

Esther loved living in New York, which she describes as the most livable place she has ever been. She paints a verbal picture of her neighborhood around 113th Street, walking up the block, taking us from shop to shop, while ticking off the products each sold, the foods it served, and the changes it has undergone over the years. Change is another leitmotif of Esther's multifaceted memoir; she always brings the reader up to date when discussing a place and even explains how our original academic field of "primitive" art has morphed into a variety of fields, one of which—pre-Columbian art history—she and I ultimately chose. In other words, she engages with "this is what it was," then follows it with "this is what it has become." Sometimes she is saddened by these changes, but others seem welcome, and all of them seem to fit with her understanding of her life as an immaterial entity in flux, indeterminate, consisting of an internal struggle, a desire to fit and feel comfortable in the places she goes.

Not every reader will personally identify with Esther's life experiences and her struggles to reconcile the seemingly disparate parts of the "mosaic"—a word she uses to describe the contents of her nonfiction writings. Many more will surely find them interesting and, I predict, insightful. This three-part memoir allows us to peek into the personal life experiences of a remarkable thinker and writer, and everyone who reads it will ultimately benefit in one way or another. The benefits, moreover, will be positive and uplifting, for the book is not only downright funny in places, but Esther makes it clear that she has no regrets about the rupture that changed her life forever. Her curiosity about the world, her sense of adventure, her ease at entering into someone else's world, if only for a little while, and her willingness not to return if that were to become necessary all combine to edify and enchant the reader. Enjoy.

Cecelia F. Klein, PhD, Professor Emeritus
Department of Art History, UCLA

Foreword

Memoir in Fiction

Is there such a thing as an archeology of the mind, where fiction, memoir and scholarship live without contradiction? The heroine of *The Maya Vase* is able like a shaman to travel between Tikal and a twenty-first-century archeology department. Pasztory's heroine is Naomi, who "in the midst of writing a romance about a girl in Indian times before Columbus" disappears "into ancient America, incarnating as her own heroine," Marigold. And, as the narrator says, "of course married a Maya lord," Night Sky. "She knew more about the ancient Maya now than Professor Brown," deceased under suspicious circumstances.

I think the reader will find an incident in the travels of Naomi/ Marigold key to what Pasztory is in search of: Marigold gives an exquisite vase—enigmatically rare because of its human figures on a black field—to Lord Sky Rain of Tikal. Lurking behind his chambers, she overhears an argument that turns into the sound of a vase smashed in a fit of anger. She retrieves a black shard near the scene and takes it back to the world of contemporary archeology. Is it part of the masterpiece? Or is it from one of those she judged mediocre that were sitting all together with ones aesthetically pleasing to Marigold? Did Lord Sky Rain appreciate the vase as did Marigold? Did Lord Sky Rain knowledgeably grab an inferior ceramic to express his anger? Back at the archeology department Naomi follows the clues, which involve the question of whether Lord Sky Rain's rash act was tempered by good taste. And suppose he simply did not want to spoil a gift? What if, without any aesthetic sense, he simply honored the time it took to mine the clay, filter and wedge it, model it, prepare the pigment, and paint it?

Time. The calendar was a Maya obsession. Apparently so was the love of time required to make things Bronze Age and beyond with stone and wood tools in a world we classify as Stone Age. The time taken to make anything of value in pre-Columbian times is beyond our ken. Perhaps Lord Night Sky would have had to value the figures on the black vase above the ordinary ones simply because the difference in time taken to make each was so obvious to him. The fundamentally different indigenous way of looking at time is still reflected in Indian life today. The Xingu, Guarani and Huni Kuin that I have shared time with do not kill birds to obtain what they call "the gift of plumes." They stun the birds with blunt arrowheads and domesticate them, gathering the feathers during the molt. The conquistadors received the Indians' gifts of feathers with disappointment and disdain. Feathers that had taken so much time to harvest.

Esther Pasztory is not satisfied with the Euro-centric classification of the classic Mesoamerican civilizations as Stone Age, when actually much of their material culture is Bronze Age or beyond in its technology or thinking. Witness suspension bridges made not of iron but plant fibres. Or think of the uncannily precise masonry accomplished with stone and wooden tools at Mitla in Oaxaca, Mexico, and Machu Picchu, Peru, where nearly seamless joints were achieved by rubbing stones together. The "bricks" themselves were the tools! These sorts of accomplishments are cited throughout and read as subtext in a dialectical conversation with text.

The long-standing metropolises, such as Cahokia, near what is now Saint Louis, Missouri; Tenochtitlán, with canals in the midst of a lake like Venice, on the site that is now Mexico City, and Teotihuacán—the ruins of whose monumental pyramids and classy residences were only a short distance away; Cuzco in Peru; these were among the engineering marvels that rivaled European cities, roughly between 250 and 1525 CE. But as the author points out, the story of the ancient civilizations of the Americas is usually written in what they lacked from the point of view of the Old World norm and thus was explained why they were so easily conquered. But we could look at them in terms of what they had and what they valued that might have been different from the Old World. While it would not have saved them from European conquest, it might help to validate them in retrospect in history. It might also throw an explanatory light on the special civilizations of the Old World. What did the Old World lack that the New had? Time.

Pasztory reminds us that for the ancient Americans, "domesticating plants required infinite patience over hundreds or thousands of years. The Indian approach was to work plants by cuttings and seed-by-seed planting. While the European farmer cast seeds by the handful, the American planter selected seeds individually to be the best possible for what he or she wanted. Without knowing the laws of Mendel and genetics, they refined each of the plants they were growing." Fortunately some of the traditional non-European horticultural and botanical traditions are vibrant. In 2014 the Huni Kuin tribe published in Rio de Janeiro, *Una Isi Kayawa* (The Book of Curing), 255 pages of their ancient Amazonian pharmacopeia passed down since time immemorial (ISBN: 978-85-86488-43-6).

In a telling personal incident, a Xingu friend gifted me some arrows and a bow. Noticing that the feathers were not aligned at an angle designed to rifle the arrows in flight, I began to twist them away from their parallel alignment with the shaft into a slight angle with it. Timei said to me, "Oh, I didn't know you hunted." I explained that I don't anymore but that I wanted the arrows to look like arrows designed to be shot by him, not just ornamental. He, in trying to please me, correctly assuming that I would not hunt, gave me ornamental arrows for show. Each of us was thinking with arrows, not just in terms of how we would use them but how each other of us would use them.

Exchanges such as these make me ask if we will ever get beyond desire to understanding? Or is desire enough? Art historians such as Esther and I are not satisfied with such a thing as the progress in the history of Western intellectualism. No, we humans of what I called in a review of the Whitney Biennial, "The Restless West and the Rest," written several years ago, deserve better: something the likes of what Esther Pasztory's "A Stone Age Civilizations in the New World" tells in its attempt to have a conversation, on equal terms, with First Americans.

And yet, if you are anticipating that this is another book of the wonders of Native American culture, no, this is not just another lauding of the glory and grandeur that was. You'll be absorbed in the parallel subtext that weaves like an Amerindian textile, warp and woof intentionally thinly veiled. At the outset Esther Pasztory says, "I haven't really known any American Indians personally. This book is about Indians, without the benefit of knowing Indians personally. It is based on what Indians did, what they left behind, what they did not do." I think this book is about the deferred personal quest of the author of *Thinking With Things* and *Conversations With Quetzalcoatl* to know the Indian through conversing with the thinking that their things did. At first I wondered if archeologists and art historians would think that Pasztory has climbed onto a limb of insupportable fantasy. But it is precisely the time-tested thoroughness of her academic career that supports the freedom to interface archeological fact with a fictional recovery of events in the personal life of Marigold the Maya, who is also Naomi, a contemporary student of archeology. Esther Pasztory's fictional Marigold is entirely supportable by what we know of the ancient Maya. Esther would that she/we know/knew people who lived "so long ago, so far away" and break through "the impersonality of archaeology and the bias of old texts." It is this false norm of European cities and things European that troubles Pasztory throughout.

Male colleagues have asked her why a nice woman like her would study these civilizations of human sacrifice. She is quick to remind us of the numbers: Stalin 50,000,000 plus, Hitler 11,000,000 plus, Uganda 800,000, Hiroshima and Nagasaki 280,000, Vietnam, and on and on. None of her detractors would rail against studying European or American civilization.

Whenever I look at art or read about it, I keep going back to the late Meyer Schapiro's advocacy of the importance of "subjective content." We all recognize the external content, the form of a work of "art." But its real authenticity lies in what he called "the subjective, internal voice of the art." The time required to achieve the many modern accomplishments of pre-Columbian America had its own internal subjective aesthetic, an illusive aesthetic of what the Akan of Ghana call "hand thought."

George Nelson Preston, PhD
Professor Emeritus
Department of Art, CCNY/CUNY
Academico, Pierre Verger Chair
Academia Brasileira de Arte, Rio de Janeiro

Acknowledgments

I am indebted to the following friends and colleagues for helpful extensive readings, corrections and encouragement: Marc Haefele, William Haviland, Timothy King, Marsha Manns, Blaise Pasztory, Valerie Reid, Ann Wallace, and especially to Wayne J. Holman III, I hope he likes it. Finally, I would like to thank my husband, Richard Eaton, who read bits and pieces as they came hot off the printer, and who was a never-ending source of possible titles.

I

MULTIPLE HORIZONS

Tales from the Life of a Refugee

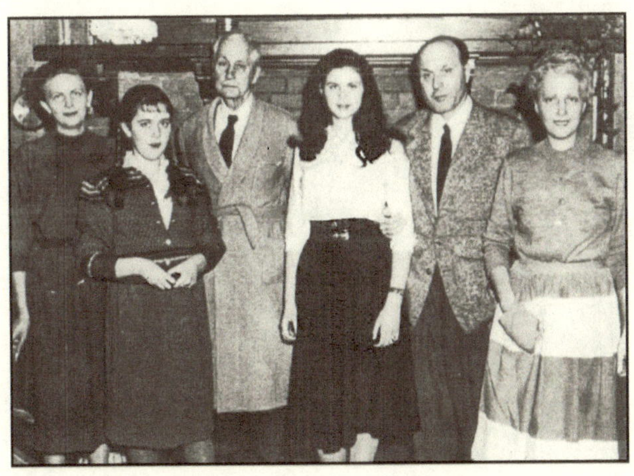

Family the author escaped with from Hungary, from left:
Klara Miskolczy, Kristina Miskolczy, Ferene Borbiro,
Esther Miskolczy age 13, Lászlo Miskolczy, Babszi Bodroghy.

To the memory of my father,

Laszlo Miskolczy

ଓ ଃ

1

INTRODUCTION
TOWARDS ASSIMILATION

It has been said, that no European ever came to America except out of necessity. Anyone who's had a halfway comfortable spot in the Old World, preferred to stay there, rather than hazard the trials or even the possible joys of assimilation to a new natural and social environment. The story of America is immigrants and assimilation. (There is then the story of those who have been born here, but that is not my story.) My story is the assimilation of an immigrant into this vast and diverse USA in the twentieth century. What do you do? How does it happen? This is how I lived it.

My family—father, mother, sister and my thirteen-year-old self—came to the US as refugees from the failed 1956 Revolution in communist Hungary. My Americanized aunt impressed upon me, in the very beginning of our arrival, that I had two tasks: to learn English and to assimilate as fast as possible. (That was in the days when hyphenated Americans were not thought of.) In a few months I learned basic English, but assimilation was a more complex proposition. To what, exactly, was I to assimilate? Where in America was "America," and what was it?

The boarding school my aunt sent me to was to hasten learning English and assimilation. The people I met there were nice, and I felt stimulated and sheltered. Evidently, I liked it so much, or was so fearful to try something else, that I spent the rest of my life in schools. First as a college and graduate student and later as a tenured professor at

Columbia University. I did not leave "school" until I retired at seventy. So, I suppose, I assimilated to the American educational system quite well. In fact, the structures of academic life were a bulwark of safety and stability at the times of personal upheaval.

The field of study I chose—pre-Columbian art of the Aztecs, Maya, and Inca—was at first sight not particularly appropriate to assimilation in the US. The word "pre-Columbian" meant that it was of an Indian time prior to the arrival of Columbus in 1492. It was ancient art. There was pre-Columbian art in the Americas from the southern US to Argentina, but the term usually referred to the spectacular ruins of the Aztec, Maya, and Inca cultures now in modern Mexico, Guatemala, Peru, and Bolivia. While those were outside of the US, they were in the Americas. When I chose them in the 1960s, I saw them as the "antiquity" of America. To me, they were the beginnings of the American story, and I thought I was starting in the beginning.

But somewhere, I knew, of course, that most Americans considered Europe their place of origins, and Greece and Rome their spiritual antiquity. Ancient Indian America was rarely taught in US schools, and as one of my professors told me early on, I might never get a job teaching it. Americans felt some guilt about their part in the devastation of Indian cultures, but in practice they preferred not to think about it. On the other hand, America prided itself on a global and universal, scientific enterprise in which all arts and all cultures were studied. I could not have studied ancient American art in any other country—certainly not Hungary or even in Paris. So, oddly enough, the study of ancient American art was "American" in spirit and in material support. I found it in America, after all.

What drew me to pre-Columbian art? It is monumental, complex, and it has been neglected by scholars in comparison to European art. And it was mysterious. One could do pioneering work in it. I ended up writing the first book on Aztec art. It was a way of discovering the treasures of the New World. And then this treasure was just over the border in Mexico, in a more-or-less modern country, easy of access. I picked the biggest, most enigmatic ruin—the ancient city of Teotihuacán—as my field of study.

I wrote half a dozen books, dozens of articles, went to conferences, organized conferences, received prestigious grants, prepared a world-class exhibition of Teotihuacán art—all using the neutral, academic English language I learned in school. I had an excellent reputation, and you could not tell, except from the name, what my ethnic background was nor how long I had been in the US. As a scholar, I seem to have assimilated completely and seamlessly.

And then, in 1997, forty years after my arrival, I came out of the Hungarian closet. I wrote a nostalgic introduction about my Hungarian origins and about Hungarian origin myths to my major book on Teotihuacán *(Teotihuacán: An Experiment in Living)*. Having held back so long, I seemed to need to proclaim who I was and where I came from. Assimilation in my private life was not easy at all. "Assimilate," yes, in principle, as my aunt said, but I was also determined to hold on to my Hungarianness in private. I intended to marry a Hungarian (and I did, Blaise Pasztory), and I planned to teach my child Hungarian (and I did). What did I have in mind? To start a Hungarian lineage or colony?

There was no need for me to start a colony, since there was already a vibrant Hungarian colony in New York—swelled by the 1956 refugees. There were Hungarian churches, restaurants, pastry shops, delicatessens, butcher shops, hairdressers, bookshops, newspapers, travel agencies, bridge clubs, scientific societies, etc., to say nothing of social gatherings. Hungarian doctors and lawyers were available in many specialties. For me, the New York colony was friendly and familiar; you could hear Hungarian spoken on the street. There was no connection between my pre-Columbian art and the Hungarian émigré community. Their orbits did not meet.

We knew that the "real" America was not in New York City, but somewhere in the countryside. We got to know a little bit of this America in the summers, when we escaped the sweltering heat of the city, into country houses. By chance, New Jersey and Pennsylvania were the first country areas my family got to know and found charming—but impenetrable.

Eventually, the émigré world began to seem narrow and vestigial to me, and I yearned to explore and live in the "real" America. Sometimes Hungarians looked down on Americans as "uneducated and dull," but I knew from my boarding school start that this was not the case. Hungarians could be dull, too. I left this Hungarian "womb" and struck out on my own, despite the daunting immensity of "America." I was forty years old and recently tenured at Columbia. Leaving my Hungarian family and community was a wrenching experience.

My hope was to marry an American who was rooted somewhere and to assimilate through him into some part of America. America was too big and diverse to assimilate to all of it, but an interesting corner of it would do. I left the region up to chance. As this did not happen overnight, for many years I was single. I moved into Columbia University housing and continued to live in New York. I traveled a lot: Mexico, Europe, the US, cruises. I dated an interesting man from Chicago and fantasized living in Chicago. All was not so simple, however, since his roots were actually in Tennessee, and he considered himself a Southerner. I tried to understand all that.

Unexpectedly, Hungary resurfaced in my life with a bang. In 1989 the Soviet Union collapsed, and Eastern Europe was liberated from communist rule and Russian hegemony. My single, American life was not going anywhere. I started to feel very Hungarian again. Many Hungarians went back not just to visit but to buy houses and start businesses. I too bought an apartment in Budapest and tried to become involved with educational institutions. My dealings with Hungarians were disappointing, and I lost whatever desire I might have had to settle or retire there. At the same time, I spent many summers in Budapest enjoying ordinary life, cultural activities and people, as an adult. This time compensated for the loss I felt in leaving Hungary as a child. Paradoxically, in Hungary I came to feel very American.

In the 1990s I met Richard Eaton, and he offered me the state of Maine. His family had eighteenth-century roots in Deer Isle, an island off the mid coast of Maine. I knew nothing about Maine. Evidently, it had beautiful natural scenery and cosmopolitan summer residents. This gave me a chance to move into a "corner" of America. I became incorporated into a lobster-eating native family. Still teaching in New York, I was a summer resident in a place with an illustrious history. Richard knew everyone at Deer Isle, and I got to know artists and fishermen.

After retirement from Columbia University, we moved to Deer Isle, but the rural isolation there proved to be too much year-round. Subsequently, we settled in a retirement community in southern Maine (Huntington Common), which has some of the life and diversity I remember of boarding school. My son and twin grandchildren live in San Francisco, California. We visit them once or twice a year. The thought occurs that we should move out there in future. Like many Americans who move around after retirement, we are exploring different geographic options. I think my aunt would say that I have assimilated reasonably well.

This book consists of what I call "ministories" (vignettes) of moments in the course of my assimilation to the US. There are high points, low points, funny points; persons of importance and no importance, celebrities, family, and strangers; famous and unknown places zigzagging in a more-or-less chronological sequence. Each colorful anecdote tells how my horizons have been continually broadened by experience, how I came to terms with being an immigrant, dropped into the US in the 1950s and graying in the twenty-first century. The aim of this book is to share the serious and the silly and noting all along how, even in this short time, things have changed in America.

2

OTTO HERMAN STREET

Otto Herman was a German Hungarian nineteenth-century naturalist and politician.

I was born in 1943 in the middle of World War II. My family survived the siege of Budapest—carpet bombing by the US and ground conquest by the Soviet and Romanian army—during the winter of 1944–45, in a cellar in Pest. My sister was born after the fighting was over in 1945. Politically, the Hungarian government was in confusion, and the victorious Soviet army had not left the country.

We then moved to a large villa on the suburban side of Budapest—Buda. It was set in the hills among trees and healthy breezes. It was a good place to raise children. It was one of the wealthiest neighborhoods in the city. Professionals like doctors, architects, engineers, and opera directors lived there. Those who were mostly not members of the Communist Party, but whose expertise was needed for the functioning of society, even if their politics was suspect.

After the war, our building was still unfinished. My father, who was an architect, made a deal with the owner that in exchange for living there for free, he would complete the building. We had the entire top third floor of a modern building with spacious rooms. After the communist consolidation in 1947, probably the building was requisitioned by the state. The communists solved the chronic apartment shortage by moving second or third families into large apartments. Several families using one bathroom and kitchen was too grim to contemplate. To forestall this, my father divided the apartment in two and gave up half of it.

My childhood home was still an indecently large apartment. A

Bauhaus-style, modern, dining-room set occupied one third of the living room. The third by the windows had two sofas facing each other across a tiled coffee table. The third between these was empty, except for a bookshelf by the wall and two large rugs on the floor. These rugs were special, in that they were designed by my uncle Feri. In the 1930s, Feri and my father founded a weaving workshop in southern Hungary to encourage the local arts and crafts that were seemingly dying out. The rugs were tufted, like Persian rugs. The flowered designs were based on folk motifs. As Bartók and Kodály collected folk music at this time, my family was involved with folk art. My father wrote a book on folk architecture. I sometimes snuck across these rugs to borrow a forbidden book from my parents' bookshelf. The communists frowned upon all folk arts.

By the time I was thirteen, I still knew very little about the economics of communism. I knew that the communists took people away, tortured them and killed them. They were unpredictable. Even children had to be careful what they said. Never praise anything American. I didn't know any communists personally. One girl in my class was the daughter of a police chief, and she might have been dangerous to befriend. I did understand the hypocrisy of communism: that they talked about equality, but the communists themselves lived like the upper class of old. People minded that almost as much as the tortures.

My father was the head of the City Planning Bureau and had to work with the communists. He planned new cities and low-income housing. He was very good at it. He received the highest prize the nation could give, the Kossuth Prize. Party officials urged him to join the Communist Party. He did not want to join, not just because he did not believe in it, but also because members of the Party were notorious for intrigues and frequently ended up executed. How do you say no to the Communist Party? My father's advice to me was: "Don't rise too high in any profession."

I also did not know much about capitalism. Communist propaganda conflated capitalists with the old aristocracy. They were all evil and enslaved ordinary people. All I gathered from my parents was that under capitalism life was richer and more colorful. They had oranges, pineapples and bananas, which we did not.

Communist Hungary was backward; how backward, we only found out later. Very few people, mainly Party members, had cars. Horse carts were common. Drivers whipped horses mercilessly to pull heavy wagons of coal or garbage. In smaller towns horse-drawn fiakers took the place of auto taxis. We had no washing machines. My family had a washer woman, who came once a week to do the laundry. There was no television; we only had radio. On the state-run radio, we only had two stations that played music approved by the Party. The chosen music was mostly classical. The Party believed in elevating the taste of the lower classes they were supposed to serve. Certainly not rock 'n' roll, which was considered decadent. My ponytail was decadent, too, because it was considered Western. The school principal told me in no uncertain terms that if I did not change my hairdo, I would not get into the university later on. The communists micromanaged all aspects of life.

My earliest memory is being shaken by my French governess, Anni, while she was yelling at me: *"Penche toi! penche toi!"* (Lean over! lean over!). It must have been in the dining room over a bowl of soup. I was bilingual from the start. I could eat European style with the fork in my left hand and the knife in the right by an early age. My parents were demanding and tried to "civilize" me as soon as they could.

I was a bookish child. My favorites were stories in which the hero or heroine go away from home and meet up with magical adventures with new people and/or animals. In Selma Lagerlöf's *The Wonderful Adventures of Nils*, a bad little boy gets turned into a Tom Thumb and flies away on the back of a goose to remote and exciting places. On his return, he becomes a regular little boy again. I cried at this. In the Hungarian *Book of the Lakes* by Albert Wass, a fairy princess leaves home to be the mistress of an underground lake full of birds and animals. I don't think she ever went back home. It was my favorite book.

I played with dolls, too, usually enacting stories. When not in use, my dolls were set on top of the armoire. I no longer remember them all, except for one exotic one, a gift by someone. This was a black, negro doll, with a skirt that had some kind of a banana print and perhaps a turban (Caribbean?). It was made out of caoutchouc, a rubber material prior to plastic and came from the West. But of course we did not get any real bananas. Once my father returned from a foreign trip with a can of pineapple, and we divided it up ceremoniously as a great dainty delight.

My parents tried to create an upper-middleclass family shelter at home against the harsh communist life outside. It was all contradictory and made no sense.

3

ESCAPE

The Hungarian revolution of 1956 was a spontaneous uprising without a leader. We first heard of it on the telephone on October 23. Various mothers of my classmates called my mother not to let us go to school because there were disturbances in the city. The disturbances were in Pest, while we lived in Buda. One of the first acts of the revolutionaries was to capture the radio station in Pest and to begin broadcasting. From that moment on, throughout the revolt, we were glued to the radio for bulletins as to what was happening.

The revolutionaries demanded fourteen points. The first and most important was the withdrawal of the Russian troops from Hungary. Others included the demand for a free press and various transparencies in government. And ending the handing over of uranium deposits to the Russians. We didn't know that we had uranium deposits. The revolutionaries didn't actually ask for the end of communism—at that time no one thought they could end communism. They wanted reform. They wanted the current puppet ruler, Rákosi, gone, but they eventually wanted another communist to take his place, Imre Nagy. Nagy had a reputation for fairness and integrity.

The beauty and mystery of the revolution was in its early days, when almost everyone wanted the same things. The Russians seemed stunned by the turn of events and did nothing except ride around in tanks. They seemed afraid to get out of their tanks. There were skirmishes only. The revolutionaries asked for help from the international community and were hoping and waiting. There were food shortages, and my mother sent us out to stand in line for bread or sugar or whatever. In the lines, we were all comparing notes about the events and the participation of fourteen-year-old boys. Imre Nagy was putting together a government. There was general euphoria. It seemed like the revolution was going to succeed with little bloodshed.

We sat by the radio and listened to the encouraging news. It was all very naïve. The student and worker revolutionaries had been idealistic and not practical. The US broadcasts on Radio Free Europe incited rebellion in the Soviet block countries and implied help. However, help never came. There was a concurrent crisis on the Suez Canal, and the French and English got involved fighting the Egyptians. That was of immediate relevance to the West and obscured events in Hungary. Was the US going to risk war with Russia over Hungary? Russia may have weighed the question of war with the US the same way. World War III? Atomic weapons? Khrushchev may have hesitated at first but then decided that he could act with impunity and little consequence from the international community.

On November 4, we woke to the sound of loud explosions at dawn. At age thirteen, I and a great many others thought that these were fireworks celebrating the revolution. But of course, they were not. The Russians mounted a major attack and were shelling the city in earnest. The radio broadcast confirmed it. What resistance there was, was easily crushed. The radio chronicled the defeat and played Beethoven's seventh symphony. We sat by the radio and cried. Not too long after, the broadcasts fell silent, and a new Russian puppet was speaking. Imre Nagy and many revolutionaries were later executed. Reprisals were taken on a great many others.

Hungary's borders to the West were opened during the revolution and for a while in the aftermath of November 4, until the Russians regained control of the whole country. Altogether 200,000 people left the country, many of them highly educated and experienced.

My sister and I didn't know that we were planning to leave the country. My parents said that we were going out of Budapest for a few days to rest my mother's nerves. We were to wear warm and sturdy clothes. We wouldn't carry any luggage, only little handbags. They did not tell us the truth in case we blurted it out and were caught. I don't know what day we left. We crossed the border on November 24, so it must have been around the 10th or the 15th. When we shut the door on the Otto Herman Street apartment, my sister and I had no idea we would never come back. We didn't say goodbye, we took no mementoes.

We went to the train station and took a train west. We were going to a small town near Lake Balaton, where relatives lived. Strangely enough, the trains ran, haphazardly, but they ran. They were full of stone-faced people—also, it seems, eager not to blurt out where they were going. The tension was palpable. In Keszthely we met my aunt's sister and their eighty-year-old father. The adults kept withdrawing and whispering. My sister and I put two and two together and figured out that we were escaping. We confronted our parents. They admitted that we were leaving the country through Austria. Our hosts were coming with us. We were going to some other distant relatives' house near the Austrian border in a town called Csepreg. We had never heard of them before.

I remember it as sort of a farmhouse. My father was in and out talking to people. He was looking for guides to take us across the border. By that time the border was not completely closed, but it was patrolled by Russian tanks. We would have to go at night. Previously, people went by cart with hay piled on top of them, but the Russians were onto that and shot into hay carts. We would have to go on foot, nine kilometers. Could the eighty-year-old man do it? He was sure he could.

The guides were local young men, and they checked us out before leaving. They took away the little handbags. There was a bit of a scene with my mother, who had soap and chocolates in hers, for quick energy and keeping clean in case they took us to prison. That was a laugh, because if they caught us they'd shoot us on sight. According to my aunt's sister, she was hysterical and urged my father to go back. I don't remember this, perhaps because my mother was often hysterical, and the moment was not out of the ordinary, or to put it another way, this moment was out of the ordinary.

We went. Two by two, holding hands. Across frozen cornfields, in the moonlight. In complete silence, frequently falling down and getting up. Scared of the Russians, scared of the new life who knows where. Once we came upon Russian tanks with searchlights by the side of a road. We hid in a ditch until they passed. They passed. A brandy flask was handed around by the guides. We went on until we came to a wider depression. It was no man's land. On the other side was Austria. The young men were paid in wristwatches and jewelry and disappeared. They did this both for money and patriotism. Our story is not unique; many others have had similar encounters and stories escaping from Hungary in 1956.

We found a small road in Austria that led to a small town. It was two or three in the morning. The town was prepared for refugees. People put us up to sleep. The local church had clean clothes available the next day. In a few days, we were in Vienna officially signing up as refugees. Hungarians were milling about in Vienna, deciding where to go. Many countries opened their doors to the brave Hungarian "freedom fighters."

My father had architect friends in Rio de Janeiro and Brussels and thought of going to Brazil or Belgium. America had a very small quota for Hungarians. However, because of the revolution and perhaps because they had not helped the revolution, America decided to admit many Hungarians. My aunt, whose sister and father came with us, lived in Cape Cod, Massachusetts. She was married to her second husband, a Nobel Prize winning chemist, named Albert Szent-Györgyi. Her children were in the US. My father talked to her on the telephone in Vienna, and she urged us to come to the US.

This was all pretty ironic since my parents hated my aunt Marta. She had been married to Dezso, my father's brother, and they had two children. Later, Marta was involved in an affair with Albert Szent-Gyorgyi and eventually married him. They came to the US. My parents never forgave her the divorce. And yet, they turned to her in Vienna, and she was extremely helpful in our getting started in the US.

By Christmas 1956, we were in Woods Hole, Massachusetts. A transport plane had taken us from Vienna to a military base in New Jersey. My aunt's son came with a van and drove us up to Cape Cod. My aunt was an extremely efficient, well connected, and resourceful woman. She got my sister and me scholarships in boarding schools. By early January, I was in the Cambridge School of Weston, outside of Boston. At the same time, my sister was in the Windsor Mountain School, quite far in Lenox, Massachusetts. My parents were in New York City looking for a job. We were all separated from each other. My aunt thought this was necessary, so we could learn English and assimilate quickly.

After the Christmas of 1956, my family never lived together again, except for brief vacations. We all pretended that this was a matter of course and that we had not been through traumatic times. But then, of course, we were alive, Russians and communists did not kill us, and we were free. We had a lifetime ahead of us to figure out WHERE we were and WHO we were going to be.

4

FREEDOM

When I went to the Cambridge School of Weston in January 1957, I was freed of my country, my family, and my language. If I ever had escape fantasies as a child, they had come true. New impressions, people and events crowded out the loneliness I must have felt. Starting with the awfulness of peanut butter and ending with the silent joy of the art studio, I waited patiently for enough English to come so I could understand and make myself understood. Knowing French was useful—the only time in my life I needed it. I had a wonderful time at the Cambridge School, one of the best times in my life.

My mother saved some of the letters I wrote from the Cambridge School. They were generally something like this: "Dear Mommy, I miss you. Today we had an algebra test and I think I did all right. I would write more, but right now I don't have the time. I must do Biology. I miss you and love you."

I remember writing those letters. They contained nothing significant because I could not possibly explain to my parents what an American boarding school was like. Besides, they would not have understood or approved of what I was doing. Things like rock and roll and boys. I always said I missed my father and mother, which was true, sort of in the abstract, but not in my day-to-day life. I felt guilty that I did not. I loved being on my own and treated as a responsible person. At thirteen I stopped being a child. My parents sensed this. There was never a separate room or space in their apartments for me. There was a trundle bed in my sister's room. I came and went and lived in boarding school.

The Cambridge School began in Cambridge, Massachusetts, but was later moved to the rolling hills of the countryside near Weston, not far from Boston. It consisted of a number of small buildings scattered about. There were about two hundred students. The girl's dormitory was called "White Farm House," because it was a converted farmhouse. The largest building was the gym that was also the theatre and place of assembly. There was a small ivy-covered administrative building and a modernish dining hall around a central quad. Further out, there was a little biology building in one direction and an art studio in the other. The house I lived in as a senior had only five students and was very intimate. The buildings were in different styles and quite modest. They were markedly different from the school I went to in Buda, which was a single, large multistory building with a yard and a wrought-iron fence around it. The Cambridge School was mostly wooded. There was a pond on which we ice skated in the winter. There were athletic fields on its perimeter. Roads and foot paths connected the buildings.

In the morning, the entire school assembled in the gym for daily announcements. The music teacher led us in singing folk songs like "Oh my darling Clementine," "She'll be comin' round the mountain," Michael rowed the boat ashore," and "When the saints come marching in." I enjoyed them. Then we went to classes. In Hungary, they emphasized memorization and oral recitation. The teacher would call on you in class and ask how many rivers there were in Argentina. We memorized Lake Titicaca or the volcano Popocatepetl. At the Cambridge School everything was in writing. I was asked "my opinion" about the things we read. In Hungary no one asked my opinion about things. Just as my father never consulted me about leaving the country. My opinion did not matter. The Cambridge school was a progressive school making me feel that I mattered and making learning fun. Once I learned English, it was a piece of cake.

The other students complained about the meals, but I thought the meals were great and abundant. I didn't even mind specialties of the time, such as chipped beef on toast, which were generally hated. We had assigned seating at meals, with a faculty member at the head of the table. A selected student went to the kitchen window and got a tray full of platters and bowls of food for the table. It was supposed to be family style. The dirty dishes were returned at the end. Occasionally some student dropped the tray to great hilarity and clapping.

After classes, in the afternoon there were sports. After an unsuccessful try with softball, I discovered modern dance and stayed with it. Hungary had no modern dance I was aware of. When I was small, I was sent to ballet class, but the teacher said I was too tall, and I had to quit. At the Cambridge School dance was a form of exercise and self-expression doable at any height and any age. That was nice about America.

I always had roommates. Some of them were peculiar. One loved the then popular musicals and had records of even the most obscure ones. I discovered *My Fair Lady* through her, which I really liked. Another one was the daughter of a famous Hollywood actor. She had problems. Once she put a large frog in my bed. (We had bunk beds and I slept on top.) She was later kicked out of the school for stealing from the local stores. She had the most beautiful clothes—colorful pleated tartan skirts and cashmere sweaters to match. Strangest of all was a Southern girl who bragged that she had sex with the bellhop of the Ritz in Boston, on the way to the Cambridge School. Periodically, she went to Boston to see him to have sex. She actually brought him to a prom or something, where he really looked out of place. Awkward in a cheap suit, he was not at all like the other boys.

In our final year, Ann and I chose each other as roommates. We had in common that we were both very shy and liked Classical music. She was blonde and petite. Her mother made her beautiful but very little-girlish clothes. My mother sent totally inappropriate clothes, like mid-calf-length fake fur coats she found somewhere on sale. She wanted me to be warm.

At the Cambridge School, I was a star. I had the lead in two plays: I was a Chinese princess in Eugene O'Neill's *Marco Millions* and Miranda in Shakespeare's *Tempest.* (My roommate Ann was Ariel.) I was voted president of the Town Meeting student government. I had been a success.

My boyfriend, Marc, expanded my horizons. He took me all over the Boston area for movies, concerts, restaurants, and museums. He knew the streetcars and buses. He was knowledgeable about music, avant-garde films, books, and even mass culture. When no one in school seemed to know where Hungary was or what it was and didn't care to know, he knew. He had gone to the library and looked it up. He understood me more than anyone at the Cambridge School. When at school, we spent the after-dinner hours wandering the many wooded paths of the school grounds. We became very emotionally attached to each other. My parents would not have understood. They met him eventually and thought he was a nice kid but totally inappropriate as a companion for me. He became a journalist.

After four years of the Cambridge School, my Hungarian side reemerged. I missed my parents and the Hungarian refugee colony in New York. I married Blaise Pasztory, a Hungarian lawyer who had gone to Harvard. Like me, he also had deep American boarding school experiences. Our backgrounds seemed to match perfectly. At the age of twenty, I moved to New York with its large Hungarian exile community. Many years later, though, I came to miss Marc and the Cambridge School days. Eventually, Marc and I had an affair, which led to divorce from Blaise but no permanent connection with Marc. My Hungarian and American sides seemed to be in unresolvable conflict.

Since the time when I was there, the Cambridge School has changed. In my day, it was progressive for being coeducational. Most boarding schools are now coeducational, and it is no big deal.. Therefore, now the Cambridge School has become more of an art school than a standard prep school. More dramatic modern buildings have been added to the campus. They are now raising money for a large Health and Fitness Center.

5

COOLING OFF

Our first summer in the US was in New York, and we were unprepared for the great heat and humidity prevailing there. By July the pavement would melt. 1957 was in the days before home air conditioners. We slept naked with a sheet. Hungary could be hot in the summer but was usually not humid and much more bearable. My father worked in an air conditioned office. The solution for my mother and us girls was to spend as many hours as possible in some air conditioned place. My parents came up with two favorite places we frequented as much as we could: Radio City Music Hall and the Frick museum.

If you went at noon, Radio City Music Hall cost ninety-nine cents. For that you got a two-hour feature film, an orchestra playing light classical music, an organ or piano solo (I can't remember which), and the Rockettes in unison kicking their legs, a floorshow that lasted another two hours. That was four hours of coolness. That summer the big hit was *The Prince and the Showgirl* with Marilyn Monroe and Lawrence Olivier. The story took place in London in 1911 during the coronation of George V. The prince was from Carpathia, an imaginary kingdom near and sort of like Hungary, while the showgirl was an American recommending democracy to the prince. Predictably, they fell in love and hoped to get together someday. It was the kind of romantic fantasy fluff the public liked; royal pomp and balls. We probably saw it a number of times. The best scene is Marilyn wrapped in a pink bedspread with the Carpathian seal on her sexy bottom. It must have been ironic to watch this Eastern European kingdom on the screen while Russian tanks were still fresh in our minds.

I have never seen anything quite like the Frick museum anywhere. In those days the Frick, prestigiously located on 5th Avenue and 70th Street, was free and cool. We spent many hours there. By New York standards, it was a relatively small, three-story building. We preferred it to the big, impersonal museums, like the Metropolitan, the Natural History museum or the Museum of Modern Art. The Frick was built as a private mansion by a somewhat unsavory nineteenth-century industrialist named Henry Clay Frick. He had been one of the richest men in the US. He began collecting old masters as a young man and always intended his mansion to be a museum after his death. Furniture, china, glass, bronzes and paintings were displayed in the reception rooms on the main floor, as in a home. There were living rooms and dining rooms. Frick, his wife, and daughter had private quarters on the second floor. Twenty-seven servants occupied the third floor. There were under two hundred paintings in the collection, but all of the choicest kinds: Rembrandts, Monets, Goyas. There was nothing modern or political in nature.

We liked sitting in the covered patio with the fountains and plants, enjoying the atmosphere of this palatial private house now available to the public. It was a luxurious home that was a comfortable way to look at paintings that were not overwhelming in number. In a short time, we were familiar with the paintings and where they were and greeted them happily on subsequent visits. There was the Gainsborough room with the paintings of aristocratic English women in gossamer gowns. There was the Holbein portrait of Sir Thomas More with a golden necklace on a meticulously rendered fur collar and a steely glance near El Greco's bearded St. Jerome in electric pink. To say nothing of the Fragonard room with its lighthearted romp of pretty women in a rococo garden. A visit to the Frick cooled the body and freshened the spirit.

When I came to teach Western art at Columbia, I always sent my students to the Frick, not just to experience the art but to see the kind of elite homes and mansions they were originally made for, even before Frick bought them. I did not have to go and check out the paintings ahead of time because I pretty much knew where they were, and the Frick did not move them about. Then.

The Frick is still my favorite place in New York, but not the same it was in 1957. Admission now is $20, although it is still free on Sunday—

for an hour. A temporary exhibition place has been carved out of the basement for things like old master drawings, supposedly expanding and enlivening the original collection. Now there is much traffic for that alone. And, yes the paintings have been moved about varying the museum-going experience. For me, the Frick was a haven of peace and stability, but it is now competing with other museums in novelty and activity in order to attract more visitors.

We sallied forth from our first, hot, cramped, little, furnished apartment on the West Side daily to fantasize about princes, mansions, art, and coolness.

6

CHARITY

One of the strange aspects of being a refugee was to accept charity. Through the connections of a Nobel-prize-winning relative, my father found a job in a large, prestigious architectural firm in New York quite soon after we arrived. He was lucky. Many other professional Hungarians had to make do with menial jobs, such as superintendent and handyman. The firm was called Harrison and Abramowitz, and its leading architect was Wallace K. Harrison.

Harrison was a relative by marriage of Nelson Rockefeller, one of the richest men in the world and at one time governor of New York. Rockefeller had presidential aspirations that in the end came to naught. He was a major architectural patron, and Harrison was his favorite architect. Harrison had his hand in everything from Rockefeller Center to the United Nations building and is best known for Lincoln Center. His firm drew up the plans for additions to Columbia University and to the airport. The critics and posterity have not been kind to Harrison's architecture—it has been panned as modern but boring. Although my father was just a small cog in this great architectural machine, he had been a leading architect in Hungary, and that was respected by the Harrisons.

Enter Mrs. Harrison, Ellen. Mrs. Harrison was a great lady in her own right. She was a Milton, from a family allied with the Rockefellers. She decided to take charge of the women in my family—my mother, sister, and myself. Naturally, she gave us big bundles of hand-me-down clothes, but more than that, she invited us into her 5th Avenue apartment facing Central Park. I no longer remember whether we received tea or lunch or any refreshment, because I was so amazed by the dining room. The dining room was full of menacing black shapes.

On one wall there was a huge, gray-black tapestry of grotesque, screaming faces. I later learned that it was a copy of a painting by Picasso entitled *Guernica. Guernica* was a Spanish village bombed by the Germans. The victims were mostly women and children. Picasso painted the twenty-five-foot original in 1937. It has been considered the most important painting of the twentieth century. The Harrisons had a somewhat scaled-down tapestry copy in their dining room. My mother said that she couldn't eat her soup in that room.

On the other side of the entrance door to the dining room, there was a huge, black, metal, tree-like construction with flat, round plates, looking like water-lily leaves on branches. It reached up to the ceiling. That turned out to be a Calder mobile. The Harrisons were in the vanguard of modern art. Since the communists forbade modern art and abstraction, all this was new and strange to us.

Mrs. Harrison first set to work on my mother. She tried to get her involved in some practical activity, like sewing or waitressing. That did not go far, because my mother called forth her aristocratic pretensions and insisted on being treated like Mrs. Harrison's equal. Mrs. Harrison saw that there was nothing to be done with my mother, who refused all her help. So Mrs. Harrison turned her attention to me. She suggested to my father that I should be sent to summer camp as a counselor to make some money. My father would hear none of it. He wanted his children at home in the summer because we were away in winter in boarding school. Then Mrs. Harrison suggested that I spend a week or two in their Long Island summer home, cataloguing their library. So I went, and perhaps even got paid for it.

The estate in Huntington was of course modern, but I only remember the swimming pool—it was big and round and had a mural on the bottom. The mural had been designed by Leger, a French contemporary of Picasso, who spent the war years in New York. I was impressed. I was allowed to swim in the pool. Mrs. Harrison was then in her fifties or sixties, a fine figure of a woman. She often treated me like a daughter—her own daughter was institutionalized in an asylum and was rarely mentioned by the Harrisons. I ate with the family and saw lobster for the first time. Then at other times I was treated like a servant and asked to fetch this or that. It was not clear where I belonged.

Then there was the library, my reason for being there. It wasn't all that big a library. I was to use the Dewey decimal system to organize it. Someone must have explained it to me because I didn't know the Dewey decimal system from a hole in the ground. However, I rearranged the books and put numbers on their spines. Sometimes I had to scrape off old numbers—evidently someone had arranged them at least once before me. But who was I to question the wisdom of the Harrisons? There were many beautiful art books, and I enjoyed the job. In retrospect it seems very unlikely that either Mr. or Mrs. Harrison would put the books back in the order in which I arranged them, so the work was probably in vain.

Mrs. Harrison also arranged that I should go on a date or two with a young man from her family. I believe his name was Fenner Milton. (Fenner was a hard name to forget.) He was a very nice young man, and the dates were unmemorable. I was sixteen or seventeen. With great suddenness, he disappeared from my horizon, and Mrs. Harrison herself stopped taking an interest in me. The reason may have been the 1959 scandal in which a young Rockefeller married a Scandinavian kitchen maid, Anna Marie Rasmussen. Mrs. Harrison wouldn't want this to happen again. It was probably safer to let me go.

7

PAPRIKA SAUCE

To avoid the sweltering New York summers, we rented a cottage by a lake in New Jersey. The cottage belonged to a Viennese doctor who thus got to spend July and August in Vienna. It was more a camp than a proper house; the rooms were cubicles, and curtains on strings closed some of them rather than doors. Lake Owassa is a medium-sized lake, and we had a large dock for sunbathing. That was before sunbathing was considered injurious to one's health.

Lake Owassa is located in what was bucolic northern New Jersey. After one left the outskirts of New York City, it was all farmland, mainly cornfields and dairy farms. We bought fresh milk on the way. The biggest event of the summer was a farm-and-horse show. By now all the farms have been sold and suburban housing has taken their place. But in the late 1950s and the 1960s, it was all definitely country. Lake Owassa had modest summer cottages. It was a delightfully low-key environment. My sister and I canoed across the lake to a little store to buy victuals when necessary.

We shared our cottage and the cost with another couple and their daughter we knew from Budapest, who had also escaped and who also lived in New York. The Szantos. The arrangement with the Viennese doctor and the Szantos worked so well we spent almost ten summers there.

Those were Hungarian summers. Exiles huddling together for comfort in an alien land. During the winter, the adults in their workplaces and the children in their schools struggled learning the English language, trying to understand American ways and tried to fit in. At lake Owassa we did not know any Americans, had no American friends. We knew no young people to socialize with. We were a Hungarian enclave, and Hungarian friends visited us from the city. It was relaxing. We could be ourselves.

We talked Hungarian, ate Hungarian, and danced to Hungarian popular songs in the evenings. My father gave lessons in the Viennese waltz and the continental tango to us girls. My father liked to barbecue, and the women made salads. They did not barbecue hamburgers, because Hungarians hated the smell of beef fat. They cooked hot dogs, chicken, and pork chops. And with the meats we had paprika sauce. Paprika sauce was supposed to be originally from Transylvania and was contributed by my mother. It was very simple to make: lots of paprika, two or three tablespoonfuls, mixed with red wine until it has the consistency of a sauce. A little salt. It's not a marinade; we spooned some over the roast meat when it was ready to eat. Everybody there loved it.

The conversations were often about trying to figure out how to get rich quick. There were stories of so-and-so making a million out of some silly gizmo. Why couldn't they make a million out of something? Here was the paprika sauce, an excellent condiment no one ever heard of in America. Unlike ketchup and barbecue sauce, it was not based on tomato sauce but Hungarian paprika. It was something new and different. Then came endless discussions of how it could be manufactured, preserved, bottled, advertised, and distributed. Suppose they went into business together. How would they raise the money? The preservation was a knotty issue—paprika sauce was best when made fresh.

The summers at Lake Owassa and the discussion of paprika sauce ended when the Szantos had saved enough money to buy their own summer cottage somewhere in Connecticut. We then saw them rarely. My sister and I were married soon after, and we bought our own summer houses in that same general area, but not at Lake Owassa. Lake Owassa became severely eutrified; it was turning green and pea-sized blobs of algae floated in it. It was disgusting to swim in.

8

LINGERIE

Edna and Bob were my parent's first American friends. My sister befriended Edna, who was a secretary at the Windsor Mountain boarding school, where my sister was sent in 1957, after our arrival, at the age of eleven. To Kristina, they were surrogate parents. Edna smiled a lot and said "nice" about everything. They invited my parents to tuna casserole dinners. Edna and Bob came from patrician families but were down on their luck. Financially, they were on my parents' level, but in their fantasies they were American upper crust. They thought Lake Owassa, where my family spent the summers, was too low class. They suggested, instead, that we should spend the summer in Lenox, Massachusetts, which was a more elegant place. My parents agreed to try it. It was all more expensive, but eventually a house was found for rental. It had the disadvantage of not being near water. There was a country club with a swimming pool not too far away, but as it turned out, it was either too expensive or they would not have us. Perhaps both.

In preparation for the Lenox summer, my mother and Edna thought up a business venture. They were going to start a custom-made lingerie shop. Assuming that there were well-heeled summer visitors in Lenox, they planned a lingerie boutique: they would sell silk slips and nightgowns, as well as hostess gowns. In those days, a hostess gown was a cross between a bathrobe and an evening gown that the hostess would wear to her own party. It was usually long. I think the idea was that she had just come out of the bedroom to greet her guests.

The silk and satin slips and nightgowns were luscious peach-colored confections with beige lace. The hostess gowns were summery, some with a lovely sunflower print. All these were designed by my mother. A seamstress in Brooklyn made them up. Edna took care of the business end and rented a room in a hotel for the shop. Their idea was that the customer would select the models she wanted, and the Brooklyn seamstress would make them to size very quickly.

This could not have been more naïve. In the 1950s, most American women did not wear silk underwear. Such silk luxuries really came in the 1980s, in the Reagan era. They were a couple of decades too early. (Now, most women don't even wear a slip of any kind.) That summer, I think, none of the beautiful things sold. In the end, my mother and Edna divided up the samples and got to wear them. By acclamation, we decided to go back to Lake Owassa the next summer, where at least there was a lake.

But not before I had my moment of teenage rebellion. Lenox did have a lot of young people from "good families," and somewhere we got to know them and partied with them. The incident I remember occurred after a party when the kids with cars were taking the ones without home. It was after midnight. I was sixteen or seventeen at the time, and I was loosely attached to a tall gangly boy named Kit. Anyway, he was going to take me home, about twenty minutes away. A girl named Marcia appeared, who needed a ride, an hour away, in the other direction. I suggested that I go along; we take Marcia home, and then he takes me home in turn. I guess you could say that I was arranging private time with Kit.

Kit and I had almost a two-hour ride ahead of us. We drove in silence for quite a distance. Then, as if on cue, he put an arm around my shoulder. I moved aside and waved him to indicate that I did not want any of that. So he shrugged his shoulders and drove on. Did he think I expected it? Did he expect it? I didn't know. I sat quiet as a mouse. It was one of the longest rides of my life. Without words, he deposited me in front of my house.

I tiptoed in, so as not to wake the household, but my mother was up waiting for me with lightning in her eyes. "Where the hell have you been? It's four o'clock in the morning!" She chewed me out good and proper. I slunk off to bed feeling very satisfied.

9

THRIFT SHOP GOWNS

Before the 1980s, there were dozens of secondhand shops on the Upper East Side of New York, known generally as thrift shops. The things in them were hand-me-downs from the rich on Park and Madison avenues. I bought all kinds of things there: furniture, Oriental porcelains, and, once, even a piano. It was an excellent piano. But mostly, I bought ball gowns. These ball gowns were custom made, or designer gowns worn probably only once. In the early years, they were made of silk, chiffon, and velvet. Many of the ones I had were strapless, whalebone waisted, with full skirts and crinoline underskirts. They were Scarlett O'Hara gowns. In the thrift shops they cost about $10. Most of the people who frequented the thrift shops were looking for everyday clothes, not the ball gowns, so there was quite a choice.

I needed the ball gowns because the Hungarians in New York, swelled by the 1956 refugees, organized balls. Some of the Hungarians who had come out in 1947, at the time of the communist takeover, had a little money. Many of the refugees were professionals such as doctors, engineers and financiers, whose skills got them jobs relatively quickly. The price of the ball tickets, especially if you just went to the dance and not the stuffy dinner, were not very high. It was not possible to go back to Hungary, so New York Hungarian life took its place. After the fearful and austere life under communism, my parents' generation wanted the trappings of luxury and dancing. We couldn't afford real luxury, hence the thrift-shop gowns. After we wore them, we re-donated them to the thrift shops.

The balls also brought out of their lair members of the Hungarian aristocracy. The communists persecuted the aristocracy—who dared not admit who they were. The least harassment was to forbid them to live in Budapest or force them to do farm work. There they were at the balls, various counts and barons and Knights of Malta, with their old-fashioned decorations and insignia pinned to their tuxes. Never mind that during the day some had jobs like superintendents and took out the garbage.

In the winter, there were Hungarian balls at hotels like the Waldorf Astoria and the Plaza. In summer, there were tea dances at Tavern on the Green in Central Park, under the stars. The Plaza was my favorite. The Plaza Hotel goes back at least a century and is a historical landmark on the corner of Central Park and 59th Street. Its grand ballroom is ornate and gilded. A throng of five or six hundred Hungarians used to dance the Viennese waltz, tango, polka, foxtrot, with a little rumba and rock 'n' roll thrown in, year after year. Those who could, danced the national csárdás, a folk dance that has been converted into a ballroom dance, perhaps in the nineteenth century. At midnight, the ballroom closed and the remaining dancers moved down to the Terrace Room. The Terrace Room is somewhat smaller but also quite fancy. There, a gypsy band or some other orchestra played popular songs from Hungarian operettas to dance to until four in the morning.

The thriving Hungarian community was mainly on 1st and 2nd avenues. There were Hungarian establishments to take care of every possible need and all imaginable specialists to take care of every problem in Hungarian. I belonged to this community. I was introduced to Blaise in the Budapest Restaurant, and we were married in the Hungarian Reformed Church. He was my escort at the first Hungarian ball I went to as a debutante at the Plaza. This community and its shops have now largely disappeared. (Blaise came from a distinguished family of lawyers and judges. John von Neumann, said to be the greatest mathematician of the twentieth century, was a second cousin.)

Early in the two thousands, the Hungarian balls ended. There were not enough Hungarians to fill the ballroom. Many of those who came in 1956 had died or retired. Children born here were more American and not interested in the Hungarian balls. After 1989, when the communist regime ended in Hungary, some wealthy Hungarians came to New York for the balls. But that did not last long. People now travel back and forth between the US and Hungary, but there is no longer such a large Hungarian community in New York. What there is meets at dinners and events organized by the Hungarian Consulate of the current Hungarian government or at the small Hungarian House.

The thrift shops ended even earlier. Rents on the Upper East Side became too high for the secondhand stores to afford. Their place has been taken by chain stores such as the Gap, Banana Republic, Williams Sonoma, and Crate&Barrel.

10

HELPING WOMEN

When my son was born, I needed help to be able to get back to Columbia and finish teaching the semester. Someone was found through the Hungarian grapevine. She had this advice to give: "You have a perfectly good maid's room in this apartment. Why don't you invite an older woman from Hungary for a year. She can get a visa for one year. She will cost much less than an American. She can take care of the household and the baby when you are working. Also, the baby will learn Hungarian from her. If you want, I will find you somebody for next September." This seemed sensible, and we agreed to it.

One day in September Klara came into our house and life. She was a sixtyish lady on the short and plump side. It turned out that she was a countess, by birth, not marriage, originally from Transylvania. She had no aristocratic airs; she scrubbed the floors as if she had been doing it all her life. Her cleanliness standards were very high. In fact it seemed as though she enacted the role of housekeeper and nanny as she herself would have expected from a maid. She had a very clear idea of what had to be done. Perhaps the only problem was that she wanted more appreciation than we gave her, and we gave her a lot. At such times, her eyes filled with tears. After we consoled her, everything went back to normal. She was a great cook.

Klara spent hardly any of the money she made. She wanted the money for her old age. She frequented thrift shops and bought furs and fancy clothes. In Hungary, she wanted to look rich and elegant and show off in the streets. A dozen or so years later, we visited her in Budapest. Strangely enough, her apartment was in a building designed by my father before the war. She served us tea in her home filled with lace doilies and porcelain knickknacks.

The following year, Klara returned to Hungary. She sent us Gaby (Gabriella). She was also sixtyish, short and plumpish. She came from the other end of the social scale; she was a tavern keeper's daughter. She too was a good cook, and she did everything Klara had done, though in a less obsessive manner. Klara learned a little English, but Gaby was unable to learn anything. On top of that, she was convinced that she understood English and responded in Hungarian, resulting in farcical misunderstandings in her daily round. Her instincts were good, and in some manner she communicated in the supermarket and area stores.

Gaby did go to thrift shops some, but most often she found things in the street: coins, buttons, t-shirts, hats, endless number of things. She always said that America was wonderful because it gave her gifts. She and Klara frequented the Hungarian churches on their off days and met many people over the dinners there. They had a separate social life from us, to some extent.

She and Klara alternated for a few years, and then Gaby decided to stay here. She loved America and she wanted to live here. She had a son, and she sent him money in Hungary, but she did not want to go back. The reason was, as she said, that there she was married to a man she did not like. Among his many faults was the fact, as she put it, that in prison he became a homosexual.

Without English, Gaby somehow managed to get her green card and stayed. It has been my good fortune to share some of my life with these indomitable women. They came for the money, to be sure, but they also came for the adventure of living in New York and doing something exciting in their later years.

11

CELEBRITY

I met Martha Stewart, the home-life celebrity-to-be at Barnard College in French class. I transferred to Barnard from Vassar after I had been married and came to live in New York City. I was twenty years old. I was new at Barnard and had no friends. I sat next to this beautiful blonde girl with high cheekbones. We both had short hair, a trendy Vidal Sassoon-style cut. She was of Polish origin, I was Hungarian. As we started to talk, we discovered that we had much in common. We were both married to young lawyers, who worked sixteen hours a day. We both went home after classes to cook dinner. We were both art history majors. Martha was interested in the elegant castles of the Loire Valley in France; I was interested in African art. It did not matter, we were friends. We gave dinner parties and invited each other. Once, Martha made a delicious beef Wellington, a fashionable dish in those days.

At that time Martha was a fashion model. One would open The New York Times Magazine on Sunday and there was a picture of Martha advertising a dress, a bag, a scent, or something. I too wanted to be a model then and went to inquire at a model agency. I was told that at 5 foot 9 inches, weighing 120 pounds, I was still too heavy and needed to lose ten pounds more. As I was already pretty thin, I never lost the extra ten pounds. Too bad, because you could make a lot of money modeling. Martha was doing very well. As she told me, however, she'd have to quit soon, because her husband was jealous that she might have an affair with a photographer. Around that time, there was a sensational film entitled *Blow Up*, about a fashion photographer who sleeps with his models.

Eventually, Martha quit modeling to become a stockbroker. She sold stocks to all her acquaintances in the fashion business and was very successful at it. Perhaps more so than her husband. So she quit that and retired to their home in Westport, Connecticut, and raised chickens. My husband Blaise once ran into her at Grand Central Station, and she gave him a dozen blue eggs.

Soon her name cropped up again at parties, where the exquisite cocktail nibblets had been catered by Martha Stewart from Connecticut. Catering led eventually to a bestseller book on entertaining and ultimately to a TV show, a magazine, designing glasses and towels at Kmart, and who knows what else. Martha undertook an amazing range of projects in the home-making arena, and she was successful at most of them. She had the Midas touch and probably made millions. Her name was a household word. Martha's secret seemed to be that she showed average American women an upscale life style for which you did not need much money or servants, only the knowledge of how to do it right. She had a huge following. When I wanted to publish a book with many illustrations, I turned to her husband, Andy, who was then head of an art publishing firm. Abrams published my book, *Aztec Art*, and that was instrumental in getting me tenure at Columbia University.

At some point in her ascent, Martha's husband left her, presumably for someone less awesome. She and I went separate ways, as our lives moved on. Many years later, when we were both divorced, I once dialed her number in my phonebook on a whim and, to my surprise, she answered. We chatted like old friends. The conversation turned to men. I complained that most men did not want to date a professor. She laughed and said, "You think you have it tough, you should see me." I saw her point.

I don't know what Martha is like in her apotheosis as a celebrity and after she has been in prison, too. When I knew her, she was a straightforward and down-to-earth person I was happy to have as a friend.

12

PRESENCE

My former mother-in-law married an Italian late in life. Lisiade was a kind and gentle man who said little in any language. Without being super rich, he had some wealth. He had some kind of a degree, but never had a job. He had a house in Milan and an apartment overlooking the Mediterranean in Alassio. He was an old-fashioned gentleman who wore a hat (a fedora) on the streets of New York. He was tall for an Italian and had an impressive Roman nose. He looked significant.

When in New York, we often went out to a restaurant together. Naturally, Lisiade felt most at home in an Italian restaurant, but preferred northern Italian cooking. However, he was no gourmet and did not fuss about his food. New York has at least half a dozen northern Italian restaurants. They pride themselves on having no tomato sauces. Tomato sauces are southern Italian and "lower class." The northern Italian restaurants were all fancy and expensive and competed with the best French restaurants.

On one occasion, we went into a fancy northern Italian restaurant and perused the extensive menu. The waiter came and we all ordered some chef's creation from the menu. When it came to Lisiade, he put the menu aside and ordered two fried eggs. We were surprised and wondered what would happen. The waiter bowed and left with the order. We all got our dishes first. Lisiade's eggs arrived last on a plate with no garnish, just two perfectly shaped fried eggs. The waiter gave it to him with a slight flourish and scraped and bowed. Lisiade wasn't trying to prove a point—he simply felt like eggs for dinner that night. He was treated like a very important man by everyone in the restaurant as we left.

13

DISCOVERY

The assignment was to write a paper about a piece of primitive art in a museum or gallery. This was in a required anthropology class at Barnard. I could have gone to the American Museum of Natural History or even to the Museum of Primitive Art if I had heard of it. But I went to a gallery owned by a Hungarian. I was staying close to home. I am not sure where it was, but it was close to where I lived, and I went by it frequently on the bus. It was the Segy Gallery of African Art.

Mr. Segy had a thick Hungarian accent. Originally his name was Szecsi, but that was unpronounceable in English. People managed to figure out that the *sz* was the English *s*, but they pronounced the rest as "sexy." Not good. The *cs* in Hungarian is like *ch* in English, as in "chair." This, however, never worked out, so he changed Szecsi to Segy. His first name was Ladislas, which was my father's first name.

I knew nothing about African or any other primitive art. I knew a lot about European art and had been to Europe. I knew something about "Oriental art," because I had a wonderful teacher at Barnard who taught Islamic, Persian, Chinese and Japanese art. I could make my way through Persian miniatures, Indian temples, Chinese bronzes and Japanese screens. The world held no secrets for me. Segy's African objects were mostly wood and very crude. Primarily masks and figures, they looked like they were carved with a hacksaw. They were rough, abstract, and angular. I didn't like them. Later I would learn, this was because that's precisely what he and his customers liked.

I was looking around for something I could write about, and in the back somewhere I found little (two- or three-inch) brass figurines, almost stick figures, in a variety of curious poses. I asked Segy what these were. He said they were Ashanti gold-weights from Ghana. The Ashanti were an Akan-speaking group. I asked him what they were for. He said they were to weigh gold dust, which at one time was used as currency in the Akan kingdoms. He showed me in a book a picture of Ashanti scales to weigh gold dust. I asked him why they had such strange positions. He explained that they all illustrated certain proverbs. It was all curious.

At that point a customer came into the gallery. Segy dropped me and went over to greet a man he called Chaim. I eventually figured out that this was the reasonably well-known sculptor, Chaim Gross. Chaim Gross had a collection of African art and was likely to buy something. Segy followed him around, saying things like, "Look, Chaim, how Kubistic!" and pointing to this or that. A taste for African art began in Paris around 1900 and inspired the geometric art known as Cubism. Artists like Picasso and Braque collected African art for its abstract quality. As I later learned, much of African art is highly polished, refined and detailed, but some Westerners like Segy wanted the rough stuff. Segy lived nearly twenty years in Paris art circles before opening his gallery in the US.

I was amazed. Kingdoms, gold dust, gold weights, proverbs south of the Sahara Desert—I had never heard of anything like that in or out of school. I was not interested in modern art or Cubism. I was interested in unknown kingdoms. I looked up some of the proverbs. They seemed wise.

> A lie can annihilate a thousand truths.
>
> Do not follow the path. Go where there is no path to begin the trail.
>
> Even though the old man is strong and hearty, he will not live forever.
>
> He is a fool whose sheep run away twice.

The books on the Ashanti showed many photographs of royal pomp. There were rulers holding gilded insignia sitting on sacred stools with attendants. They were wearing complex silk robes. Further reading indicated that these were known as "kente cloths"—

imported European silk fabrics had been unraveled and rewoven in African designs. There was nothing "primitive" in any of that. I was impressed.

After my visit to the Segy gallery, I asked myself what other wonders there might be in the world that I knew nothing about? It was to answer that question that I decided to study primitive art in graduate school at Columbia University. And the answer was, there were many more wonders.

14

THE SIXTIES

The "sixties" were actually the late sixties and the early seventies. The era didn't last long. It was the time when an American youth culture expanded its horizons and shocked its parents with Beatle music, psychedelic drugs, Eastern religions, back-to-the-land subsistence, communal living, and promiscuous sex. The youth culture found and admired the small, communally based, primitive tribes who were still living in Africa and the islands of the Pacific. Until recently, those people had been called savages. All of a sudden, they were emulated. Maybe it had to do with the Cold War that was still going on with Soviet Russia, with the fear of the proliferation of the atom bomb and total annihilation, and more specifically, with the Vietnam War. Primitive peoples still existed on the margins of advanced societies, following lives thousands or even millennia old. Perhaps they had the secret of good living.

Unrelated to these trends, a small artistic elite had already picked up primitive art on their own. Since 1900, modern artists like Picasso admired the art of such tribes and used them as inspiration to create modern abstract art. A small group of collectors followed. Nelson Rockefeller founded the Museum of Primitive Art in New York City in 1954 (a few years prior to my arrival there) and donated his private collection for the edification of the public.

These various streams came together by the mid sixties in the study and appreciation of primitive peoples and their art in a few colleges and universities. It was something new and exciting. While generations of scholars had studied the Italian Renaissance or even Impressionism, only a handful had studied primitive art. Not only was it as beautiful and as inventive as modern art—or even better—it was built into the everyday life of the people. The arts were their churches, schools, legal courts, entertainment and philosophy and they could not exist without them. A Western artist could only envy such a central role in society for his work.

As a young Hungarian refugee, married woman, I was not a part of the wild counterculture of the sixties. But some of these ideas must have been in the air when I "discovered" the Ashanti gold-weights in Segy's gallery. I also discovered that in primitive art history you could be a pioneer, the first to write about it. Little reliable information was available. The two professors at Columbia University, Paul Wingert and Douglas Fraser, were the first to teach the subject and had messianic zeal, which they imparted to their students. It wasn't just a field of study, it was a mission.

When I started graduate school, there were many, six to a dozen, students studying primitive art for their master's or doctorate in any one year. (More recently, there has been only one a year.) All of them as eager and enthusiastic as I was. Four of us became particularly good friends. Wingert had seminars in his house in Riverdale, and the student with the car, George Preston, would drive us there once a week. Wingert taught art from the actual masks and figures in his collection.

Since there were so many primitive peoples and so few scholars, we could each have a "people" of our own. George Corbin (who later taught at Lehman College), did fieldwork in the Pacific area of Melanesia. In his cups, he often repeated, "I know all about the Baining, and I don't know anything about the Baining." The Baining were his. George Preston was initiated and became a chief among the Akan of Ghana. I admired his aquiline nose when I first met him and asked him which part of Africa he came from. "Harlem," he said, happy to deflate me. He taught at the City University of New York and established his own African art museum in Harlem.

Cecelia Klein and I were both interested in pre-Columbian art, the art of Middle and South America, prior to the arrival of Columbus. She pursued the intricacies of Aztec mythology and imagery at UCLA, where she later trained dozens of West Coast enthusiasts of primitive art. I was trying to figure out the meaning of mural paintings from the ancient Mexican site of Teotihuacán. We were an impressive group.

Circumstances have changed a great deal since then, although it has been only a little more than fifty years. Globalization and modernization have arrived everywhere, and few traditional customs and arts survive in the primitive world. Tourism is all over. Almost all the traditional art is gone or is in museums. The sixties are gone, and only a very few students are interested in primitive art. The name "primitive" has been dropped altogether as too pejorative. We now speak of "African," "Oceanic," "Native American" art and study them separately.

All over the world, formerly "native" people are familiar with Western and modern art and create new hybrid arts of the traditional and Western for sale. This new, often fantastic art is avidly collected by museums and galleries now, and this is the art that fires the imagination of current students. The old art we studied in the 1960s has now been called, ironically, "classical," or even "extinct."

15

TENURE

In 1965 I entered graduate school to study primitive art at Columbia University. There was a dynamic young professor there in that field. Douglas Fraser had recently got tenure. He taught everything: African, Melanesian Polynesian, Indonesian, Native American, and pre-Columbian art. He had a global vision, which was as rare then as now. He was a charismatic teacher, and his students had jobs in museums and universities all over the country. He was good looking and high principled. He was married and had three children. Great things were expected of him.

In April 1968, student demonstrations erupted at Columbia. The underlying cause was probably the Vietnam War. More directly, however, it was the discovery that Columbia was secretly involved with the Defense Department. Certain papers had come to light. And, even more locally, Columbia's relations with the neighboring black community of Harlem were in trouble. Columbia was in the process of planning a grand gymnasium in the adjoining Morningside Park. Morningside Park separates Columbia from Harlem. Significantly, Columbia is on a hill overlooking Harlem below. The park itself is a rather abandoned bit of nature with a high crime rate, but it belongs to Harlem. Columbia wanted to take some of it over for the gymnasium. In order to make this more acceptable to Harlem, they planned to have a "back door" and some kind of facilities on the lower level for Harlem residents.

It was the sixties. The students rioted. They occupied administrative and classroom buildings. Eventually there were two leading groups, one black, one white. They took hostages. The students were joined by outside extremist revolutionaries. At one point, Columbia called the police to break up an occupation, which they did with brutal force that incited the demonstration even further. The rest of the semester was pretty much cancelled. I was supposed to have my oral examinations at the time, and my four examiners and I went from building to building to find a classroom unoccupied by protesters. When it was all over, Columbia severed its relations with the Defense Department and the gym was not built in Morningside Park. (It was built underground on campus.) Smaller student disturbances continued in the next two or three years.

Like other young faculty members, Fraser joined the demonstrations. His interest in African art made him sympathetic to a black cause. According to friends and family, he got so intensely involved that he stopped sleeping and talked incessantly. It became evident that he was having a nervous breakdown and had to be hospitalized. He was diagnosed as manic depressive. In those days, depression was treated by electroshock therapy, and he underwent extensive treatment. Subsequently, he was in some rehabilitation center. All told, he was out a year or two. He was eventually stabilized on lithium, which was a new experimental drug at the time. Taking too little was ineffective, taking too much could be toxic. Frequent blood tests established the right level. All of Fraser's illness was public, and he openly talked about it.

When he came back to teach, he was a different person. He was still a good teacher. But, gone was the cheerful, optimistic young man. He was bitter, cynical, sarcastic. He put on a lot of weight. He often wore ethnic, African shirts with big prints that did nothing for him. His marriage fell apart. He started to go out with admiring female students. He was unpleasant.

At that time, on his recommendation, I was appointed assistant professor, a junior untenured job. The rule was that I could be there eight years, and if there was a line available, I could be put up for tenure for full professorship. But, of course, there was no line available. There was only one line for primitive art, and Douglas Fraser had it. After eight years, I would have to find another job. We worked together more or less harmoniously. He was not always nice to me. I always knew that he had chosen me and had a high regard for me underneath the jabs.

Sometimes he complained that students liked me more than they liked him, which was no wonder.

Periodically, some member of the senior faculty would pull me aside and ask in whispers, "Tell me the truth, how crazy is he?" or, "He is crazy, isn't he?" and they'd wiggle their fingers in a circular motion near their heads. I would try to explain that he wasn't "crazy," that he was stabilized and sane. He was just difficult or obnoxious. And I mentally added to myself, *as difficult and obnoxious as you, senior faculty, also often are.* But I never managed to get it across. If Fraser was angry, he was thought to be "crazy." He was treated like a crazy person. They did not have him head committees; certainly they did not want him as chairman of the department. They were reasonably cordial to him, but he became a pariah. I told myself that if ever I had a mental problem, I would tell no one about it.

Fraser continued fieldwork, writing, went to conferences, and organized symposia after his recovery. In 1982, after a conference, he became ill. It was entirely unrelated to his mental problem. He caught legionnaire's disease from the air conditioning system in a conference. Legionnaire's disease is an often fatal form of pneumonia. Suddenly, he became very ill, perhaps terminally. I visited him in the hospital. He said acidly, "So you're here to see me die so you can have my job." He never allowed me to express my concern and affection. All I could do was to stay and let him abuse me verbally.

Shortly afterwards he did die. He was fifty-two years old.

The following year I got his job.

16

BAG LADY

One of the most unusual persons I came across at Columbia in the field of primitive art was Monni Adams. I first asked her why she carried her belongings in paper shopping bags rather than suitcases? "Because they're light," she said, as if that was the most obvious answer to a silly question. I got to know Monni in 1965. We sat in the grass on campus a warm spring day and talked. She was strange looking. In her forties, she looked like fifty. Under five feet, thick semicircles penciled for eyebrows, with blue or green eye shadow smeared on her eyelids, she looked like a clown. Her hair was in a bun and looked like it needed combing and/or washing. Her voice was high and sharp. Our professor, Douglas Fraser, was on sabbatical, and she was teaching an introductory course in his place, so she must have been all right. I was a new graduate student and somewhat lost. She took an interest in me. I was trying to find out what planet she was from.

It was obvious that she was very smart and well read, and I could talk to her about anything. Her special area of interest was Indonesian textiles. In one of those bags she carried Indonesian textiles. It was never clear where and on what she lived. A lot of her things were in Douglas Fraser's office, which was temporarily hers. The office staff was suspicious of her and kept asking her to remove the "dirty cloths" that were all over the place. They were very happy when Douglas Fraser came back.

Monni was supremely uninterested in what people thought of her, so long as she got to do her work. She was very careful of her person, so she would not get ill or fall down. One day, talk was about skiing and whether she had ever skied. Her comment was: "I have too much invested in myself to risk skiing," by which she meant that with her PhD and grants and work plans, she literally could not afford pastimes of that sort. She didn't drink tea or coffee, preferring plain hot water and a slice of lemon. She watched over herself like a precious jewel. Once, when she came back from Africa, she complained about our hard, asphalt sidewalks. She had got used to walking on earth paths, and her body preferred it.

She eventually found her niche at the Peabody Museum at Harvard. After some years of fieldwork in Indonesia, she started to do fieldwork in Africa. She did much of her work among women, because as a woman they were more available to her. She was always sensible. She wrote about women and masking. It was at that point that the attitudes of feminism found her. Here was this brilliant, eccentric, tiny little female scholar. Articles and exhibitions followed. She was still writing at the age of ninety.

She kept track of me over the years. She sent me notices of books or exhibits I might be interested in. They were written on reused open envelopes, torn catalogue pages. She did not waste money on paper. Perhaps she saw me as a pupil from back in 1965. Was I a close friend of hers? I don't know. Her life before graduate school and her forties she shrouded in secrecy. Was she ever married? Did she have children? Did she have lovers? No one ever knew. All her conversations were about ideas.

She wrote me long letters when she was doing fieldwork on the island of Sumba in Indonesia in the 1970s. Did she not have anyone else to write them to? One letter in particular impressed me: she described how she entertained a local chief by singing him songs. She once told me that at one time she had been an agent for opera singers and thus perhaps could sing herself. But the vision of strange-looking Monni singing a cappella to an Indonesian chief is one I treasure the most. I can't imagine anyone else doing it.

17

ZONA ROSA

In the 1960s the art of ancient America was classified as "primitive art." It didn't require exotic fieldwork; all you had to do to see some of it was to go to Mexico. Mexico was near, inexpensive and modern. You didn't have to have a grant; you could go as a tourist. Starting around 1966, I went to Mexico at least once or often two or three times a year. In the years when you could not go back to Hungary, Mexico was a substitute. A great, backward country with fantastic antiquities and folk art.

From the beginning, I stayed in the Zona Rosa, a district off the great Reforma boulevard. The Reforma goes diagonally across Mexico City, bordered by beautifully landscaped parks. There are a number of roundabouts, known as *glorietas*, punctuated by various monuments and statuary. Near the Zona Rosa is El Angel, a gilded figure of an angel symbolizing Mexican independence on top of a tall column. The Zona Rosa was reminiscent of Greenwich Village in New York, in that it was a residential and tourist district at the same time. People lived in attractive houses and shopped in a big covered market. The market had eggs, onions, squash blossoms, and other Mexican culinary fare. At the same time, there were a number of hotels, night clubs, and gift shops for tourists. Beautiful silver jewelry from Taxco. Batik textiles. Lovely craft things.

The big hotel was the Hotel Geneve. It may have had over a hundred rooms, all furnished in colonial décor. Sometimes I stayed there for as long as two or three months, for four dollars a night. The Zona Rosa was originally populated by foreigners, and its streets had the names of European capitals: Londres, Liverpool, Hamburgo, Varsovia, etc. A single woman did not feel safe in all parts of Mexico City, but I always felt safe in the Zona Rosa. Because of my height, I was sometimes followed on the street by short Mexican men. Politely not coming too close. Sometimes they would exclaim things like: "¡Qué tamaño!" which translates roughly as "What size!" or " how big!"

By the 1980s, the nice balance of the Zona Rosa tipped in favor of the tourists. The covered market stopped selling eggs and sold cheap tourist souvenirs instead. People must have moved out. The Hotel Geneve was bought by a chain and "modernized" its entrance with ridiculous balustrades and whatnot. Men's clubs opened their doors, as well as pornographic movie theatres. And of course crime and prostitution. The area went downhill. In later years, I found a different hotel on the other side of the Reforma, but the area did not have the same charm. In the 1990s, the Zona Rosa underwent further changes. It now has the biggest gay community of Mexico, and oddly, cheek by jowl, a large Korean community. I am very grateful that I started to go to Mexico City when the sky was still blue (not gray from pollution), when the population was fifteen million (not twenty million), before the crimes of narco-trafficking, and when the Zona Rosa was at its best. But even in the good old days, Mexico was Mexico.

On one occasion Blaise and I were driving a rented car from the Zona Rosa to the airport. Near the Angel glorieta, we were stopped by a cop. (The police have been notoriously corrupt in Mexico since time immemorial.) He said we went through a red light and needed to pay a fine. We argued that we did not go through a red light and anyway were on the way to the airport. He said, "Do you want to pay the fine here, or do you want to go to the station house?" Well, of course you don't want to go to a Mexican station house. So we paid whatever he wanted—$50? $100? Then he motioned us to follow him. He got on his motorcycle and got in front of us. He waved the stream of cars to part. As if we didn't know where the airport was, he gave us a motorcycle escort all the way. He slowed down the traffic on both sides, as if we had been foreign dignitaries. It was a nerve-wracking ride. At the airport he waved and peeled off.

18

COLOSSUS OF THE NORTH

Educated Mexicans were always delighted to hear that I was from Hungary—*húngara*—which made me more human in their estimation. They all liked the US—they had investments in the US; they went to school in the US; some spent part of the year in the US, but nevertheless, the US was oppressive in its power and bigness right across their border. A Mexican might call the Coke he was drinking "the black waters of imperialism" *(las aguas negras del imperialismo)* and laugh.

US scholars were no exception to this Mexican ambivalence. They were better educated, better funded, and had more time to do whatever it was they wanted than their Mexican counterparts. The US scholars came to Mexico wanting access to the ancient ruins and artifacts, which they were going to study, write up, and acquire fame and fortune. With some exceptions, they were less interested in the Mexicans' scholarship. The Mexicans were there to store and protect the material only, and they were often criticized for not doing a good enough job of that. Sometimes Mexicans dealt with that by official denial—they would deny permits or lending, even if only to slow up the process and frustrate someone from the US. On my first trip to Mexico, I got the runaround. I had to get papers from the US Embassy guaranteeing who I was. Then I got a permit to photograph ruins, *"sin usar modelos."* When I asked what that meant, I was told "without girls in bikinis." In the end, I went as an ordinary tourist with a camera, without any permit.

I was all too much the US scholar, when with Kathleen Berrin I tried to organize a Teotihuacán exhibit at the De Young Museum of San Francisco. We went to Mexico with a shopping list of items we wanted for the exhibition. I had a clear idea of what message we wanted to convey. We hit a wall. Not surprisingly, Mexicans prefer to organize their own exhibits with their own messages and travel it themselves. We didn't know that, in the beginning. In the end, the Teotihuacán exhibit and catalogue was a collaborative effort with Mexicans, but still with the overbearing help of the US Embassy. We got everything we wanted. It was a great exhibit; I'm not sure it was a great diplomatic process.

I loved Mexico, but my stomach didn't. From my earliest trip, I became quite ill with "Montezuma's Revenge." I followed the advice not to drink the water and not to eat raw fruits and vegetables, and it didn't help. Back in New York, I was diagnosed with amoebic dysentery by a tropical medicine specialist. Mexican doctors I saw said I got so sick because US food is too sterile—it was the fault of the US.

I would get cured and go back to Mexico. Each time I was cured, the cure took longer and longer. When the cure took over six months, I realized that I had two choices: not to go to Mexico or not to eat anything there.

I devised an eating scheme that would work, from canned and packaged foods I took from New York and could also buy in Mexico. For breakfast, I had a peanut-butter-and-jelly sandwich and a can of orange juice. For lunch, I had a peanut-butter-and-jam sandwich and a coke. For dinner, I had a small can of Vienna sausages or ham, a wedge of aluminum-wrapped cheese, a can of peas or mixed vegetables, and a piece of chocolate. I had straws, little paper plates, and a bottle of alcohol to wash my hands, and my Swiss army knife and spoon. I could carry five days' worth of food in a bag on my shoulder. This system worked for me for many years. Sometimes, on my last night in Mexico City, I would have a real dinner, figuring that by the time I got sick I would be back in the US. My favorite place was Fonda el Refugio on Liverpool Street, where I'd order the Chicken in mole sauce—a sauce of chocolate and chili peppers with a dozen other mysterious ingredients. Yum.

19

EXOTIC TEXTILES

I have done my share of needlepoint, embroidery, knitting, sewing dresses and even misshapen sofa-cushion covers in my life, but I was never really any good at any of them, because I lacked patience. I admire the patience textiles require. Unlike ceramics, textiles do not break. You can fold and stuff them into a paper bag. They keep you warm and can become an intimate part of you. They are good to look at and good to touch. I love textiles of all kinds, from rugs to mittens.

Some of the most beautiful folk textiles in the Americas were still being made and worn in the twentieth century in the Guatemala highlands. The area was near Lake Atitlán and the town of Chichicastenango (Chichi for short). When I was about thirty, a generous travel grant paid for a three-month trip all through Mayaland, that was something of a National Geographic adventure. I wasn't doing any in-depth research; I just went to see as much as I could, especially in out-of-the-way places not visited by tourists. Including the Guatemala Highlands.

One of the great moments of that trip was a motorboat ride on the Usumacinta River. (The Usumacinta separates Mexico from Guatemala in the tropical forest.) We were going to the ancient Maya site of Seibal, where the carvings record dates just prior to the Maya collapse in AD 900. It was largely overgrown and romantically mysterious.

Another moment was a car trip along a dried-out riverbed (no road), to the ruins of Copán in Honduras, by a daredevil Maya driver five feet tall. The over-life-size sculptures of Maya rulers set up on a court made every spine-bounce of that trip worthwhile. Almost as well preserved as if made yesterday.

In Mérida, Mexico, I chartered a plane and pilot for $80 to fly me over to the sites of Yaxchilán and Bonampak, which as yet had no road. It was the first time I had flown over the undifferentiated tropical forest until the little Maya buildings came to view. I, who am normally uncomfortable about flying, found it exhilarating. The famous murals of Bonampak were a sad sight; a milky white layer of calcite, leached out from the limestone building, covered everything. I knew that was likely to be the case, but I had to make my pilgrimage to that Maya masterpiece anyway.

But I digress. Ruins are cold and impersonal, however much one imagines an ancient life in them. The real highlight of that trip for me were the modern Maya people, who were dressing in folk costumes in the Guatemala Highlands around Lake Atitlán and the town of Chichicastenango. These are the descendants of the people who built the ruins. By then the men wore western clothes—jeans and shirts. But the women went to church, market or stayed at home in garments whose shape is ancient. The skirt is an uncut piece of fabric wrapped around the body, held in place by a sash at the waist. The blouse—known as a huipil—is an unfitted square shirt, big enough to cover the upper arms. The huipil is colorful with figurative and abstract designs in the weaving, the embroidery, or in tie-dyeing, sometimes all three. The colors are bright and modern. To us, these colorful huipils look like modern art.

In the Guatemala Highlands, each village has its own designs. When you went to the market at Chichicastenango, you could identify which village each woman came from by her huipil. I was fascinated by these garments and bought a couple of dozen from various places. It was only a matter of time before women would stop making and wearing them in favor of store-bought clothes. Already there were some ugly machine-made huipils. Mine were all nice older ones. (Not too old; in the tropical climate, textiles do not survive for a long time and simply don't exist to be collected. I collected my textiles in the 1970s, and perhaps they dated back to the '60s or '50s.)

My guide took me to a textile workshop, where women dressed me up as a native in the skirt, sash, and huipil and put a folded cloth on my head as a headgear. I must have been a giant compared to the tiny Maya women. Unfortunately, the photos of this did not come out, because in my excitement over this trip, I bought the wrong kind of film—indoor rather than outdoor film—and did not have enough sense to buy the right film in Guatemala City, when I started out.

Instead of modern paintings, I hung some of the Guatemalan textiles on the walls of my Riverside Drive apartment. The most striking piece was an oversize wedding huipil from Solola village. A bright red all over, it had tie-dyed white dots in a syncopated pattern, emphasized, here and there, by patches of embroidered primary colors. Red silk outlined the neck opening. This stunning piece I had above the (nonworking) fireplace in the living room. I moved the huipils around, so none would get overexposed to light and lose its glorious color. When I retired, I gave them to the Brooklyn Museum, where they are well cared for and sometimes exhibited.

People have often asked me whether I've ever worn the Guatemalan huipils. The answer is yes. In the early seventies it was fashionable to wear ethnic dress from many parts of the world. I once wore the red Solola wedding huipil with black silk pants to a New Year's Eve party. But starting in the 1980s, it no longer feels right to wear the clothes of exotic peoples. I do not know why. We no longer express our inner selves by masquerading in the clothes of others.

20

SILENT CITY

"Mom, what are those things on my pillow?" asked my thirteen-year-old son, Adam.

"Scorpions, dear. They fall from the thatched roof."

We were renting a house in the village of San Juan, Teotihuacán, Mexico, next to and partly over the ancient site of Teotihuacán. (Teo. For short). A large, sixteenth-century construction by appearance, the house had a thatched roof and more-or-less modern plumbing.

Almost a decade before, the San Francisco De Young Museum was given as a bequest of about seventy Teotihuacán mural fragments by a local architect named Harald Wagner. Obviously the murals were looted, cut out of walls. It was clear that the murals came from Teotihuacán, and there was nothing like this quantity in any other museum. It was very sensitive for an American museum to have such looted materials. After many years of discussion and negotiations, half the murals were returned to Mexico in 1986. But before that, San Francisco wanted to study and publish the murals. I was called in, because I had written my doctoral dissertation on the murals of Teotihuacán and was one of the few people who could be considered an "expert" on the subject. In the summer of 1984 we were in Mexico with René Millon, the archaeologist who had already found the place at the ancient site where the murals were looted.

René Millon was one of the most distinguished Mesoamerican archaeologists. He had previously mapped and surveyed the entire site of Teotihuacán and showed that it had been the largest city of its time with a population over one hundred thousand, which is huge for a pre-industrial city. The two great pyramids had long been known. The Pyramid of the Sun is as big in mass, though less tall, than the largest Egyptian pyramid. A wide—forty meters wide—and three-quarter-mile-long avenue connects the Pyramid of the Sun and the so-called Pyramid of the Moon. René Millon's map demonstrated that at one time the people of Teotihuacán lived in well-built multifamily apartment compounds near the pyramids and the avenue. There were about two thousand of them. Each apartment compound housed about sixty to a hundred people. Rooms were arranged around inner patios. Many of the apartment compounds were covered with mural paintings. The subjects were some gods, water and fertility and weapons of war. The chronology of the city was established as lasting from about 1 AD to about 600 AD. A long time, by the standards of any civilization.

The question about Teotihuacán was, what kind of a place was it? Good or bad? What kind of government did it have? In most Mesoamerican cultures there are representations of rulers, wars, and conquests. At Teotihuacán there are no representations of rulers and conquest. Because Teotihuacán is located less than an hour outside Mexico City, the original area of the Aztecs, Teotihuacán was believed to be sort of like the Aztecs, only earlier.

How did I get involved with Teotihuacán? It all began a long time back, when I was visiting the Sistine Chapel in Rome. The great Michelangelo frescoes on the ceiling. The crowds below. The deafening noise of the crowd. Someone in a corner started shushing—sh! ssh!—and shortly everyone was shushing his or her neighbor until the vast hall fell silent. There was a moment of silence while everyone looked up at the ceiling. Then the chattering noise began anew and rose again to a full roar. The crowd went through this several times before I left. European art is much too popular. I wanted to be somewhere just as grand, but by myself, as if I had been the first person to come upon it. When I saw Teotihuacán, that was it. The ancient city of Teotihuacán actually has a million visitors a year, but it is so vast that the tourists disappear in it. One can be alone in many parts of the site with just cacti and a few local children for company. I liked that.

Compared to Aztec and Maya scholars, Teotihuacán scholars were few, and most were there that summer. The Mexican archaeologists included Ruben Cabrera Castro and Linda Manzanilla; the Japanese,

Saburo Sugiyama. The Americans were René Millon, George Cowgill, the ceramic expert Evelyn Rattray, and the figurine specialist Warren Barbour.

Warren seemed to know something about scorpions. He claimed that the scorpions whose sting is fatal are in the American Southwest or far northern Mexico—not to worry about. The one-or-two-inch local scorpions at San Juan Teotihuacán could "stun you," whatever that meant, but were not lethal. He got rid of the scorpions for us, and none of us got stunned. Housekeeping in the village was not easy. Besides my son, a student came with me. We cooked our own food and bought supplies in the open market. The meats looked unappetizing, so it was mostly vegetarian—a lot of eggs and poblano peppers.

René's archaeological team found that the San Francisco murals had been looted from two exceptionally large apartment compounds. In the process of excavation, they found new murals, still on the walls in a pristine state of preservation. These were representations of the Storm God—god of lightning and rain—particularly important in an agricultural civilization. Many images of the Storm God had been found before; he was recognizable by goggles around the eyes. The new murals were a beautiful green in color. The color green in Mesoamerica symbolized life. Teotihuacán murals were mostly a maroon red with accents in green, blue, and yellow. Early travelers compared them to Aubusson carpets. Stylized and decorative, their meaning is still enigmatic.

The new murals created a problem—there was no point in removing them because they'd end up crumbling in a storeroom; leaving them open to sun and rain would fade them. It was necessary to hide them, so looters would not get at them. Luckily, most collectors don't want murals—they are crumbly and messy. In René Millon's archaeological excavation, they were reburied until a decision could be made about them in some future time.

How much is there still underground in that great metropolis?

21

MYSTERY

How do you explain a great, ancient civilization that had no writing, except for a few glyphs, and had no European eyewitnesses because it collapsed eight hundred years before the sixteenth-century conquest? You don't know their language or ethnic group. The mounds were named by the Aztecs, who came six hundred years later and also didn't know. Most frustrating is the fact that the arts don't depict the rulers, the court, the enemies, and their glorious deeds. With a few exception, their arts don't depict their everyday activities, either. No burial of a great ruler has ever been found.

Teotihuacán (the Place of the Gods in the Nahuatl language of the Aztecs) is a mystery. We don't know what its inhabitants called it. It was a mystery when I started my research, and it remained a mystery after I finished.

There are the ruins of the city itself. The two largest pyramids in the New World. Almost everyone who has tried to explain Teotihuacán has done so with the pyramids. They were erected more or less in the beginning of the life of the city, and it is generally assumed that some powerful, absolute, pharaonic ruler ordered them built. Teotihuacán is seen as a totalitarian place. This is the view that my Teotihuacán scholar colleagues, starting with René Millon, have of the city as a whole.

I did not start out with the pyramids but with the murals, and I had a different vision. While I was working on the San Francisco murals, which came from apartment compounds, I saw Teotihuacán from the bottom up. Everyone who tries to explain Teotihuacán starts from a few key observations. Mine were the apartment compounds on a grid plan with mural paintings, and the lack of the images of a dynastic ruler in any medium. Both of these were unique in Mesoamerica. The two thousand or so apartment compounds indicated high standards of living and high status. Actually, status and wealth seem to have varied within and between compounds. The rulers, whoever they were, evidently kept a low profile or did not rule through their images. The murals glorify the fertile natural world with its major deity, the Storm God, and emblematically war and sacrifice. The arts generally seem to be positive reinforcements of things like flowering trees dripping with water, birds and butterflies. (The Aztec arts were mostly negative reinforcements like skulls and fangs.)

There were a few enigmatic feminine images that Millon named the "Great Goddess." I thought I could find many more. As she could be related to a lot of things, including water, vegetation, fertility, maybe she was a major deity, too. Perhaps a major female deity personified communal ideas, away from competitive, male-dominated politics.

It therefore seemed to me that Teotihuacán might have had a more "corporate" or "communal" organization surrounding its rulership, or, somehow, had a consulting body for the rulers. This was unusual and heretical, and I wrote it up hesitatingly for the San Francisco murals volume. I showed a draft of it to René Millon, who was a senior scholar I respected. He disagreed with me most vehemently. Therefore, I toned down the chapter to fit with the orthodox view. Some months later, we were both giving talks at a Teotihuacán conference in Washington, and to my surprise René was talking about more "corporate" aspects of Teotihuacán, without giving me credit for the idea. To my knowledge, he did not pursue the subject further. The scholarly world is highly competitive.

In the book I was subsequently writing about Teotihuacán, published twenty years ago in 1997, I presented my hypothesis of a collectively organized city with greater emphasis, knowing that I was out on a limb. I did not know what that organization might have been like in detail, but I had a strong sense of its basic nature. This has not been received well by the Teotihuacán scholarly community, who have closed ranks around the pyramid-great-ruler theory and left me sort of out in the cold as an idiosyncratic voice.

Subsequently, I haven't tried to fight for my theory in print or in person, but I haven't stopped thinking about it. I haven't been retreading the old arguments. I've been thinking in a more general way about it. Most people are astonished by the achievements of ancient Americans, considering that they used stone tools, had no beasts of burden or practical use of the wheel. How did they manage to build great cities like Teotihuacán? Mesoamericans did not work with slave labor. The elite had to convince their own people to spend at least half the year (the other half doing agricultural work) on vast architectural projects. Obviously, religion is a good persuader and has been extensively studied by everyone. But it had seemed to me that American Indian societies, not just Teotihuacán, but those of South America, had ways of persuading their people to do work by ideas like "redistribution," rather than the whip. Why couldn't Teotihuacán have had a persuasion system, perhaps by rank and class up and down the social scale, by some form of participatory social and political organization built into the social fabric itself?

The term "councilor government" has been used recently for some Mesoamerican sites (Chichén Itzá) and means that a ruler may have ruled with a council or that a council ruled by itself. I think Teotihuacán had a councilor government with the participation of ten, twenty, fifty, a hundred, who knows how many lords representing segments of the city. One or two persons could have been the symbolic top. (According to sixteenth-century sources, some Mesoamerican cities in the sixteenth century had dual rulership.) The exceptionally large compounds could have been some of their residences. Besides the people on the top, there were the headmen or chiefs of the multifamily apartment compounds—which numbered about two thousand. That's too many for a "council." But some could have been more important than others. As a ranked place, all up and down the social scale, many could have had a stake in Teotihuacán's activities, including building and labor. Here the arts glorify common values, such as bountiful nature and the community.

As it turns out, the apartment compounds were not at Teotihuacán from the beginning. They were being built from AD 300, halfway through the history of the city. So my "councilor government" idea may fit best the second half of the city's life. That is the time of the mural paintings. It is not the time of the great pyramid building. In pyramid building times, housing seems to have been perishable. Perishable, poor and more modest and might suggest a more authoritarian government. All of us scholars may be right to some extent for different times and circumstances. There is no reason why Teotihuacán should have had the same organization throughout its long history.

I have now found an interesting parallel that might make sense for Teotihuacán, in ancient Rome. The long-lived civilization of Rome underwent many changes in its history: at first it was a kingdom; later it became a republic. The republic had a senate consisting of a hundred wealthy men led by two consuls. Then it became an empire with an emperor. Teotihuacán could have been a kingdom to start with, when the pyramids were built, and a participatory government later, when the apartment compounds were added, and an empire at some time or another.

These issues are not just quibbles among archaeologists. It is how we think about ancient America. Is it just a place of bizarre rituals and unpredictable kings? Or might it be also a place of participatory government experiments, like Greece and Rome?

As I proofread these pages in 2018, Teotihuacán archaeologists have decided that Teotihuacán had a collective organization, after all. A new wrinkle of the recent excavation is the discovery of sacrificial victims in some of the pyramids, who were "foreigners." The new excitement is about Teotihuacán's conquests, possibly of Maya Tikal, and an empire of sorts. Still, it is good to have been right twenty years ago.

22

SACRIFICE

Teotihuacán was difficult to teach. There was little factual information. It was supposition on top of supposition. Students had nothing to hold on to; they were frustrated.

The Aztecs were a different matter because there were abundant sixteenth-century sources written by eyewitnesses like the conquering Cortés and by missionaries. Myths, royal histories, religious rituals, everyday life activities, even the speeches of parents to their children and the words of songs were recorded. The great art of the Aztecs was powerful basalt sculpture with a lot of death imagery. But what everyone knew about the Aztecs was the human sacrifices. I knew that if I gave a course on Aztec art, only a few students would come. But if I gave a course on Aztec art and sacrifice, there would be many. All these wholesome and good-looking Columbia boys and girls came for the sacrifice. Ghoulish.

So by the second class, I assigned the monthly sacrifices as recorded by the missionary Sahagún, in all their grisly detail. He hadn't witnessed them; they were described to him by Aztecs after they were no longer practiced. The saddest was the young man who impersonated a god for a year, was well treated, even given mistresses, before being sacrificed. He was to play a flute and break it at each of the four stages of a pyramid. We discussed the basic rationale of Aztec religion, the fact that the gods were believed to have sacrificed themselves for humanity, and humans had to pay the debt with the most precious thing they had: life. The best story that expresses this is the *Creation of the Sun* myth.

After the last destruction of the world (the Aztecs believed in multiple worlds), the few remaining gods and beings got together at Teotihuacán (then an impressive ruin) and built a huge bonfire. The god who would jump into the fire would become the sun. A rich god sacrificed jades and feathers but could not throw himself in. A poor, sickly god jumped right into the fire and became the sun. The rich god was ashamed and jumped into the fire next. But by then the fire was not so hot, and he became the moon. However, the heavenly bodies would not move in the sky until all the onlookers jumped into the fire.

The next theme was violence. Because the Aztecs wanted sacrificial victims for their rites, their warfare was conducted to get live victims for sacrifice and not so much to kill on the spot. Not an easy task. Their body counts were low. We are horrified by the sacrifices because of the way people were killed; we accept much larger body counts in our wars whose violence seems acceptable to us. From that it is just a short mental step to the devastations of A-bombs at Hiroshima and Nagasaki that would have been beyond an Aztec's imagination. Even the Roman gladiatorial deaths put on for entertainment would have been beyond an Aztec's imagination.

The class was usually relieved and surprised when we turned to Aztec poetry. Aztec poems were recited with music at the feasts of the nobility. Many were said to be written by the rulers themselves. About fifty to a hundred survive. Most are philosophical and questioning. They could have been written by anyone at any time. So what were the Aztecs really like?

Will I have to go like the flowers that perish?
Will nothing remain of my name?
Nothing of my fame here on earth?
At least my flowers, at least my songs!
Earth is the region of the fleeting moment.
Is it also thus in the place
Where in some way one lives?
Is there joy there, is there friendship?
Or is it only here on earth
We come to know our faces?

Aztec culture: c. 1350–1521, capital city Tenochtitlán, population c. 200,000 (under present-day Mexico City).

23

FISHING

The property in Dingman's Ferry was the first land we owned in the US, and that was momentous. We were really a part of the country. Dingman's Ferry is about fifteen minutes from Lake Owassa, on the Pennsylvanian side of the Delaware River. A ferry must have existed there a long, long time ago but was long gone. In my time, there was a noisy, wooden bridge that connected New Jersey with Pennsylvania. The US Army Corps of Engineers had an ambitious plan to dam up the Delaware to create more hydroelectric power for Philadelphia. The area was only sparsely inhabited, anyway. The Army Corps of Engineers bought up most of the land on both sides of the Delaware. Riverside settlements were moved. Dingman's Ferry, once by the river, was moved up the hill. There was a great deal of local discontent about this. The construction plans were very much in flux, and people had to sell their lands cheap. Red ribbons on some trees indicated the mysterious intentions of the Army Corps of Engineers on the property that interested us.

There were sixteen acres of more-or-less wooded land with a small pond. A long, winding driveway led to the house, which was modern without being arty. The house was on a little hill overlooking the pond. Every direction you looked from the house was your property and was wilderness. How wonderful! Total privacy was assured on one side, because it adjoined a five-hundred-acre forest preserve. All this wilderness was only two hours from New York City.

It was paradise. More precisely, it looked virginal, as if this land might have existed in this unspoiled way even before the Europeans landed in the sixteenth century. Or, perhaps even before, in Indian times. As if emphasizing this romantic view, Mr. Miller, the previous owner, pointed out a big rock that according to him had an Indian petroglyph carved on it. It was an arrow pointing north. Subsequent examination of the rock by us revealed the date 1914 carved below the arrow, so if it was an Indian, he was a modern Indian. No matter, it was a petroglyph and a part of the atmosphere of the place.

The previous owner, Mr. Miller, was a local heating oil contractor who loved nature. He had built extra-large windows on his house, so he could watch animals at all seasons. There was an abundance of deer, wild turkeys, and occasionally bear. Mr. Miller stocked the pond with trout. He didn't hunt or fish. He fed the trout from a big sack of fish-food pellets, some of which he left for us. The pond was spring fed and very cold. It had little vegetation growth. It was translucent enough to see the fish.

My husband Blaise and I bought the property. We figured that the dam might not be built, or if it was built, it would take a dozen years, and we would have time to enjoy. Environmentalists were fighting the dam on the ground that at springtime each side of the river would have huge mudflats. In fact, the dam was never built. The land bought by the US was turned into a recreational park.

At first we could only go to Dingman's on weekends, and we noticed each weekend that there were fewer fish in the pond. Evidently the neighbors were busy fishing them out when we weren't there. We didn't really want the fish; we wanted to swim in the pond. So we thought we should fish them out, too, before they were gone. Neither of us was a fisherman, so we wanted to invite someone who was. My boarding school roommate Ann had recently married an older (fortyish) psychiatrist, whose hobby was fishing. We invited them to come and fish, and afterwards we'd have a great fish dinner.

With expertise, Larry, the psychiatrist-fisherman, caught one fish very quickly with some ordinary bait. He then took that fish up to the kitchen and gutted it. He found some little flies in its belly. Then he spread out all his fishing gear on the dining-room table and proceeded to create a similar fly out of bits of thread, feather, fur, and whatnot. He was at it for an hour or more as we watched in fascination. It seemed to take a long time. Finally the artificial fly was finished to his satisfaction, and he went back to the pond to try it on the fish. But the fish were not biting anymore.

In the meantime, my sister arrived from New Jersey with her son and a black Fresh Air Fund kid on his first vacation away from a city. The kids were about eight to ten years old. They too wanted to fish. In the meantime Larry was getting progressively more angry as the fish were not biting the fly he had created. He was in a white-hot fury. To make matters worse, trout were being caught by the Fresh Air Fund kid using a string with a bit of raw hamburger meat as bait. We had the trout dinner. Memory fails me as to how the fish got cleaned and gutted, which is probably just as well.

Once the fish were pretty much gone, the pond was available for swimming. It was clean and clear but so cold none of us could stand it. It was beautiful to look at in all seasons. On very hot days, an occasional bear would come and splash around in it. We went to swim in the Delaware.

24

PERFECT LITTLE TOWN

The first little American town we got to know well was Milford, Pennsylvania, eight miles from Dingmans Ferry. It was the place where we did our shopping. Population two thousand. Commercial Milford is mostly an intersection with one traffic light and a few blocks in either direction. Within that small area there was everything we could want: supermarket, drugstore, Leonard's five-and-dime, a beauty salon and a barber shop. Most surprising was Bloomgarden's Department Store, where you could buy everything from sturdy shoes to men's and women's basic underwear and outerwear. I still wear a lovely fleece robe I got at Bloomgarden's in the 1970s. There was an antique store where I got a tea set. There were two restaurants, Faucheres, a New Orleans French restaurant run by two elderly sisters, and the Tom Quick Inn serving steaks and burgers. Let me not forget the bakery, run by a handsome man with a fat wife and two delightful children. Their donut holes were to die for.

The thing about Milford that was so striking to us in the late sixties and seventies was that it was neither upper class nor lower class. It and its merchandise were thoroughly no-frills middle class. The other thing is that it was minimal. It had everything one needed, and it was compact. There was even a courthouse, a library, and a movie theater. A utopian town planner could not have done better.

Milford had a "European" aspect because of a great stone castle on its western periphery, overlooking the town. Named Gray Towers, it was built by the Pinchot family in the early nineteenth century. The

Pinchots were a well-to-do French family who supported Napoleon. After he lost the Battle of Waterloo, the family left France and eventually came to the US. They bought large tracts of land in the Milford area and went into various businesses, especially the lumber business and wallpapers. Originally, the Eastern US had huge trees, like the redwoods in California. The Pinchots of Milford cut down the great aboriginal forests around them. As they became wealthy, they had a grand home built imitating a French castle of the Loire Valley, with three round towers at the corners. It was designed by the architect Morris Hunt.

The third generation Gifford Pinchot grew up at Grey Towers and was horrified by his family's and others' destruction of America's forests. Mountains were denuded and rivers silted up. Already his father James had begun a conservation movement and funded a forestry school at Yale. Gifford went to France to learn sustainable forestry techniques. He was appointed the first chief of the newly created Forest Service by Teddy Roosevelt, and forestry classes met in Milford. Later on he was governor of Pennsylvania for two terms. Grey Towers was eventually given to the nation and is administered by the National Park Service. It is now a major tourist attraction. Although it copies European designs, it is built entirely of local stone and other local materials.

My admiration for Milford as the perfect little town in the 1970s did not take the town's history into account, which I did not know, except for the Pinchots. I had been there and admired it just for a short phase of its history. Milford kept changing since the eighteenth century when it was founded. It changed also between the 1970s and the 1990s, when I went back after a long absence. I was disappointed by what had happened to Milford. The courthouse, library, and forestry buildings were still there, as well as the restaurants. But all the practical shops—Leonard's five-and-dime, Bloomgarden's Department Store, etc., or their equivalents—were gone.

All the shops now sold antiques. Patchwork quilts, butter churns, vintage clothes, old dolls, cranberry glass, and Victorian furniture were everywhere. There was an orgy of them inside the great hall of the Pinchot forestry building. Milford had turned into the antiques capital of eastern Pennsylvania. Probably Milford had two choices for development—to go downscale to Burger Kings and Pizza Huts or to go upscale to antiques. There was no middle road open to it.

For ordinary things, people shopped seven miles away in the strip and malls of Matamoras.

The old movie theatre in Milford, once showing ordinary Hollywood films, had been "renovated" for a yearly Black Bear Film Festival. It brings in avant-garde filmmakers, critics, elite intellectuals, artistic people, and fundraisers from New York, California, and other places. Milford is now a player on the national art scene and not just a small town in Pennsylvania. It has become gentrified.

I am glad I saw it when it was a town for everybody.

25

KILLER

All the time I spent in Milford I never asked who Tom Quick of the Tom Quick Inn was. I knew that he was considered an "Indian killer," but that seemed hardly surprising, and I never thought twice about it. If you go far enough back in the history of American towns of the Northeast, sooner or later you come to Indians. And, it is also obvious that these Indians were somehow killed or gotten rid of before whites settled. In the Northeast, Indians are largely gone, having left picturesque words for rivers and settlements, like Narragansett, Massachusetts, Passamaquoddy. I presumed that Tom Quick was just one of many "Indian killers."

In 1997 Tom Quick made news in The New York Times because his monument in Milford was vandalized. I had not been aware of this monument and its story. Evidently, Tom Quick was the first white child ever born in Milford, in 1734. His father was the first white settler. According to legend, Tom saw his father being killed by an Indian and vowed to slay as many Indians as he could. In revenge. Depending on the various stories that were told about him, he killed under ten or as many as a hundred Indians. Some believed these to be factual killings; some thought that they were grandiose tales told by Tom Quick himself. There are no accurate facts.

The really interesting part of the story was that in the nineteenth century, people believed them to be facts. In 1889, a zinc monument was erected in Milford to glorify Tom Quick as an Indian killer. By then there were no Indians around Milford, although elsewhere in the

US there were Indian wars, moving Indians to reservations. "A good Indian was a dead Indian."

In 1997 the monument was seen in a different light. It had been vandalized by presumably pro-Indian persons. In those days, I was not in the habit of visiting Milford. My information came from newspapers. After it was vandalized, the monument was removed. The town was divided between those who wanted the monument removed permanently and those who wanted to keep is as a "historical object." Town officials and Indian spokesmen discussed the issue, which remained difficult to resolve.

The story of Tom Quick puts a face and a name on the early days of US towns dispossessing Indians. What has Milford to do with this legacy? Should Milford have a monument to a killer of anybody?

26

BRIEF FAME

My sister found the Red Fox Inn and the Liebs. The inn was located on the old road somewhere, between Dingmans Ferry and Milford, Pennsylvania, in the middle of nowhere. The largish building was furnished with lovely antiques. Alan Lieb did the cooking, which varied with the availability of local foods. Ronnie made the scrumptious desserts (something chocolate and hazelnutty comes to mind). She also chose the wines. I don't remember any particular meal I had there, but generally the Liebs had a European style of cooking mixed with the unusual combination of flavors and textures just beginning in American cooking labeled as "nouvelle." Whatever it was, it was delicious. The Red Fox Inn was the best kept secret of the three adjoining states near the Delaware River: New York, New Jersey, and Pennsylvania.

The Liebs were not only great cooks but also charming people. They chatted with us while they were preparing the meals. After everyone finished eating, we sat around with them discussing the problems of the world, the goings on in Milford, their children's schooling, and our various travel experiences in Europe. We were all cosmopolitans who ended up in a small US town and relished it.

The Liebs were European exotics. Alan's father was Austrian but had a restaurant in Spain, which is where Alan learned to cook. His mother was English and sent him to school in England. That accounted for the British accent and mannerisms. Was he Austrian, Spanish or British? Ronnie was Latvian; I have never known any other Latvian.

That accounted for the eclecticism of their cooking. They probably told me how they got to Milford, but if I ever knew I had forgotten. Their children grew up in Milford. Nor am I certain what their plans were. They seemed like a local fixture. But they informed us that they had put up the Red Fox Inn for sale. (It needed repairs? They needed the money? They were going somewhere? I don't know.

We were not the only diners who became friends with the Liebs. Of the two dozen or so diners a night, not a few became friends. Among them was a well-known writer frequently published in *The New Yorker*, John McPhee. John McPhee became so enamored of the Liebs that he wrote a paean about them in *The New Yorker* in 1975. Well-traveled New Yorker that he was, he wrote that the Red Fox Inn was the world's best restaurant he had ever eaten in and that its owner was a culinary genius.

He told the Liebs of his intention of writing such a praise review. They were ambivalent about it. On the one hand they welcomed the recognition; on the other hand they feared its effect on their settled rural life. They asked to be made anonymous. They asked that he not even mention the state they were in. So, in the article, McPhee called them Otto and Anna, names the Liebs chose for themselves, and merely said that the restaurant was two hours from New York.

One of the things that most impressed John McPhee was that the Liebs ran their restaurant mostly without a staff. Their children served the dishes to the diners, and on the weekends when it was busy, they employed a dishwasher. Otherwise Alan and Ronnie did everything themselves, relaxed and cheerful. (Any fancy New York restaurant would have a staff of fifty). That casualness was a very sixties ideal.

The article on "Otto" was not just a sensation, it was even a challenge to the New York food establishment. John McPhee suggested that The Red Fox Inn was as good, if not better, than the reigning French restaurant in New York, La Grenouille (The Frog). The chase was on to unmask Otto.

In the meantime, the Red Fox Inn sold and closed. While they wanted to remain anonymous in the article, the Liebs were also human enough to realize that they might have extra diners as a result of it and probably wanted a little fame and extra cash. They planned to open a temporary little restaurant very quickly. The small restaurant they found for this purpose was even more out of the way than the Red Fox Inn and had all the charm of a diner. In a pique of thumbing their noses at the hoity-toity New York food establishment they named it The Frog. Alan may have had a British accent, but they were rebels.

The search for the Liebs was led by Mimi Sheraton, the formidable food critic of *The New York Times*. She took it personally—no great chef could exist without her knowing about it—Otto must not be great. The critics ran their quarry down as if they were wild animals. They consulted all food people and diners in a two-hour radius of New York City. In a short time—was it a week?—they found The Frog and turned up to sample the fare. Following Mimi Sheraton, they did not think the food was extraordinary at all. Otto's cooking was panned in half a dozen newspapers. OK, but nothing special. From anonymity they were catapulted to notoriety or even disgrace. Although contrary papers like the *Village Voice* published positive reviews, the general reception was negative.

I remember that the Liebs were greatly crushed emotionally by the experience of being raised so high and dropped so low in such a short time. At that point, my own life was messy, and I lost track of the Liebs. They did leave the area, that's certain. My sister thinks they went to California, but that could be a rumor. Did they open a restaurant somewhere? Did they change their name? The Otto incident is on the web in great detail, but there is no information on the subsequent doings of Alan and Ronnie Lieb in the public eye.

There is a lesson in this story, but I am not sure what it is. It's tough to be a rebel and a success at the same time.

27

PARIS

I was in Paris when I had a nervous breakdown in 1976. I was to give a talk on masterpieces in pre-Columbian art at the International Congress of Americanists. I sat through several sessions feeling ill: restless, dizzy, unable to concentrate. Soon, I left and never gave my talk.

A day or two before I went to Paris, my lover had broken up with me, and I was awash in tears. I felt as if the ground had been pulled out from under me. I was separating from my Hungarian husband, and I was relying on his helping hand to ease me into the comparatively foreign American world. In retrospect, I may have felt dropped into outer space.

For hours, I wandered around the streets of Paris in a strange frame of mind. I thought I had become clairvoyant and could understand what people said, even a block or two away. My French had long become totally fluent. When I got hungry, I had a delicious omelet in a café. At one point a man followed me and proposed marriage. I think he was Vietnamese and wanted to go to the US. I told him I'd think about it. I was on a high.

When I got back to my hotel room, the mood darkened. An "inner voice" suggested that I would now have to die. Obediently, I put on my nightgown and got into bed. I closed my eyes. Nothing happened. I lay there waiting for death to come for a long time. Eventually, there was nothing to do but to get up. I wasn't dead. I realized that I must be mad.

There was a ninety-year-old close family friend, "Uncle," somewhere in Paris, and I found his phone number. I called him and asked him in a hysterical voice to come and take me to a hospital because I had gone crazy. He was a little man sporting a French beret. He came and took me to a hospital where a white-coated French doctor listened to what I told him—whatever that was—patted me on the shoulder and told me to go home. Although, I remember that I had done some impressive screaming.

Uncle took me home with him. Back at his home, I developed a new panic. I was convinced that my carryings-on would be too much for the ninety-year-old and as a result he would have a heart attack. I will have killed him. I was getting hysterical again. To stop my restless fidgeting and incoherent words, Uncle brought me his own tranquilizers. I had no idea what the proper dosage was, so I took a handful. It then occurred to me to call my psychiatrist in New York to ask if that was too little or perhaps too much. (I had consulted a psychiatrist the year before for depression.)

Amazingly, despite the time difference and whatever day it was, she was in and answered the phone. She told me to double the dosage I took of Uncle's tranquilizer every twelve hours and take the first plane back to the US. Somehow or other, I did. She concluded that I was bipolar (manic depressive) and had had a psychotic "episode." She put me on lithium and little gray antipsychotic pills. She said the tendency for the illness was genetic but was brought about by circumstances.

I was crushed. I thought my life was over. I was thirty-three years old. I was afraid I'd end up in a sanatorium weaving baskets for the rest of my life. She assured me that the little gray pills would prevent any new episode. And that I would always know if something was not right. From then on, I have always been on some amount of medication. In time, I picked up the pieces of my personal and professional life and learned to live with it. Well, not quite. I was terrified of the return of being out of my mind and habitually monitored my words and behavior. I avoided certain tasks, like being chairman of my department, where I was too much in the public eye and could not guarantee that I would always be well.

Was there a silver lining to my experience of insanity? Very small. I had been interested in insanity earlier, read about it in books, and wondered what it was like. Now, I knew and had experienced it. In the end, whatever the cost, knowledge is knowledge and a part of you forever. Certainly, I didn't want to go there again. No marijuana cigarettes for me.

In the Paris incident, I was very lucky. Wandering the streets, it could have turned out much worse. Uncle did not have a heart attack because of my carryings on—he lived for several more years. He was actually delighted that at ninety he could help a young woman in distress and that a young woman kept him company overnight in his apartment.

28

SEX

My marriage broke up and my affair wound down. I moved into a splendid Columbia apartment at Riverside Drive. My thirteen-year-old son stayed with me every other week. Willingly and unwillingly, I was out of the Hungarian exile society. I would have to make new friends wherever I found them.

One day, I saw a woman I recognized on my street. She was tall, very thin, and somewhat stooped. Her facial features looked too big for her face. She could never have been pretty. She wore a pleated skirt and a silk blouse and walked energetically up the hill, the pleated skirt billowing behind her. I knew her quite well as my editor at Abrams art books.

She was a wizard who turned my sentences upside down and inside out, making my first book, *Aztec Art*, better than how I wrote it. She understood that it was the first book on Aztec art, and I wrote it because I could not find a book with all the illustrations and information in one place. She saw that it was going to be a useful book for a long time. She stood up for me in editorial meetings where they wanted to cut down the number of illustrations or quantity of text. She was a peach.

I said hello to her and discovered that she was my neighbor across the street. She lived in the house with the grand glass awning (1910–1920?) that features in many movies that take place in New York. She invited me for a drink the next day. Meg was seventyish, and I was just a little past forty.

She put away a couple of martinis, while I sipped my diet coke. She had never been married and had no children. Her apartment was small and full of books. Eventually, she came to the revelations she wanted to impart to me. For the past twenty or twenty-five or whatever years she had had an affair with a well-known professor of classical studies in my very own department at Columbia. Of course, I had known him. He died not long before. I felt that I was supposed to be surprised, and I was.

Meg reminisced. This had been the best thing she could have done with her life, she said. He was a fascinating man. (And she was no slouch herself, I added mentally.) He would meet her at five when she came home from work; they would have a couple of drinks, talk and make love until seven. Then he would go home and have dinner with his wife. Now that he died, Meg was lonely. To fill up her time and interests, she traveled to places like Iceland and New Zealand.

I realized that she was trying to educate my newly divorced self. As neighbors, we met occasionally. She could talk politics, art history, travel, clothes, and sex. I most remember one of our last conversations before she moved into a retirement community outside New York City. She told me how her best friend had died recently and she had gone to the funeral. Afterwards, she and her dead friend's husband were consoling each other with a couple of drinks. They ended up consoling each other so successfully that they went to bed together and had sex.

"Well," she added by way of explanation, "I was curious to see if at our age it still worked." I must have looked questioningly at her, because she added: "It worked."

This time, she was definitely trying to shock me. But then again, at forty, I could not imagine being seventy.

29

SAILING

Skip, a former Columbia graduate and Santa Barbara professor, invited me to go sailing with him in Puget Sound. He had a very nice thirty-two-foot ketch. I had never sailed before. Hungary is a landlocked country. I loved the wind, the water, the luxury of a private boat. I had such a good experience that I thought of taking my fourteen-year-old son on a boat trip. He said yes, he'd like to go but not to someplace hot like Mexico. So I said, "OK, we'll go to Alaska."

The cruise ship to Alaska was neither elegant nor exclusive, but we did see glaciers and have outdoor salmon barbecues. I learned two important things on the Alaska cruise: one, that every ninth person has a plane in Alaska because there are few roads; and two, on a cruise you need a different outfit every night. I had come in jeans.

Soon after my return, I received an invitation from Columbia to lecture on a four-masted schooner, the *Sea Cloud*, sailing in the Caribbean. I was ready. The *Sea Cloud* had been was the largest private yacht in the world. It was built for Marjorie Merriweather Post in the 1930s. Marjorie was the richest woman in America at the time. Subsequently owned by a consortium, it was converted to a cruise ship for about sixty to seventy passengers. The crew and staff also came to about sixty to seventy, a one-to-one ratio. It was lavish. (She still sails.) The passengers on the *Sea Cloud* were mostly millionaires. On this cruise, beyond the price of the trip, there was a hefty donation to Columbia and other Ivy League schools. There were businessmen, judges, opera singers, and other intelligent, talented, successful and wealthy people on board.

I was invited to give a one-hour lecture on the Maya, since the tour included a stop to see the site of Tikal in Guatemala. They wanted a light, entertaining talk. There was also another invited lady, who was to talk similarly on fish. Otherwise we were supposed to mingle and socialize. This time I brought a splendid outfit for every night. For the last night, I had a gauzy, embroidered Mexican Native garment—a huipil—that added an exotic touch.

As I was embarking on the *Sea Cloud*, a gentleman came over to me and said, "When do we get to try the hallucinogenic enemas?" Did I hear that right? "When do we get to try the hallucinogenic enemas?" What a line! It took me a minute to take this in. It was the latest shocking information about the Maya. My first reaction was, *Good god, are these people so knowledgeable? What about my "light" lecture?*

The ancient Maya used to be compared to the Greeks; they had beautiful naturalistic representations of their rulers, as well as sophisticated writing, mathematics, and astronomy. This idealized depiction of the Maya had changed recently, because of the decipherment of some hieroglyphic writing. Now the focus was on bizarre rituals such as self-bloodletting to the point of seeing visions and the taking of hallucinogenic drugs. A pottery vessel depicting people and strange little pots supposedly containing hallucinogenic enemas had been widely reported in the news. There was no absolute proof that these were enemas, but the idea of hallucinogens was popular at the time. The media jumped at the story.

I need not have worried: the passengers on the *Sea Cloud* cruise knew nothing about the old, new, or any views of the Maya. The clever gentleman with the humorous line was merely teasing the Columbia lecturer, who probably took herself too seriously, with a bit of kinkiness recently picked up from the media. Wayne was otherwise a brilliant mathematician.

To my disappointment, most of the time the *Sea Cloud* motored at a gentle speed to make its scheduled ports. Only a few times did the captain turn off the engine and let us experience sailing just with all the sails. It was fantastic. One of our stops was a luncheon picnic on Roatán Island. Yummy looking seafood, shrimp, and salads were set up on an outdoor table waiting for us to arrive. I took one look at the groaning board and thought of my bad tropical food experiences in Mexico. I didn't eat a bite. That night almost everyone on board was sick. Next morning was the side trip to Tikal, by small plane. Only a very few passengers turned up for it. My mathematician either abstained at the picnic or had a cast-iron stomach, because he was there.

I did not have to lead the small group through the ruins, because a local guide had been hired for that purpose. I could explore the ruins on my own. I had been to Tikal before, but this visit was still a treat. In those days, the tropical forest was largely uninhabited. The trees are about a hundred feet high. Looking down from the plane, the treetops look like an ocean of moving greenery. The five Tikal pyramids, about 120 to 145 feet, thrust up suddenly from the trees, looking like the monuments of an alien civilization. In movies like *Star Wars*, they have been used to represent extraterrestrial cities. How many people have seen Tikal from the air?

I made for the Central Acropolis and Temple I. Temple I is a soaring, vertical pyramid with a tall roof comb capping the little building on top. Going up the steep stairs, one had to hold onto a chain and not look down. The pyramid was the burial place of Tikal's most powerful ruler, known to archaeologists as Ruler A. His descendants, Rulers B and C, were responsible for the other pyramids. Since then, tourists are not allowed to climb the pyramids of Tikal. Tourist feet have been eroding the limestone steps and destroying the ascent.

My mathematician followed me to the top of Temple I. We sat in the doorway of the temple and looked out across the plaza to Temple II—no one quite knew who was buried there. Behind it, peeking out from the jungle foliage, were the roof combs of the other temples. It was peaceful and quiet. We didn't say much. The view was breathtaking, but at that point, neither of us really cared a fig for the ancient Maya. The present moment was splendid enough.

30

MY NEIGHBORHOOD

I decided that the number 13 must be lucky for me because for many decades I lived on the 13th floor of a New York apartment building on 113th Street. (Built by a French contractor in 1916, the building did not have an 11th floor, for which no one had an explanation.) 113th Street divided exactly in half the local community that ran from 116th to 110th Street. It was called Morningside Heights, and the central avenue, one block from my house, was Broadway.

People outside New York have often commented on how exciting it must be to live in a city full of museums and theatres. Others have wondered how I survived such constant cultural stimulation. The fact is, like other New Yorkers I went to museums and the theatre only occasionally. I have been to the Empire State Building and the Statue of Liberty once to take visiting friends there and once to take my son when he was four. I wouldn't be caught dead on Times Square at New Year's Eve or at any other time. When people ask me what I like about New York—if not the above—I always say "the neighborhoods." New York is the most livable city I have ever known.

The six blocks between 110th and 116th Street were my little world, and sometimes for months I did not set foot outside Morningside Heights, because everything was there in easy walking distance. North of 116th Street was Columbia University, where I taught and walked to most mornings. I went past the house-wares store and the hardware store, owned by the same man. Next came a nail salon, where I got my pedicures from young Guatemalan girls. That had only been there a few years. Before that, it was a jewelry store, where I got batteries for my watches. Then came a big restaurant called the West End, with a big noisy bar. It was famous as the hangout of the beat poets Jack Kerouac and Alan Ginzburg in the 1950s. Recently someone bought it and renamed it Havana Grill, serving beans and pork. Next was Mondel's handmade chocolates, made in the back room. My favorite was no sugar almond bark, a chocolate that nearly broke your teeth when you bit into it and then melted into deliciousness. The end of the block had a bookstore with half-priced children's books laid out on the sidewalk.

Then in no particular order, there were two supermarkets, two drugstores, two stationary stores, one dry cleaner, one shoe repair, one optometrist-eyeglass store, and two delicatessens on the practical side. There was a post office, a branch of the Public Library, and a church—I think Methodist—with a soup kitchen. The area had a lot of eateries, many with outdoor cafés. A French, an Italian, and a Greek restaurant. A Chinese and a Japanese restaurant. Two hamburger places and two pizza places. Something Mexican and an ice cream place. As the area gentrified over the years, the number of restaurants multiplied. A farmers market came twice a week at 114th Street selling local vegetables as well as fish and sausages. My favorite stand was the sprouts—these were six types of sprouts, one, I think horseradish, was peppery and pungent. There was also the branch of a major bank on one corner. I have heard that after I left, the building burned down. Whether it was rebuilt or not, I am sure a bank found a space nearby.

I was fond of the assortment of businesses in my neighborhood, but I have lived in other parts of Manhattan and there was similar diversity and practicality everywhere else. In fact, Manhattan is a series of similar neighborhoods blending into one another. It looks as if some great central intelligence designed the fact that there is always a dry cleaner and a florist near you, but it seems to be the decision of a lot of separate and independent minds. Businesses come and go, not necessarily repeating their services exactly but in their way adding to the needs of the area. If they don't, they don't make it. When I go back, I will find it much changed and much the same.

31

STREET LIFE

New York streets, especially the wide shopping avenues, are full of people going at a brisk pace. After a vacation somewhere else in the country, the pace seems very fast. Like in a skating rink, you have to join the given speed as soon as you enter. After a while, the pace seems normal and you don't think about it.

You're moving along let's say uptown at a good clip, while many others are coming at you going downtown. The trick is finding open areas on the sidewalk between the uptown and downtown people without slackening your pace. You don't want to touch anybody. If somebody is touched, that leads to many "excuse mes" and actually looking at the person who may get angry. You want to avoid eye contact as much as possible, so everyone has his or her own space on the sidewalk. Privacy is very important. In those few seconds you pass by, you size up everyone: short, tall, thin, fat, dressed as a slob or up to the nines. They are sizing you up, too. Knowing this, you are conscious of how you are dressed before going out. The greatest sport in New York is watching people on the street. One can do so more leisurely at the many sidewalk cafés.

Of course, occasionally you meet a neighbor, a colleague, a student, and Broadway dissolves into a small town as you exchange some gossip. But most of the time the stream of human traffic consists of strangers. Where do they come from and where are they going? You don't know. They are obstacles to avoid. The couple of times I have fallen on the street, four or five individuals emerged from this stream to come to my aid immediately. It's not true that New Yorkers are indifferent.

One night I was walking home from a party dressed to the nines. By ten o'clock Broadway is empty. But there are still people coming and going at all hours, which is reassuring. As I was walking up Broadway, a figure emerged from the shadow of the bank's entrance and came towards me. I saw him out of the corner of my eye. In less than a second he kicked me in the shins and said out loud, "Rich Bitch!" I regained my balance as soon as I could and redoubled my pace in the direction I was going. I did not look back at my assailant. Luckily, he did not follow me. In the annals of New York crimes, this was no big deal. I did not even have my purse snatched.

It dawned on me that I elicited this reaction because I was wearing a fur coat. I acquired the coat in my mid fifties. I had been brought up with the idea that a woman does not buy herself a fur; a man gives it to her as a gift. But no husband or lover ever gave me a fur, and it did not look like anyone ever would in the future. So in one ebullient moment, I bought myself a fur coat. Not something my grandmother would wear, but a sporty three-quarter-length mink. It was something called "sheared mink," and it was on the cheaper end of the scale. It was unbelievably soft to the touch and a mellow mahogany brown in color. But it was a mink.

Women rarely wore fur coats in my neighborhood. They are more popular in the posh parts of town, such as Madison Avenue. There, every other woman is in furs in the winter. In my neighborhood, they wear down jackets, and most of the time I did too. So, in fact, I did not wear my mink coat very much and felt conspicuous in it when I did. After this incident I wore it even less. It hung in my closet taking up space. When it came time to move and downsize, I gave it to the Salvation Army.

32

COLUMBIA APARTMENT BUILDING

New York rents are so high and faculty salaries are so low that Columbia University has been buying up the old buildings in its neighborhood for subsidized faculty housing. Some of these buildings date from around 1900, when the area was fashionable. There are stained glass doors and windows, and in my building a covered driveway entrance—a *porte cochère*—where the elite used to drive in protected from snow and rain. The house fronts Riverside Park, and from the higher floors one can see the Hudson River and beyond that New Jersey. The rooms are large with beautiful parquet floors. The ceilings are over ten feet high.

Some of the plumbing and heating is turn-of-the-century, too. The radiators hiss ominously and sometimes explode. I was luckily in the bedroom when my living-room radiator exploded, spewing greasy black steam in every direction. I grabbed my keys and rushed down to see the superintendent, Mr. Garcia. Out in the corridor, I listened to what sounded like a gushing oil well, while several men went in and shut it down. When I asked what I could have done, they just shook their heads and said, "Nothing, sometimes they just explode." Yes, there was a mess.

On my thirteenth floor, there lived a retired English professor and his musicologist wife, who were often up early playing tennis in the park. In regulation white tennis gear. There was an older lady from somewhere in the Balkans, who let out rooms to her compatriots and, according to some, exploited recent arrivals. A small apartment was a revolving door for middle-aged, single women, the last of whom was an Italian. She could be heard arguing vociferously on the telephone in our hallway. You could not hear what she said, but the intonation was Italian. Whatever it was, you could tell that she was very unhappy about something. The ambulance came once and took her away. The rumor was that she had tried to commit suicide. Eventually she was back, talking on the telephone. Not everyone on the floor was teaching at Columbia. One small apartment was inhabited from time to time by a couple who had been living there before Columbia bought the building and had the right to live there as long as they lived. The man was an artist. We said hello in the hall and in the elevator and commented on the weather but acquaintanceship did not go further.

There was a tenants committee, who decided on the color of the hallways (a sickly green) and other minor matters. It was run by Gladys, a lady who made herself in charge of the building, and even Mr. Garcia was afraid of her. It was rumored that her handsome European husband had said to her that she could remain his wife, but he wasn't going to sleep with her anymore. He had others. There was a graying Central European with a lame leg, who always greeted me warmly, making me think that he liked me, special—but never said another word. If I said something, he rushed out of the elevator like a speeding bullet. Once, when I said, "Good morning!" he said, "I have a girlfriend in Germany."

No Latin American dictator had more power than Mr. Garcia in the building. He terrified everybody. The doormen lived in the building more than in their real homes. Nick, the overweight Irishman on day duty, planted with flowers a barren island of dirt in front of the building. He paid for the plants himself, until Gladys got the tenants to chip in. It was Nick's garden, and he kept it looking nice. Alberto, the night doorman, was a dark Puerto Rican. Once he got arrested as a result of a burglary in the Columbia gym. He was not the burglar, but he either knew the burglar or was somehow associated with him. He went to jail. The building raised money for his wife and kids while he was in jail and petitioned Columbia to give him his old job back when he came out. Eventually he was back on the job.

My housemates included two ginger-colored cats I got as kittens from my sister. They were brothers. My son, then twelve, said he didn't want them to have silly cat names and named the gorgeous longhaired one Howard and the runty shorthaired one Robin. Did we call them that? Of course not. He started calling the longhaired one Fuzzy and the shorthaired one Skinny. Skinny had a skinny tail. Skinny seemed to need special attention. The first day I went to work after getting the cats, I was very nervous about all the doors and closets and made sure to close them tightly before I left. When I came home, I was greeted by Fuzzy but could not find the other cat. A faint meow came from the kitchen closet. This was the closet that had all the glasses and breakables. Sure enough, in my zeal to keep them out of trouble, I had locked Skinny in the closet. No harm came to him, but the closet was full of broken glass. It had to happen to Skinny.

The scariest event with Skinny was later in his life. He tended to be wild and jump around, and the pigeons outside the window drove him crazy. One warm summer day, we had the kitchen window open, just with the screen, to find that Skinny had jumped through the screen. He landed on the window ledge at the thirteenth floor, nothing protecting him from the street below. (That was probably a turn-of-the-century screen.) Luckily we managed to coax Skinny back into the kitchen, and he did not fall off. I will always think of that Columbia apartment with Skinny sitting on the ledge thirteen floors above the traffic.

33

THE TAO OF VOICE

Not being sports-minded, I got out of organized sports at the boarding school by selecting modern dance as a form of exercise. As far as I knew, Hungary did not have modern dance, only folk, ballroom, and ballet. Modern dance appealed to me in its freedom from stepping two to the right and two to the left, and being able to move sinuously up and down from the floor. I found the story of Martha Graham inspiring, especially her partnership with her husband, Eric Hawkins. That is how I hoped to live.

I continued to look for dance classes after I left school. When I became interested in non-Western art, I thought I'd take up some kind of non-Western dance. What I found available in New York was classical Hindu dance or Bharatanatyam. A small group of us met in a scruffy studio on 9th Avenue, a decidedly unfashionable part of New York, and danced with bells on our ankles that jingled with every step. In Hindu dance, your knees stay bent, you stomp with your feet, and your arms and hands make complicated designs in the air. I even got the hang of moving my neck from side to side. It was great fun, and we were practicing for performances in nursing homes. Unfortunately, my knees and feet began to hurt quite seriously, and the doctor suggested that I give up Hindu dancing.

When I moved to Riverside Drive, I did not find nearby dance classes. I thought I'd take up singing as a "sport." I got a list of singing teachers in my area from the music conservatory Juilliard and consulted several. My repertory was very small—mostly I knew Christmas carols and auditioned with "Silent Night." The teachers had me sit with them on the piano bench and sang along with me. They suggested that I could "put out more" with coaching.

On the list, Stephen Cheng lived closest to me in the next block. He was an Asian American of indeterminate age—fifty or maybe eighty. He had me sing standing up, raising my arm and pulling it slowly towards my belly. He told me that this was to "pull in the chi." Evidently the chi was some kind of vital spirit that moved around in the body. The second time he had me sing "Silent Night," I could tell that I was already "putting out more." He taped the session and told me to listen to it at home. I signed on with Stephen and had classes with a growing friendship, or as my limits became clear, friendship with classes. His method is elaborated in his book, *The Tao of Voice*, that has a lot to say about the chi.

He asked me what I wanted to sing, and I answered: Austro-Hungarian operetta. I grew up on the melodies of Lehár's *Merry Widow* and *The Land of Smiles*, and Kálmán's *Csárdás Princess*. I knew many of the lyrics—the men's as well as the women's songs—by heart. I had no one to share them with in America. When nostalgic, I sang them at home by myself. A light tenor, Stephen had recorded a number of operetta pieces and knew what I was talking about.

I used to think that I was an alto, but Stephen decided that I was a lyric soprano. I did not have an operatic voice, but I was good enough for the "living-room circuit." My specialty was the "Vilja Song" from *The Merry Widow*. In English it began, "Vilja, oh Vilja, my nymph of delight, haunting the woodlands, enchanting the night." It ended with, "Vilja, oh Vilja, I'll die for you," and then it went up, "I'll die foor YOOOOU," up to a high C, and on a good day I could do it—Stephen had his students do recitals at Carnegie Hall—well. Not THE Carnegie Hall, of course; some small Carnegie Hall auditorium in that building. I did "Vilja."

He had me sing all kinds of things from, "I Could Have Danced All Night" to Beethoven's "Alleluja." Once I performed with a chorus, again somewhere in the bowels of Carnegie Hall, with the Hebrew Chorus from Verdi's *Nabucco* and Beethoven's *Choral Fantasy*. I still get goose bumps when I hear the *Choral Fantasy*. Just once, I sang operetta arias to a party in my living room, and they were gracious enough to clap.

When I told my friend Edda, who was in Hungary, that I was taking singing lessons, she barked: "What for? What's the point of taking singing lessons when you will never be any good."

I was taken aback. "I am doing it for pleasure and to learn something."

"You are just wasting your time and your teacher's time," she said.

"It's just a hobby, a pastime; I know I won't be a professional," I demurred.

But she was adamant that it was a stupid thing to do. Evidently in Hungary, it is not customary to take classes to sing and play music unless one has serious potential or serious plans and is really good at it. Eventually, she smiled at me indulgently when I made her listen to my cassettes. She thought they were terrible. In the US we do such childish things.

I lost my voice after I had radiation treatment for breast cancer. It is not just that my weak but precious high C disappeared; often I managed to get only an uneven, croaking sound out. I even have trouble with "Silent Night." But what a pleasure it all was! I managed to combine my nostalgia for Hungary with my interest in exotic people. I got the pesky chi to work for me. Stephen taught me several Chinese songs in the process. To say nothing of Carnegie Hall . . .

I never learned much about Stephen Cheng, except for singing. He was secretive about his origins, his family, his history. Once when I had a cold, he recommended a Chinese cure—a soup with ginger and watercress. That's about as intimate as we became. After I stopped singing, I saw him frequently in the neighborhood or in a local Chinese restaurant, mixing hot-and-sour and egg-drop soup together. Better for the voice.

34

STALKER

When I was a teenager, I heard a thirtyish Hungarian refugee doctor brag to my parents, "I showed them how to take out tonsils!" and by "them" he meant the Harvard Medical School! I was amazed by such self-confidence. Recently, I was curious to find out what happened later to the arrogant Dr. Geza Jako. I looked him up on the web. Evidently, he did have something to show the Harvard Medical School, because that was the start of an illustrious career in medicine that led to a major White House award. He was referred to as "the father of laser surgery."

Arrogance, merited or not, is very Hungarian and also very European. Emese, a remote cousin, and her boyfriend Zsolt found me in New York in the 1990s. They had no intention of staying in America. They came to learn English and to make enough money to buy an apartment in Budapest. They were in their low twenties, fresh out of university. In no time at all, they judged America severely.

They sort of loved New York (who doesn't?), but they were disappointed by America. They said Americans were "dumb" and were kept dumb on purpose, so they would not criticize their country. The American educational system (including what I did), was utilitarian and vocationally oriented. Bad. There was no searching for ultimate truths. There was no profundity to it.

They asked if I had seen the movie, *Stalker.* I had never even heard of it. Evidently, that was an example of profundity. It was made in 1979 by a Russian filmmaker, Andrei Tarkovsky. They wanted to complete my education by showing it to me. It wasn't playing anywhere in the New York area. Emese and Zsolt took me to see *Stalker* the next time when I met them in Hungary. They said that in Budapest, *Stalker* is almost always playing in one or another movie theater. I was curious.

The title, *Stalker*, was a misunderstanding of the English word by Tarkovsky. To him it wasn't a stealthy pursuer, but a kind of a metaphysical guide. The film is a long and slow meditation on the human condition. It is a fable set in a science fiction terrain of industrial debris that looks like the result of an atomic blast. Within that is a guarded "zone" within which there is a mysterious "room" that grants wishes. But, as it turns out, it only grants subconscious wishes. Three persons search for the zone: a writer (artist), a professor (scientist) and their guide, the stalker. The stalker also searches. The film is a journey. The three characters discuss philosophical issues and interact according to their personalities. In the end, no wish is fulfilled.

Much of the film was confusing in a mystical, Russian way and gave rise to endless debates about its meaning. Europeans like this sort of thing more than Americans. The film reminded me of Thomas Mann's book *The Magic Mountain*, in which the philosophies of three men, a liberal Italian, a totalitarian Jesuit and a vitalist Dutchman vie for the intellectual and emotional allegiance of a young man close to death. That book had Germanic clarity. The philosophical fable is a European form of adult inquiry. It is rare but not unknown in American literature. Herman Melville's *Moby Dick* is also a philosophical saga, a sea voyage in search of a white whale with a vengeful Captain Ahab and his multiracial crew. The "white whale" is a mystery, perhaps God, perhaps Nature. The destruction of the ship is a parable. Whole academic industries try to figure it out. I was happy that I was introduced to my generation's "profound" movie, but there wasn't much I could do with it.

The Soviet authorities persecuted Tarkovsky for this film. They saw something spiritual, perhaps even Christian in it. Tarkovsky defected and made his last film in Sweden with the help of Ingmar Bergman, another mythic filmmaker.

The European critique, represented by Emese and Zsolt, of American education made me think about what we, in the Ivy League schools, assign to students to read. In higher education, we usually assign the latest book or article on a given subject, assuming that the latest is bound to be the best. Except in core courses, which are special, we don't necessarily assign the work of great, seminal, older thinkers—the equivalents of profundity. So I began to assign some selections from great thinkers such as Freud or Marx in my classes, even if they seemed only tangentially related to the subject at hand. Students were invariably grateful. They said that they often heard such names mentioned, as if they knew all about them, but have rarely had the chance to read and discuss them in class.

35

THE BOUGHT PAPER

After more than thirty years of teaching, I pride myself on being able to spot a bought paper. One can usually tell, because the bought paper is so good. Too good. I have had several instances where an undergraduate student who did poorly on the exams and was vague in oral answers turned in a well researched and clearly written paper, sometimes good enough to be published. The odd thing with such papers is that they show no signs of having been in my class—no ideas I have presented, no authors I have cited. They're just out of the blue. These bought papers are usually written by graduate students hard up for cash. I think they cost a couple of hundred dollars. They do an excellent job.

I would sit down with the suspected student and discuss the paper to determine whether it was bought. I would ask his or her opinion about the authors cited in the bibliography and ask them what the gist of the paper was. I would try and see whether they could talk intelligently about it. Since it was usually the weaker students who bought papers, sadly, they did not have enough sense to understand and to be able to talk about their "own" paper. I would then have to ask if they wrote the paper or whether someone else did. This was a serious offense, and after my initial encounter it went to the dean who dealt with it.

Recently, I had an undergraduate student in a seminar, who was doing adequate but not stellar work. Like a typical undergraduate, her ideas and reasoning were vague and awkwardly expressed. She worked hard, and I pegged her to be a B student. She wanted to write a paper on Maya astronomy, which seemed above her grasp but showed a romantic interest in the Maya. I prefer students to write on easier topics that I think they can handle, but seeing her commitment to the subject I told her to go ahead. I myself am not especially knowledgeable on Maya astronomy. But I see enthusiasm when it's there, and I encourage it.

The paper wasn't done on time, and she asked for an "incomplete." I thought, *Oh, oh.* She turned in the paper six weeks later. It was superb. In order to talk about Maya astronomy, the writer had to understand astronomy in general, and the discussion of the solstices, equinoxes, Venus and the Pleiades were clear and excellent. My first reaction was that it was a bought paper, and I would have to face her. So after a few preliminaries, I came right to the point.

"Did someone help you write this paper?"

"No, no, I wrote it myself," she insisted over and over again.

I tried quizzing her on the authors cited and the ideas, and though her answers were fuzzy, she clearly knew what she was talking about. I had to backtrack and say that I doubted her authorship because the paper was so good. And I would have to study it in greater detail. Was I wrong? Did she write the paper, and I accused her unjustly? If she wrote the paper, it would have to be an A or even an A+. I took the paper home with me and read it carefully. Here and there, I recognized an awkward phrasing that sounded like the student and eventually figured out how she got to the clear passages. There was no doubt; she had written the paper. It had taken her that six extra dogged weeks.

I had egg on my face. I had to apologize that I had thought that she had not written the paper. The paper was excellent and deserved an A+. I fumbled my apologies, which she accepted with no fuss at all. She asked me whether I would help her turn it into a senior thesis the following year, and I did. She taught me a lesson, but I was just as glad when she graduated.

36

RAKOCZI BOULEVARD

Francis II Rákóczi was a Transylvanian nobleman who led an unsuccessful Hungarian rebellion against Austria in the early 1700s.

In 1989 the Soviet empire collapsed. The Berlin Wall and the Iron Curtain were dismantled. The Red Army withdrew from Hungary. The new democratic government in Hungary gave citizenship to all the five million Hungarians living outside Hungary. I became a dual citizen, which entitled me to purchase property in Hungary. I revisited Otto Herman St. in the suburban district of Budapest, where I used to live as a child. At first, I was full of nostalgia. In time, however, I became more interested in the new Hungary happening right then and there than in the Hungary of my childhood. People I knew, including my ex-husband, were buying apartments and houses, inexpensive for Americans. At least part-time, they were going back. A part of me was yearning to go back, too.

I went to meet the current scholars at the university who were interested in ancient America. They were all anthropologists, because in Hungary art historians only study Western art. As it happens, they were also all men. They were very enthusiastic about me and asked if I wanted to come and teach there for a semester. There was a great desire for Eastern Europeans to mix with the West. I said that I would love to come. So they told me that the way to do it was to apply for a Fulbright teaching fellowship, and when I got it, they would arrange things at their end. We agreed for the following January.

I was very excited. To think that I would go back to my homeland and teach there! In Hungarian, no less! That was actually a daunting prospect. Although I spoke fluent Hungarian, I did not really have the language skills for the level of university teaching. But I would try. It would be a great experience.

Where would I stay? My childhood friend Edda explained that Budapest had hardly any rental apartments; everybody owns. I knew that you could buy an apartment quite cheaply. My dual citizenship allowed it. I wanted it. Edda and I went to look at apartments for sale. To make a long story short, I ended up buying the first apartment I saw. As the old hotel joke says, it had the three necessary things: location, location, location. It was a few blocks from downtown on a busy boulevard. It was near stores, theatres and restaurants. As a single person, I did not want to be stuck in the suburbs. The apartment was a small studio with a large eat-in kitchen. Its major flaw was that it was dark. Even when it was sunny outside it, was dark. On the other hand, I wasn't going to live there permanently.

As I talked to the owners, they mentioned that they planned to move to New Zealand. In that case, I asked, could I buy their furniture too? Sure, why not. Could I buy the dishes, pots and pans, and silverware? Sure, why not. Wastebaskets? Everything as is? Yes, everything, as is. I decided that the convenience of a fully furnished home outweighed the lack of light. I wouldn't be there full-time. But I could come in January and move right in. Edda could buy me some pretty sheets and towels.

Back in New York I filled out the Fulbright application. I got a semester's leave from Columbia. I told everyone that I had an apartment in Budapest, and I was going to teach there. In due course, I got the Fulbright grant.

And then the incredible happened. I called the Anthropology Department in Budapest to let them know that I got the Fulbright. The person at the other end of the line hemmed and hawed. Someone else came on the line. There was some difficulty. Their committee had turned me down. The reason was unclear. I asked to speak to someone else. This person was nice and blamed it on the committee but still had no reasons. I was unable ever to find a reason.

I had to turn the Fulbright down. I agonized over possible reasons for this change. Perhaps I was not famous enough. Hungarians are after big fish like Claude Lévi-Strauss or Marshall McLuhan. I wasn't big enough. Maybe they wanted a "real" American and not a "half-Hungarian." Maybe they disliked art historians and art. Maybe they didn't like women. But most likely, they substituted someone who was someone's friend or someone they expected favors of. The summer before, I had been much in demand to correct the English grammar of their foreign grant applications, but it was evident that I didn't have the power to get them the foreign grants. There was also the possibility that I was too good and threatened someone's prestige and position. As a "half"-Hungarian, I could take someone's prestige and position in the country. There were plenty of reasons to choose from.

Eventually, I recovered from the shock and disbelief. I decided to go to Hungary, anyway. I was too embarrassed to tell people that I was rejected by my homeland. I didn't need to teach anywhere; I could have a free semester. My new apartment awaited me with pretty sheets bought by Edda.

37

FLOURISHING

The communists did not have the money to build tall, modern buildings in central Budapest, hence the city still has a late-nineteenth-century look and feel. It could almost be a stage set. On one side of the Danube, there is a big Neogothic pile that is the Parliament Building; on the other side a medieval to Hapsburg layer cake that is the Castle. Hugging Castle Hill is a turreted fairy-tale fantasy called Fisherman's Bastion. Except that now, once-elegant shopping streets have vendors selling souvenirs to scruffy tourists with backpacks. The seven bridges connecting Buda and Pest remain scenic time after time. The food is good, and you can drink the water. The water bubbles up from hot and cold springs, and you can swim in it, too, at many local pools. There are very few signs left of the 1944 carpet bombing. Budapest is a delightful city.

Having grown up in Buda, I did not know Pest. I started out by exploring my new neighborhood on Rákóczi Boulevard. I explored the shoddy goods in the department store to my left and the more expensive German boutiques on my right. Mid-calf-length dresses were in that year. I explored the secondhand bookstores and print shops. I bought and had framed prints for my apartment; old Hungarian kings and nineteenth-century peasants in folk costume.

I put on one of my new dresses and went to the opera. It was an especially fulfilling experience to be able to see an opera by a Hungarian composer, sung by Hungarian singers in Hungarian, in an audience of Hungarians. Some of the operas were unknown outside

Hungary; some were world famous. Béla Bartók's *Bluebeard's Castle* was a high point. It is a mysterious story of a duke who brings home a new wife, and she wants to know what is behind the doors of his castle. The duke keeps telling her she doesn't want to know and tries to stall her, because those are the remains of his former wives. She insists, of course. "Give me the keys!" she says over and over. The mournful base of the duke and the shrill soprano of his bride are both moving; the listener does not know with whom to sympathize. There is no agreement as to what it means, since 1918 when it was written. The story is based on a French folktale, one of those grim ones. The music is modern: my parent's generation could not listen to it. My generation has found eerie melody in it.

I was especially interested in Bartók because in his later years he lived in New York and worked at Columbia University. He was transcribing Eastern European folk songs in what was to be called ethno-musicology. Although he was well known among musicians, he was not famous. A few donors helped him out of poverty. He died a few years before I came to New York.

My Hungarian language skills, which I had nurtured over the decades, turned out to be inadequate. My intonation, my choice of words, my lack of current slang immediately pegged me as non-local. As soon as I opened my mouth, people knew I was foreign. Going to the hairdresser was always ticklish. "Where is the lady from?" they always asked, using the formal form of address. If I said, "The US," they immediately thought that I must be a millionaire. In New York gold pieces lie on the ground; you just have to bend down and pick them up—right? No amount of tip was ever enough.

Sometimes I said I was from Canada. No reaction. If I went more than once to the same shop, I was asked if I had a job in Hungary. That question meant, "Did I take a job away from a Hungarian?" I can't say that I was welcomed home by ordinary people. The general attitude was: Come, visit and enjoy Hungary. Come spend lots of money. Then, go home. Once, you left—you traitor, coward, opportunist, etc. Now stay away. We can manage without you!

I enjoyed Hungary, despite some of the Hungarians.

38

THINKING WITH THINGS

Returning to Hungary and living there in my own home for six months was a great sense of fulfillment, after the rupture of having to leave the country as a child in 1956. People asked me whether I'd retire there, and I said I didn't know, but probably not. I was not returning for good. Still, I felt that I had done something momentous in going back temporarily. Something was healed.

When I came back to my apartment in New York after that trip, I was quite disturbed by how it looked. My apartment looked ugly and all wrong to me. I hated it. However, I was exhausted, I dropped my luggage and went to bed. Next morning, I woke up at dawn and before unpacking, dressing or breakfasting, I began to put the place to rights. Tired and jetlagged, this seemed important. I moved armchairs and rugs, pictures and textiles off the walls, not knowing what I was doing exactly. I climbed step ladders and carried heavy frames from one room to the other, sort of on an automatic unconscious. A couple of hours later, I realized that I had moved almost everything and could now have breakfast and unpack.

At that point I looked around to see what I had done and tried to make sense of it. The apartment had been organized originally in sets on the basis of similarity—similar chairs together, similar textiles or paintings together in separate categories and spaces. It made for a very peaceful look. There was nothing wrong with it; it wasn't really ugly. It just didn't seem right anymore.

What I had done that morning was to create a more dynamic order of dissimilar things. I found a way to integrate my things—chairs, textiles, and paintings. Things were in new relationship to each other based more on subtler features than complete similarity. It seemed to reflect my inner self better; it was more multifaceted: I picked up colors here, shapes there, in otherwise dissimilar things. Apparently, by going to Hungary and picking up the pieces of my childhood, I broke down the barriers between various parts of my life. From someone who was separately Hungarian, American, and pre-Columbian in bits and pieces, I cobbled a more integrated whole. Hungarian, American, and pre-Columbian elements found harmonious echoes in one another and in the art on my walls. The apartment seemed "wrong" when I'd reentered it after a long absence, because it did not match my new sense of self. This new jazzy apartment did. Perhaps not coincidentally, I began to write fictional stories with greater seriousness, besides scholarly studies.

Organizing one thing led to organizing others. I was doing the sweaters—getting rid of some to give away, keeping others—I discovered that I seemed to favor wine color and softness of texture. I chuckled to myself, "Here you go again, thinking with things." And that phrase stuck with me. While in Hungary, I had been writing a book on the nature of art and things in general. I argued that art and things are not just to be looked at as "beautiful" but something to think with. In fact, I had been unconsciously thinking with objects before I realized what I was thinking consciously. I concluded that things are important to the workings of the mind.

I entitled the book, *Thinking with Things.*

39

FICTION

I always wanted to write a historical novel that took place in pre-Columbian times. I had been writing stories from time to time since I was ten. Now that I had a free semester in Budapest, it gave me the time and leisure to try fiction again. I'd curl up on the bed with my laptop in the evenings. I knew I would call it *Daughter of the Pyramids*, and it would start with a young girl, fourteen or so, as I was when I entered the US. I thought of the "pyramids" in the title as the overwhelming figures of my mother and father. Of course, the heroine would come from Teotihuacán, and I would try to imagine what that was really like. It was to be a romance, and she would be searching for true love. A conventional pre-Columbian girl would have married young, had babies, and stayed put. I wanted my heroine to move from city to city and have adventures. So I made her a "dancing girl," sort of a courtesan, attached to different powerful men. The goal of her journey was to go to the Maya city of Tikal as a "gift" to the ruler. (Silly stuff and an impossible undertaking, given the five-hundred-mile distance, but then this was a novel.) I named her Marigold after the flower. The plot was vague.

I had finished about a third of the novel in Hungary when I went back to New York. I was busy teaching, writing scholarly books and articles, and planning a major symposium for the year 2000, entitled all too cleverly and enigmatically, West by Nonwest. There was no time for *Daughter.*

In July of 2000, I married Richard. In November 2000, I was

diagnosed with breast cancer. That was followed by lumpectomy, chemotherapy, and radiation. Just like everyone else who goes through that treatment, my hair fell out, I was nauseous and exhausted. And, of course, I faced mortality. I was fifty-seven years old. If this was not it, the cancer could recur. A node was removed from my armpit, and I was told not to lift anything heavier than a gallon of milk with that hand, for fear the hand would swell up. I was not to have manicures. I was to take a drug for five years, whose possible side effects were heart attacks and strokes. Everything the doctors discussed was lethal.

However, I slowly recovered. Richard and I spent the following summer in Deer Isle, Maine. I reexamined my life and decided that my foremost ambition was to finish *Daughter*. I did not want to die without having written a novel. I reread the portion I had written in Hungary and didn't much like it. It's harder to write a historical novel than a scholarly book. You have to know or create all kinds of trivia for which there is no information. How did people travel in those days? Archaeologists know from the distribution of artifacts that they did. But, where did they eat? Where did they sleep? What was in the mind of a young girl? I had to make it all up.

I also made up imaginary Indian names. Bloody Jaguar, Serpent Shield, Coyote Power. The minor characters got names too, like Strong Cactus and Bubbly Spring. After a while, I myself could not keep track of the names. As a beginning writer, I gave everybody names, and the names clotted up the story. Readers have found the names a stumbling block. A greater problem was that the story meandered, since I did not know where it was going. On the other hand, these beginning chapters were not all that bad in my estimation, and I decided to keep them as is and move on. I would finish from where I had left off.

I had the bright idea of introducing a modern character, an archaeology graduate student named Naomi, who is ostensibly writing the first part of the novel. Through some hocus-pocus she falls into her own novel and becomes her heroine, Marigold. Her mind, of course, is that of a modern graduate student, and I had no trouble dealing with that. The big bonus of introducing Naomi was that I now had a plot. Of course Marigold was still on her way to Tikal, but Naomi, trapped in the pre-Columbian world, was desperately looking for a way back out to the real world, her home in Morristown, New Jersey. Eventually, she finds the way to Tikal; she finds the way to Morristown, too, and the question is: which world has a man for her, and which world does she choose to live in?

This second part of the novel went zap, zap, zap. No meandering. I wrote it in no time. I wanted to get it done and I did. I didn't fully realize it, but through these changes it became a science fiction or fantasy novel, not a romance, which I continued to call it. I did not think anyone would publish it and published it myself. No publicity, no press, no success. A handful of people read it, and some really liked it. They urged me to write a sequel. Some thought it was too difficult. Some thought there wasn't enough steamy sex in it. Some thought it was disgustingly pornographic.

I did write a sequel to *Daughter*, a few years ago, entitled *The Maya Vase.* In it Naomi leaves the pre-Columbian world to investigate a murder in Morristown. It takes place mostly in the US, although it goes back and forth. It's is a whodunit. An illegally looted Maya vase is involved. This too is science fiction, and the few readers who I hesitantly asked to read it thought it was a lot of fun and much better than *Daughter.* One of the things I tried to do in other fiction writing, as with the stories in *Conversations with Quetzalcoatl*, was to find some way of combining nonfiction and creative writing. Still working on it.

I don't know how it happened, but in the process of writing fiction, I got to like the English language. I had to learn in my teens. It was necessary to learn it, and I didn't think twice about it. If I really thought about it, I used to think that it was really ugly. Words like "throughout," for example, or "thought," were hideous—how lovely the French *pensée* or the Hungarian *gondolat* are for the throaty "thought." But the fact is, that now my French and Hungarian are rusted beyond repair, I couldn't write much in them. I still think English is ugly, but now it doesn't matter anymore. It is now my language, and I swim, play and splash in its generous medium. It is now something rich, fluid and joyful. I relish the zillion ways I have to say things in it. I can't wait to see how thoughts come out in words.

40

OWL CASTLE

There were once four Miskolczy brothers. The youngest was born in 1900. They came from Baja, a medium-size town in southern Hungary on the banks of the Danube River.

One died young in the First World War.

The eldest, Dezso, became a successful doctor, neurologist, with a reputation throughout Eastern Europe. He lived mostly in Transylvania, in Romania.

The youngest, my father Laszlo, became a successful architect. He lived in Budapest.

The next to the youngest, my Uncle Feri (nickname for Ferenc or Francis) did not do so well in the estimation of my family. He was an artist.

Uncle Feri went to the West (Paris and Munich) to study in art academies. He had fellowships as well as extra funds provided by his successful brothers. He came in contact with Cubism, Abstraction, Surrealism, and whatever "ism" was around. For exotic local color, the brothers suggested he go to Spain, where Dezso had studied medicine. Despite all that, he never became a great international artist. Not only is he not known outside Hungary, he is not even known inside Hungary. He is known only in his birthplace, Baja.

After his travels, Uncle Feri settled in Baja. He specialized in small watercolor views of the Danube. *The Danube at Sunset. The Danube with Bathers. The Danube with Fishing Boats.* Local people liked them and bought them. In order to fit in under communism, he called his style

Social Realism. The city Museum/Historical Society collected them. He became a well-known local artist.

As it became obvious that Feri would stay in Baja, the brothers claim that they helped him to buy a striking, modern, Bauhaus-style house overlooking the Danube in the 1930s. The two-story flat-roofed house had a terrace or two and a dramatic turret on top. Next to the one-story, tiled or even thatched houses of the rest of the street, it looked like a castle. At one time, owls nested in the turret, so it acquired the name, Owl Castle (Bagoly Vár). Feri looked after the old folks and the family graves in the cemetery, much to everyone's convenience. In the summer, we children were sent to Baja for country holidays, and Feri took care of us and acquainted us with our ancestors.

Uncle Feri may not have been a great artist, but he was great at befriending the people who ran the town of Baja. He received church and town commissions. As he became older, he was venerated as a great man and received an Honorary Citizen of Baja Award. In turn, Uncle Feri, who had no children, left his house, Owl Castle, with all his remaining artwork, to the town of Baja, with the stipulation that after his death they turn it into a memorial museum for him.

And that is exactly how it turned out. Uncle Feri died at the age of ninety. The Owl Castle Museum opened its doors in 2014. An impressive webpage lists all of Feri's works and accomplishments for all to see. In the end, he did the best of all.

The neurologist brother, Dezso, is recognized in medical schools and books in Romania and Hungary.

My architect father has left the least behind. His major architectural work of the 1930s, a luxury hotel in the northern mountains of Hungary (Kékes), was featured in German architectural magazines of the time. It was in the then-modern Bauhaus style. It has now been turned into a sanatorium and is deplorably dilapidated. Under the communist regime, when he was the head of City Planning, he received the Kossuth Prize. The Kossuth Prize was the highest honor that the state could give. (I think it was for something like reinforced concrete prefabricated housing construction.) In the US he worked in a large architectural office and not on his own and had no major commissions.

To be sure, he had some bad luck, but his lack of a legacy was also his choice. He didn't even leave a list of his buildings behind, anywhere. His curriculum vitae made in America merely lists that he designed the following, mostly in the 1930s: three apartment houses, ten "villas," one hotel, and two factories. (Which is not a bad accomplishment for someone under forty-two.) He didn't mention any names or addresses for any of these. He must have figured that in America those details did not matter. Those details are not known in Hungary, either. He is all but forgotten. Maybe some Hungarian researcher will find these in the future.

The moral of the story is, it sometimes helps to stay in your birthplace.

41

THINGS

We left Budapest to escape from Hungary while the revolution was beaten down but still active. Gunshots could be heard near us. When we left home that day in November 1956, we left everything as it was. My sister and I did not know if we would ever return. My parents knew and assumed that it would all be gone, let it go and did not cry over it. They never expected to see it again. Our lives were more important than our things.

Forty years later in the 1990s, my sister found out that a great deal of our furnishings were saved by Uncle Feri. When he heard that we had left Hungary, my uncle hired a truck and took some of our possessions to his home in the town of Baja. Rugs, furniture, china, etc. My sister made a list of what there was and claimed a right to it. When my uncle died in the 1990s, I was in my apartment in Budapest. His widow let me know that I could now take my things back. I hired a truck and brought everything to my Rákóczi Boulevard apartment. I put one of the folk-art-inspired rugs on the floor, the Biedermeier round table and the armchairs on top of it. They looked great. What luck.

The most unusual piece of furniture was a so-called drop-back table, put together like a puzzle without nails. (I recently saw a smaller version of it at a friend's house. He told me that "drop-back" was its name.) My table top consists of a very large, old and heavy piece of wood, whose weight holds it in place. When removed, two foot-wide uprights on the sides are held in place by a horizontal bar. When that is removed, all the pieces of the table come apart. It can be put together in the reverse order. This kind of table, made for traveling, was evidently made in Europe in the sixteenth and seventeenth centuries. One can see it in old paintings.

The table may have been wholly or partly that old and perhaps valuable. My father used it as a desk. The top wood was gnarled, showing perhaps centuries of use, and gorgeous. Big as it was, it fitted the space under my window in the Rákóczi Boulevard apartment. I used it as a desk, but there was also room for the TV and phone on it. The room had high ceilings and did not look overcrowded. (The old furniture that was in it originally I gave away.)

My mother's ornate Venetian mirror went above the bureau, and cute little night stands found their places near the bed. The transformation of the room was wonderful. In a small way, I had recreated my childhood home. I had not planned on this, but circumstances made it possible, and I made it happen. The elderly lady down the corridor had an upholsterer son, who recovered the somewhat wobbly Biedermeier armchairs. I had the rug cleaned. I was at home.

I enjoyed the Rákóczi Boulevard apartment for about half a dozen years in the summers, away from New York. In the end, life moved on and I gave it up. (A second cousin now has it.) Edda, my caretaker, had health issues. I got remarried in the US. There were other priorities. It was time to ship the family things to the US. It's not that they were so valuable, but they reconnected symbolically our lives in Hungary and the US, making it whole. They helped cover over the rupture.

When the things arrived in the US, my sister and I quarreled over the spoils. We both wanted my father's table. Technically, the things were half hers and half mine. I argued that if I hadn't gone to Hungary and got them and shipped them to the US, there would have been nothing to divide up. Therefore, I wanted first choice. I got the table. The rest we divided, but I got more because some things she didn't want. It was bad between us. She didn't talk to me for years afterwards. I loved living with my share of my family's things. I got to live with them for about a decade. At first it was very awesome; later on, I took them for granted. That was the best.

In 2013 I was retiring and moving to Maine. The table was too big for the Maine house. I offered it to my sister. She didn't want it. She said I should give it to her son. So I did. In a little while, two strong guys came, and I watched for the last time as they took off the heavy top of the puzzle table. It went to Massachusetts. Some of the wobbly armchairs wobbled into oblivion. I still have the folk-art rugs, but I don't know what I will do with them. The family doesn't want them. They will never mean anything to anybody else. It remains to be seen whether I can find a meaningful home for them. Beyond that, I can't control where the things go in the future.

Such is the way of things.

42

COLD WAR

As I planned to retire in 2013, I spent the previous couple of years getting rid of many accumulated things in my New York apartment. I gave my professional library to the Abbe Museum in Bar Harbor, my Mexican research materials to the Metropolitan Museum, my textile collection to the Brooklyn Museum, and my papers to the Newberry Library. I had a lot of Hungarian books, many inherited from my father, and I was giving them to a Hungarian Society in San Francisco. I had to cull the English language books from among them. One of them was a book I remembered that my father very much liked. It was entitled, *The Passover Plot.* I was curious as to what it was and decided to look at it.

It was clear from the cover blurbs that it had to do with a plot to fake Jesus's resurrection by giving him a narcotic that would make it seem that he had died and then seeming to bring him back to life. In other words, Jesus did not die on the cross, and his resurrection was faked. My father was born a Catholic, but later in life he had doubts about the death-and-resurrection story. I opened the book, and a small brown packet fell out of the flyleaf. In red letters it said, "TOP SECRET." It was about twice the size of a passport.

I was awestruck. On the front it said, "For the immediate attention of," and listed five people, including the foreign secretary and the director general of MI5. It was printed in England. MI5 were spies; what did my father have to do with spies? Inside it there were ten documents, mostly letters reduced to packet size. Some were from the

White House, some from the Pentagon and the CIA. After I read and reread the documents a dozen times, I came to the conclusion that the material was genuine and not some kind of game or hoax.

Everything was dated 1967. The issue was that China would not join a mutual nuclear deterrence treaty, because the Chinese believed that they could survive an atomic war. Because China was then rural and had few large cities, fallout would be spread over less densely inhabited areas. The Chinese calculated this on the basis of fallout numbers published by the US for atomic explosions over the Bikini Islands and New Mexico, as publicized by the US Government.

These numbers, however, were much lower than reality, because the US did not want the world to know how destructive the bombs really were and wanted to continue testing.

The task of the booklet was for the US and the UK to come up with a plan to let the Chinese know how bad the fallout figures really were and scare them into compliance. The trouble was, relations with China were very bad at the time, and China would not believe anything the US said. Some indirect way had to be found for the information to be leaked to the Chinese without apparent US involvement. The booklet only says that this transfer of information would take place in Paris. It does not say by whom or how. The Chinese are to be given scientifically correct information, as well as pictures of the atomic bombers in their readiness, information on anti-contamination suits, as well as data from Hiroshima. Sort of a combination of sharing information and threat. Most striking in the booklet, is a map of China showing the hypothetical US bombing targets and the fallout areas in red.

What did my father have to do with all this? His name is not mentioned anywhere. Why did he have the packet, and why was it in the *Passover Plot* book? The only explanation I have come up with is that perhaps he was the courier who took the sensitive documents to Paris. Suppose the US decided to plant the documents in a communist Eastern European country; the Chinese might accept them from there. My father knew and had worked with a number of communist leaders in Hungary and could have contacts. (The US authorities would have known all this from vetting him in Austria in 1956.) He was not a known spy who would have been mistrusted by any foreign country. He was a distinguished Hungarian architect. He could have carried the documents quite innocently and have handed them over in a café in Paris. He spoke excellent French. He had been to Paris before.

I don't have a shred of evidence for this, except for the fact that my parents went to Paris around that time. Between 1956 when they arrived in the US and 1974 when my father died, my parents only went on that one trip abroad, to Paris. They didn't have the money to travel. Who paid for this two-week tourist trip? The only thing I remember my father saying is: "I'll show your mother Paris."

If this reconstruction is true, then it changes my assessment of my father's years in the US. So far it seemed to be an anticlimax—he was working as an employee in a big architectural firm, not designing anything of his own. His private commissions consisted of remodeling restaurant kitchens after health violations. Pretty petty stuff. At best, he made a very modest living. But if at one point, late in life, he was tapped on the shoulder by America's high-ups to perform a delicate mission, that would have made up for a lot. My father was smart and had nerves of steel. He was or would have been a good choice for this. My father would have known how to keep a secret in his lifetime. Perhaps he put the Top Secret information booklet in the *Passover Plot* book, and it could have just been forgotten when he became ill with Parkinson's.

For me the booklet is a personal view into the Cold War.

43

THE RUSSIAN MOVE

Moving from New York to Maine was an overwhelming undertaking. I wrote this account of it to the amusement of the Deer Isle Writer's Group.

Me, hesitant: "Of course the big tables don't go. I am still trying to sell them."

Wassily: "You mean the refectory table? Don't worry, I'll buy it. Consider it sold."

Me: "It's sixteenth or seventeenth century."

Wassily: "Consider it sold."

Me, bolder: "My nephew may want it. I'll let you know. But there is the Victorian dining table with two extra leaves that seats twelve."

Wassily: "Consider it sold. My men will pick it up tomorrow."

Me: "It's a hundred dollars." The table is worth a thousand.

Wassily: "Consider it sold. I don't see any problem with the move, no pianos, no crystal statues. We pack it up Thursday and Friday and move it as soon as you want."

I make arrangements to be driven from New York to Maine for the following Saturday, after the packing Thursday and Friday, and have the furniture delivery for Sunday. Everything has to work just right for a smooth move. It's been worked out perfectly.

Wassily made the lowest bid and seems reasonable. Other movers made painstaking lists of what goes and what stays, but with a grand gesture Wassily says, "Everything goes, we won't count the boxes." I pay the deposit.

We are madly organizing closets, books, kitchenware; there is a lot more to do in a household that has been lived in for thirty years.

The Sunday before the packing, Wassily calls: "My men are coming to pack on Monday."

Me, confused: "I thought you were coming on Thursday; we're not ready."

Wassily: "We're coming on Monday to check out the place."

Monday Igor, a big mountain of flesh, comes with two little Latinos, and they attack the pile of books and stuff on the floor. Igor does most of the work and orders the little Latinos around to make boxes. Zip, zip is the constant sound of pulling tape. I see that they're seriously packing, not just checking out the place. What is going on? Igor brings forms to fill out and says that they want to be paid in cash on arrival in Maine. Over three thousand dollars. I say that's impossible and stick to it.

Wassily calls Monday night: "My men will be there on Tuesday."

Me, plaintively: "We agreed you'd be there on Thursday and Friday."

Wassily: "It has to be Tuesday. Too much stuff."

Me, unhappy: "Well, if it has to be, it has to be."

My husband: "You are such a ninny; you should have said a definite no to Tuesday. They must abide by their agreement. You must call back. I don't want them on Tuesday."

I don't call back, let it happen as it will happen.

Next morning all is quiet.

My husband: "Don't worry, they won't come. I called their number on the form at midnight and left a message on their answering machine that there was a family emergency, and we were called out of the city and they must not come. We're not here."

I can't believe my ears: In a couple of hours the doorbell starts ringing insistently.

My husband: "Pretend we're not here. Don't answer the door."

The doorbell goes on ringing periodically. I cover my ears.

My husband: "Don't worry; in a little while they'll go away. They will see my message. We're in the clear."

There is a period of silence. Maybe they gave up.

Then the phone begins to ring at the same time as the doorbell.

My Husband: "Don't pick up the phone! Remember we're not here. It's probably Wassily."

Then the phone rings and the doorbell rings at the same time with rapidity and intensity.

My husband: "Don't worry—they'll go away soon."

I moan in pain and embarrassment. It's clear that they know, sense, that we are there and never got or believed the message he sent at midnight.

We can now hear the movers talking and ringing with great intensity. They want to get in and pack desperately! We shouldn't fool around with these Russians; maybe they are a mafia and will break my husband's leg if we get them really angry.

Then there is quiet in the corridor at last, and I begin to calm down.

In twenty minutes there are voices and renewed bell ringing. I hear the super and the doorman's voice; they call out our names, but we remain silent.

Then the voices come from INSIDE the apartment, and there is a knock on the door of the room we are hiding in.

Super: "Are you all right?"

Me, totally flushed: "We are fine."

My husband: "There was a family emergency . . . I left a message . . ."

Me: "We are fine . . ."

The Super: "We thought something happened to you because the movers insisted that you were there but not responding. We had to cut the chain off the door to get in. We might have called the police and the ambulance—"

Boris: "Can we pack now?"

My husband and me : "No, absolutely not."

Phew.

Wassily on the phone: "Can they come tomorrow? Wednesday?"

Me, exhausted: "Yes."

With the help of a normal-size black man, Igor packed us all up on Wednesday and Friday in a whirl of intense activity, as agreed. They never came on Thursday as originally said.

Boris drove the truck delivering the stuff to Maine, as agreed, without any problems. Neither he nor we mentioned the incident on Tuesday. But I never got the $100 for the table.

44

LOBSTER PLACE

I was having a power lunch in an upscale New York restaurant with a donor and the chairman of my department. In a casual moment, the donor asked me where I was planning to retire to.

I said, "Deer Isle in Maine."

He had never heard of it. Then a woman at the next table piped up: "Deer Isle! I have a house on Deer Isle. On the Dow Road."

A lot of people have not heard of Deer Isle, but it is amazing how many have. You meet them everywhere at cocktail parties, conferences, concerts. Skip, who lives in Santa Barbara, California, had sailed those waters. He said, "You lucky dog. I envy you." Deer Isle comes with a reputation.

I heard a lot about the natural beauties and interesting summer, (and increasingly winter) inhabitants of Deer Isle and Maine from Richard. On license plates Maine is billed as "vacationland." The first time I came to visit was in August; I alighted from the plane wearing a flowing long skirt, a wide-brimmed straw hat, and sunglasses. People stared at me in wonder. They were all wearing tough and camping gear. Something was lost in translation; I had no idea what Deer Isle was like. I was looking forward to getting to know some corner of America outside of New York. I had no preference where. Life provided Maine, and I was willing to explore it.

Deer Isle is not near anything; you don't go by it; you have to want to go there. You fly to Bangor, and it is almost two hours from there. It is twenty minutes from the nearest small town, Blue Hill, and an hour from shopping and malls in Ellsworth. A beautiful, slender bridge connects it to the mainland. After the bridge opened in 1939, most island stores closed because people preferred to shop on the mainland. The bridge is fragile and, it seems, only the yearly repainting layer keeps it up. Some people won't cross it. The population of Deer Isle is only about two thousand in winter and swells to over four thousand in summer.

When I first arrived, I rented a house in Stonington, a village at the southern tip of the island. It is a picturesque fishing village on the side of a hill overlooking the harbor. Stonington is so lovely it is featured in most Maine calendars. Although there are some yachts in the harbor, and often a big schooner stops by, most of the boats are lobster fishermen's diesel boats. Stonington is still a working fisherman's harbor, and that is its charm. That can't be said about the village—most houses have been bought and lovingly restored by summer residents and are vacant in winter. There are hardly any businesses, only one restaurant is open year round.

Some of the islands in front of Stonington have had granite quarries since the nineteenth century. Deer Isle granite has been highly valued and built into many Washington monuments on the Mall, like the Lincoln Memorial. At one time, Stonington bustled with quarry workers. There is still a little bit of granite quarrying left, but Stonington granite is too expensive for ordinary house builders. Carpenters recommend similar-looking Chinese substitutes.

Deer Isle has no center. Not too far from Stonington, there is a supermarket/variety store/pharmacy/gas station all by itself. About the middle of the island are the remnants of the once-flourishing Deer Isle village, now consisting of a library, a few art galleries, a novelty shop, and a seasonal hamburger-ice-cream stop. A post office. For some unknown reason, Deer Isle has four post offices.

Richard's parents owned a restaurant called Eaton's Lobster Pool on Little Deer Isle, at the north end of the Island, near the bridge and one of the post offices. It, too, was open only in the summer. It was in a very beautiful setting. Hidden away by circuitous routes if going by car, it was also approachable by boat, and one could moor in front. A functional modern building with big windows, the restaurant was cantilevered over a cove and looked over the water at romantic little islands.

The fare at the Lobster Pool was superb seafood: local scallops, tiny local shrimp, clams, and of course local lobster. There were various complaints about the instant mashed potatoes and the iceberg lettuce salads that didn't seem to bother anybody. The Eatons were teetotalers and did not serve alcohol. They allowed people to bring their own bottles. The area had been strictly religious once, their local church, the Reorganized Church of Latter Day Saints, was of Mormon derivation and strict. For some time, the Eatons were shunned for operating their restaurant on Sundays.

Deer Isle is all about lobster. The fishermen fish lobster. The fanciest food of restaurants is lobster. People eat lobster when their pocketbook allows it, though it is much more affordable in Maine. The Eatons sometimes had lobster at Christmas or Thanksgiving. Sweet and chewy, I like the big claws the best. I don't know exactly how lobster became such a delicacy. As late as the 1930s, lobster was considered trash and used as fertilizer in the fields. In those days, fishermen fished fish: herring and haddock, cod. Now those fish have been largely fished out and the emphasis is on lobster. (Haddock in the local stores comes from Massachusetts.) Huge quantities of lobster fished here, filling big rigs that hog the local roads, are not for local consumption but for export, especially to China.

For our wedding, the Eatons gave the party a lobster dinner in the Lobster Pool. I met Richard at Columbia on the recommendation of a mutual friend of my sister's. By chance, both my sister and Richard's live in Bethlehem, Pennsylvania. We got married outside, at a lovely spot, on a point of land, a peninsula, overlooking the water and a little island covered with fir trees. A string quartet from a summer music program at Blue Hill, Kneizel Hall, played. It was a windy day, and later that night the wind tore the wedding tent to shreds. All about nature, it was a very American wedding.

According to Richard, a lot of famous people ate at the restaurant over the years. Among them, TV anchor Walter Cronkite, the presidential candidate Governor Ed Muskie, the actors Jason Robards and Ellen Burstyn, the writers Mary McCarthy and Elisabeth Hardwick, the golfer Arnold Palmer, not to mention the whole cast of the TV show *General Hospital.* Waitresses sometimes dropped full trays while staring at some personality.

After forty years, the Lobster Pool was sold in 2004, because the Eatons retired. It was bought by a wealthy man from Little Deer Isle, who planned to run it himself. The original restaurant was a seamless mixture of the high-class and the down-home local. The new owner improved the mashed potatoes and the salads, got a liquor license, and put a gift shop near the entrance. Business remained about the same. In three years, he tired of running a restaurant and closed it. The space is now being used to build boats.

45

PEOPLE FROM AWAY

When the word "native" is used on Deer Isle, it seldom refers to the Indians, who once of course were the only inhabitants, but to the descendants of Europeans, some of whom came as early as the seventeenth century. According to local history, the first to start a "settlement" was Major William Eaton in 1762. There are many Eaton descendants on the island and neighborhood. (They called it Deer Island, but the name was later changed to Deer Isle, to distinguish it from a Deer Island near Boston that was the location of a reformatory.) The Indians called it Lobster Island. Relatively few Indians were left because they had been decimated by European diseases or died in conflicts with the new colonists. According to local romantic tradition, Mrs. Eaton was part Indian, the child of a white woman who in captivity became the wife of an Indian chief. Whether or not the story is true, it indicates the early proximity of Indian groups.

The "natives" were mostly fishermen, now with a few successful plumbers, carpenters, electricians, store and restaurant keepers among them. Their houses are often small and old. Fishermen's houses are often surrounded by lobster traps, old cars and old boats, seen either as scenic or a mess by outsiders. Their houses are mostly inland, since shore property has been bought up by people from away. "People from away" is the term that natives use for non-natives. Their number is increasing. There are maybe two dozen native family clans on the island, their surnames immediately identifying them as such, including Eaton,

Billings, Haskell, Weed, Greenlaw, Thompson, Hardy, Hutchinson, Scott, Stinson, etc. Genealogy is a major pastime, and some families trace themselves back to the Mayflower. When two Deer Islers meet, they chat long enough until they trace themselves to a common relative or ancestor. Ancestral pride, poverty, drugs and domestic violence often mix. Disputes are settled locally—the police are one hour away on the mainland in Ellsworth.

Richard is fond of listing the notable people from away, who had houses or rented on or near the island, such as Frederick Law Olmstead, the designer of Central Park in New York, Buckminster Fuller, the inventor of the geodesic dome, E. B. White, the writer and Scott Nearing, the guru of the back-to-the-land movement. Artists have long come to the island: John Marin, Fairfield Porter, Leonard Baskin, Karl Schrag, and Stephen Pace, among many. Haystack, the art-and-craft school, brings hundreds of potters, weavers, and jewelry makers to the island every summer. As a youngster, Richard made friends with the Pulitzer Prize-winning poet George Oppen and the much anthologized poet Richard Eberhart. In the summer particularly, the island hums with openings and creative activity.

I can attest to the fact that this island attracts well-known people, that is, even well known to me, from personal experience. I went to a lecture on Indian canoe routes around the island at the Parish house of the Congregational church. The speaker wore a t-shirt with TIKAL on it in big letters. His name was William Haviland. The name was familiar to me from books I had read on the Maya site of Tikal. Sure enough, it was he. He had retired to Deer Isle on property already bought by his father. He now researched the Etchemin Indians who had lived on the island, for his book *At the Place of the Lobsters and Crabs: Indian People and Deer Isle, Maine, 1605–2005.*

At a Deer Isle cocktail party, I met Hank Millon, who was one of the most powerful men in art history in my day. He was the director of the Center for Advanced Study in the Visual Arts (CASVA), located at the National Gallery of Art in Washington, DC. Hank Millon had just built a striking, new architect-designed house overlooking a cove. He gave a talk at the local library on Michelangelo's architecture. It so happened, that Hank was the brother of the archaeologist René Millon, whose work at Teotihuacán was of primary importance to me. Unfortunately, René and I were never visiting the island at the same time.

Last but not least, George Kubler, the internationally respected art historian and one of the first to study pre-Columbian art at Yale, who I knew well, summered here before his death a decade before. Stories were told about him, from his latter days with Alzheimer's. His daughter, Elena, runs the most prestigious art gallery on the island. And those are just my acquaintances.

Besides illustrious inhabitants and visitors to the island, there is an increasing flow of retirees who don't mind the cold and isolation in winter and complain about the tourists in summer. They join book clubs, writers groups, exercise classes, and other activities. Educated and well-to do, they have lovely houses with beautiful water views. Many million-dollar-homes are built on the shore and are best seen by boat.

These people from away refurbished the Stonington Opera House, and a company puts on Shakespeare and avant-garde theatre throughout the year. Sometimes they try to involve some members of the native community. But the natives have their own cultural and social life: their own churches, church suppers, and charity drives. Sometimes the natives seem to act as if the people from away are not there. Natives and people from away need each other, but there is also anger and mistrust between them.

The rich people from away have created a land trust to buy up Deer Isle land for common use, when it comes on the market. Lands, such as beaches and boat landings, to keep the island beautiful and pristine for everybody, which is obviously a good thing to do. However, many natives see it as a way of removing useful lands and land decisions from their hands, and they too have a point. In a subtle way, Deer Isle is being managed.

(Actually, one wonders about the State of Maine in general, which seems perhaps artificially kept as a poor, natural paradise, without development. Canada next door, is highly developed and industrialized. How has this happened?)

46

ATYPICAL MOTHER-IN-LAW TALK

"We came out of the take-out place with these gigantic ice-cream cones—I almost dropped mine—you know, the take-out place across from where Aunt Louisa's house stood before it collapsed and where her son Mickey put up that trailer and a tree fell on it during the last bad winter storm? It is all fixed now, you can't see it—

"Mickey lives there with his man friend—he is quite good looking for a black man. I hear they are married—he comes from Georgia, but I guess he likes the weather in Maine, not that we have many blacks here—

"Aunt Louisa had five sisters—I don't remember all their names—there was Cheryl, Augusta, Therese . . . Poor Therese, no one ever found out what happened exactly in their basement. They seem to have shot each other to death. That boyfriend, Shirley—yes it's a man's name—was probably not in his right mind. You know, Flossie and Cal, his parents, should have never had children—they were too close as cousins. Poor Therese . . . awful story . . .

"Augusta married a good fisherman, Paul, and they had two children, Nora, and let me see what was the boy's name? It will come to me. Tony—and he lives in that white house on the corner.

"No one ever knew what happened to Paul. He was found drowned next to his boat.

"Then there was Barbara and Deirdre—they were schoolteachers. In them days, their father, Percy, didn't want girls in his business, so he adopted a boy, Bill, to be his heir.

"Bill is a good electrician—"

"Oh, is that why they always say 'Bill, the adopted'?"

"Yes, because Bill was adopted and not real—but there is so much work on the island these days, you can't get him fast enough."

"What about the man who got hit by lightning?"

"I don't know anything about that. Not here."

47

NATIVE WAYS

Mainers in general and Deer Isle natives in particular can be generous, kind, friendly, as well as ornery, stubborn, contentious, sensitive, and a law unto themselves. The following story of a curious man was in the newspapers recently in California: "Arrested for a minor crime, the man was given a court appointed lawyer. He dismissed him. He was then given five lawyers, one after the other, and he dismissed every one of them. The judge would not give him a sixth lawyer. The man represented himself, lost, and went to jail." I said to the person who told the story that the man must have been a Mainer. We looked at the newspaper account more carefully. He was a Mainer.

The natives of Deer Isle are inclined to feel that the law does not apply to them. They can trespass on anyone's land. This is now fiercely resisted by people from away who own most shore property, but they can't do much about it. Intense battles and generations of enmity arise, especially over boundary lines. This is partly due to old deeds that describe unrecognizable landscape features. Such as "old oaks" that no longer exist or point to "a devil's stone," which no one can now recognize. We ran into this when a neighbor was building a driveway and a postage-stamp-size property of ours was in their way. After much cursing, yelling and a lawyer, the neighbor bought the patch of land for a minimal sum and then proceeded to obliterate it with the driveway. Boundary lines are an issue in the ocean as well, as most fishermen know. Even Richard's father ran into the law and jail by disputing the boundary of legal scallop-fishing territory.

Because of high demand by people from away, real estate on Deer Isle is expensive. We found a reasonably priced house that had that most important of Deer Isle qualities, a lovely water view. The sea view included three spruce-covered islands—small, medium, and large—framed by the Cadillac mountains on the horizon. Quite special. The sea passage, known as the Reach, was a thoroughfare for boats ranging from canoes to large cruisers. Spectacular sailboat races take place there every summer. Once we built it, we could watch them, from our deck. Our view to the water was excellent, but it was obstructed here and there by trees and bushes.

The house was a solidly built native dwelling, built and owned by Jerry, our neighbor on the right, who had sold it as a result of a divorce. It had gone through several owners and renters, and as a result floors and walls were in deplorable condition. It was a mess. We built decks, a bathroom, a kitchen with granite countertops, put in skylights and bay windows, and in general transformed it to the kind of house people from away like. We were an odd couple; Richard was a native, and I was from away. We were working on it a bit at a time for all the years we had it.

One eyesore in the view was the charred remains of a burnt-out boatyard shed in the front, to the left of the house. (We assumed that in time it would be cleaned up, and it was.) Two or three years prior to our purchase of the house, the boatyard, owned by Jerry, had burned down with all the boats in it. It was considered to be an accident, and the insurance company paid the loss. The boatyard was rebuilt, but in two years it had burned down again. This time arson was suspected, and Jerry had to go to court. When we got there, he was waiting for a judgment.

Our first night in the as yet un-renovated new house, Richard reverted to native ways. In the middle of the night, he went out and cut down some of the bushes that impeded our view, which happened to be on our left-hand neighbor Roy's property. Richard probably didn't know whose property it was. He thought no one would see him, but someone did. He told me about it at breakfast next morning. I burst into tears. I was sitting there crying that I had such an idiotic husband. Our right-hand neighbor, Jerry, came by and asked me why I was crying. Jerry was a handsome man, perhaps in his mid fifties. He had the reputation of being a rascal and a ladies' man.

So I told Jerry what happened. He said not to worry; he would fix things. He went back to his house and came out with a chainsaw. What was he going to do with a chainsaw? He walked over to the bush next to the one Richard had cut down and cut down some more with a lot of noise and action. Evidently, that bush was on his property, but it was adjoining his son's land with the bushes cut down by Richard. His son, Roy, was probably watching this from his house. Jerry cut down his own bush to please me by giving me a better view (he misunderstood my tears), while he wanted to irritate his son for whatever private reason. At that time, he and his son were on the outs. As we learned later, Roy was a straight arrow and generally disapproved of his father. Jerry put us on his side by befriending us so and implying that Richard was a rascal like him. We even went out to dinner together one day. But the evening of the chainsaw, a policeman arrived from Ellsworth and told Richard not to do it again. I apologized to Roy and sent him $100. Awkward, was an understatement. We got in between father and son.

Shortly after that, Jerry lost his court case and lost all his wonderful, inherited, shorefront, family land. He moved somewhere inland and went back to the lobster fishing he was apparently good at. Some of his land was later sold to a couple from Alabama, who come up for the summer and lead a musical program on the island. They rebuilt his old house with a dramatic interior.

We slowly made friends with Roy, who was a law-abiding lobsterman and carpenter. I asked him to be our caretaker, because our house was built by his father, and he grew up in it and knew all its ins and outs. He was wonderful at the job. But because of that unfortunate start, sometimes we were all awkward.

A decade later, when we moved in, we thought, permanently, something went wrong with our relationship with Roy. I think Roy got insulted at something, though I never found out what it was. Roy returned our keys by leaving them on our driveway but explained nothing and refused all attempts to talk to us. There he was, our neighbor and former caretaker, who pretended that we weren't there.

A few years ago, fireworks were legalized in Maine. On one July evening, Roy and his friends set them off in front of their house quite close to us, across the street. The sprays fell over our house, clattering on the roof and the booms sounded like artillery. It was like the

Soviet shelling of Budapest. It was scary. On an unexamined impulse, Richard called the police in Ellsworth. They came out eventually to tell him that fireworks were legal until 10:00 p.m., and he'd have to put up with it. After that, any improved relations between Roy and us were impossible.

I never realized what problems this would cause. I knew by then that the island was sort of divided informally by native family districts, including by old and newer settlers, which you could tell by the names on mailboxes. We were interlopers from another district. Richard's family district is on Little Deer Isle. Jerry and Roy were old families in the district we bought "their" house in.

Something similar also works on the tasks people do, such as snowplowing and mowing. As our caretaker, Roy used to do our plowing and mowing, but now we had to find someone else. There were plenty of plowers on the island, and we called many of them, but none of them wanted the job. First of all, they let us know that Roy was THE plower in our district, and we should have him. They would not muscle in on his territory, and they had their own territory, which was enough for them. We got through that tough winter, when it snowed every other day, by begging various people to do a plowing job "just once, as an emergency," so we could get out. Not something I care to repeat.

We did find another mower, as it turned out, the only fulltime mower on the island, Frank. He came and mowed the lawn on two occasions. The third time I called him he yelled at me, perhaps drunkenly, that it was too long since the last time he mowed, and the grass was too high. He refused to come. He kept repeating, "I am not at your fucking beck and call! I am not on your fucking beck and call!" That was the end of that.

Richard felt that people (natives) were lurking around the house at night looking for mischief. I thought he was ridiculous. But at times I wasn't sure. As an artist, Richard sometimes made sculptures out of found materials like wire clothes hangers. Here, he made vertical columns out of piled-up fieldstones in the garden. Sometimes these were delicately balanced and fell down. At one time, there were half-a-dozen stone columns all over the garden. One morning, I looked out the window and saw that they had all collapsed, and it was hard not to think that they had been intentionally knocked down. A practical joke, perhaps? Of course, we never knew.

Perhaps one of our problems with natives was that we were neither fish nor fowl—Richard was a native, he knew people from school, through family; he could chat native-speak with the best of them. But he had gone away and was an unknown quantity. He seemed to have some native flaws and some native graces but could not be "trusted" entirely or perhaps at all. I was from away, from another planet. The only thing that seemed comprehensible with people from away, from a native point of view, was money. Lots of money. It didn't look like we had lots of money, judging by the piecemeal renovations on a native house. And in all those assessments, there was some truth.

Despite these difficulties, I am delighted to have gotten to know this corner of America. Deer Isle turned out to be more complex and special than I ever would have thought. I enjoyed its history and variety of people. Some people prophesied that in time all of the island would be inhabited by people from away, and the natives would move to and blend in with the mainland, losing some of their identity. Perhaps, perhaps not. I am happy to have known Deer Isle as it is now.

48

QUESTION

I was sitting around at lunch in the Broadmoor senior residence in San Francisco, talking with a group about travels. Which one of us had traveled the most? It was a cosmopolitan lot. As I was listing the places I had been to, I came out on top. In Europe, I had been to Ireland, England, Portugal, Spain, France, Switzerland, Germany Sweden, Italy, Hungary, the Czech Republic, and Romania. I forgot Greece. In the Americas, I had been to Canada, Mexico, Guatemala, and Peru. In Asia, I had been to Bali and Hong Kong, and elsewhere I had been to Australia, Bermuda, the Bahamas, and the Cayman Islands. (Puerto Rico, if that counts.) My first husband loved to travel, and we went to many places.

Then someone asked the following question: Which of all those places was the strangest, most unusual or unexpected, whether good or bad?

I had to think for a while. I was most familiar with Europe and Latin America and knew very little about Canada and Australia. I hadn't been to Africa or most of Asia. What was the strangest? To my own surprise I said, "The US."

To have time to think, I added, "It seems very ordinary and everyday, but it's really unusual." The table was waiting for me to say something profound. I didn't know why I had said this, I'd just said it.

I groped my way around my own statement. "It is like this," I said. "When I am in many foreign places, like Europe or Mexico, they don't feel strange to me. They all remind me of Hungary, never mind the communists. I understand exactly their social structure—the upper class, the lower class, the intelligentsia—and where I fit in or would fit in, if I lived there. It feels comfortable and easy because I know it."

Then I thought about it some more. "I understand the corruption, the crime, the pessimism. I even share the pessimism. This is the way the world is, a difficult place. An attitude of a somber, intelligent realism I find in most of the world.

"There is corruption, crime and evil in the US, too, but people believe in a benign universe nonetheless. And because enough people believe in it, they behave in an honest and hardworking fashion that in fact makes American society more benign. It is circular. At first, it's hard to fathom. Are these people on drugs? They keep smiling like idiots."

The origin of this may be the constitution that seems to guarantee equal opportunity. Other people have constitutions, sometimes copied from the American one. But Americans created their constitution out of and with the benign world view that went with it. It is now a sacred text. No other people I have met have the optimism of Americans. (Canada, Australia, I don't know.) The optimism of Americans can be foolish and even ridiculous—their attempt to export democracy is usually a failure. That in itself proves the point of how much Americans have faith in and value of their system, which is the secret of their success. Other people don't have such faith.

I once read a little story about a European woman who was distraught at an airport, because she missed her connecting flight due to an airline delay. Her luggage was going who knows where, and she didn't know what to do. She was having a meltdown. She expressed these feelings to a man standing by, who happened to be an American. He said to her: "Have faith." And, according to the story, that advice calmed her down.

Now when I first came across that story, I said to myself, *What should the poor woman have faith in? God? The airline?* I guess the American man meant that she should have faith that things will work out, because in his world they always do. Or mostly do. In America. He had faith. She couldn't possibly have had that kind of faith as a European. Things there don't always work out.

Although religions are big in America, the aim of life is not another world after death. It's all about this world. People are busy creating a perfect world, utopia, in this world. First of all there is the belief that however far we may be from it, a perfect society is achievable. America is a vast sociological experiment. In big ways, and little people strive to ameliorate discrimination, poverty, disorganization, stupidity—we could say sin—in the home and the workplace, with an eagerness the Puritan ancestors would have understood.

People may have totally opposite ideas on how to do it and bump into racism, corruption, greed and evil intent along the way, but if nothing else, they will reorganize the paper clips in a more efficient way in the drawer, to help the path forward. America can't be bothered with profundity, because everyone is building utopia, which is more important. It is perceived as a utilitarian task. My work is not abstract; I am finding a space for the recognition of American Indian achievements. A worthy goal among many other worthy goals. That is the utopian bit I am working on, and I am valued for it. (In Europe, that would just be personal, exotic oddity.) Nor is it because the American Indian is of historical and present political concern in the US. I could be studying the mountain villages of Burma, and it would be a part of the universal undertaking.

Another unique aspect of the US is that it equates itself with all humanity. The US is searching for universal values and a universal utopia. That's why, to the irritation of especially Latin America, the US usually refers to itself as "America," and the people are "Americans." America is bigger than the US. (It's not the same as Europeans calling themselves "Europeans.") I am not a "USer"; I am American.

Will it last? I came to the US in the late fifties at the height of American power and wealth. A rich middle class. I was too young and too foreign to understand it. I have been experiencing the polarization of classes and political parties since. Watching the rise of Asia and especially China, along with everyone else. Could the US fragment along red and blue state lines? Will it stay unified? Powerful? Teotihuacán lasted over six hundred years. The US just had its two hundredth anniversary. Empires decline and fall and reemerge transformed. Who knows.

I consider myself very lucky that my father brought me here in 1956. He knew nothing about America and was surprised by what he found—it wasn't like any other place he knew. I can't think that there is another place that would have been as interesting to live in, at this time in history. More may yet come, but I got to experience America at its height. And I added my bit to its great social experiment.

As Skip said about Deer Isle, "lucky dog."

49

MINI-STORY

Stories I had written before coming to Huntington Common's Writer Circle did not go over very well there. They were too long and had to be read in parts. The same people were not there every time to hear it. The stories were too complicated or too obscure. I was going to have to write differently for this group. But I didn't know how.

Then one day a new arrival named Lorraine read a simple story about her dog, Tillie. She said that this was the first story she ever wrote. It was a straightforward account of how they got Tillie, how they enjoyed Tillie's company, how eventually Tillie died and was buried. There was nothing bizarre or unusual about it. It was a surprisingly moving story. Everybody liked it.

So I thought why don't I write a short account of something that had happened or I saw in my life that would interest people here? I thought of describing my neighborhood in New York and why I liked it. It was one typewritten page. And all of a sudden topics were rushing into my mind, not just about New York, but about the Hungarian exile community, about the pre-Columbian ruins I studied, the places I got to know in the US, the interesting people I came across. It was sort of an autobiography in a mosaic of short pieces.

At about the same time as I was wrestling with the stories, I met a brilliant new resident, George. He announced from the first that he was in the last stage of renal failure and at the age of eighty-seven had declined dialysis. He had months or perhaps a year ahead of him. He was a medical inventor, who had invented something very important and complicated for cancer research and/or cure. I never quite understood what it was. Other inventors were consulting him while he was here. He was also an artist.

He said he was not afraid of death—nay, he was looking forward to it—because some years past he had had a near-death experience. He was outside his body looking at it. He was looking forward to having the experience again. He became close friends with a delightful younger woman who had also had a near-death experience. In fact, he made friends with a number of people, including me, because he was a curious and friendly person who enjoyed life to the hilt.

Hearing that I wrote books, he looked me up on Amazon and purchased one of my books. Not only did he buy it, he read it and had no trouble understanding it. He said he liked my writing style and wanted to read more. So I gave him my various books of fiction, one by one, and he commented on their quality, what was good, what was not so good. His taste was unerring; he was the perfect critic I needed. Next I gave him the manuscript of a book I had my doubts about, lying around in a drawer, and was delighted to have him give his seal of approval.

Finally, he had read everything I had written except the little "mini-stories" I had begun for the writer's circle. I had done about fifteen to twenty and called them *Multiple Horizons*. I was eager to know what he thought of them. His reaction was very positive, and he said that he was looking forward to the rest as soon as I could write them. When he liked something very much, he'd pass it on to his wife. I felt some urgency about writing the rest, since I was hoping George could read them before falling ill or anything happening to him.

Multiple Horizons is now written in draft form, and George seems to be quite well.

50

ORIGINS

The shortest version of the history of Hungary is this: The ruling Hungarians came from the East. They were quite successful in the Middle Ages. Later they were conquered and controlled by the Turks, the Austrians, and the Russians successively. In the process, they lost two thirds of their territory. They liked the Austrians the best. Hungary is now an independent democracy.

Below is a somewhat expanded version.

Present-day Hungary is about the size of Rhode Island in the US and has about ten million people. Its capital is Budapest, a city divided in two by the Danube River. The Buda side is hilly and suburban. The old royal castles are located there. The Pest side of the city is flat and is a densely built. The Parliament Building is situated there. Seven bridges connect Buda and Pest. Budapest has been called the Paris of the East.

The people call themselves Magyars, but their European neighbors call them Hungarian, *hongrois*, *ungarisch*, all derived from the word "Hun." The Huns were a nomadic horde from the East, who terrorized late Roman Europe in the fourth century, led by their ruler Attila. The Hungarians were mounted nomads, who came to Europe much later, about 900 AD. Their leader was called Arpad. They were probably somewhat similar to the Huns. These Hungarians came from somewhere in the Ural Mountains of Siberia, moved along by various ethnic displacements there. They spoke Hungarian, a language not related to the other European languages. Recent research is showing that the conquered population was also Hungarian speaking and may go back thousands of years before 900 AD. Hungarian has been compared to Sumerian. There is some uncertainty about the origin of Hungarians.

At first the 900 AD Hungarians wandered around Europe plundering its rich cities. They went as far as Paris. (Many Hungarian quips have added, "If only they had settled there !") In the end, they were routed and settled further east in the Danube basin, encircled by the Carpathian Mountains. Although this was rich agricultural land, the geographic position was in other ways unfortunate. Hungary was wedged in between German speakers on the west and Russians on the east. Both of these peoples vastly outnumber Hungarians, have been militarily expansionistic, and have played an aggressive role in Hungarian history. Hungary is surrounded by small Slavic-speaking groups, sometimes inside sometimes outside its borders.

Arpad's grandson accepted Christianity in 1000 AD and changed his name to Stephen. Eventually he became a saint. He had a choice whether to join the Eastern Orthodox Church or Roman Catholicism. He and all other Hungarians since have chosen to belong to the West. (The Eastern Orthodox Church was popular with the Slavs.)

The Middle Ages and early Renaissance were the best times Hungary ever had. The kings married into various European royal houses, pursued local wars and alliances as they did. Hungary's borders were three times those of present-day Hungary and included a portion of the Adriatic Sea. This was what is called Greater or Historic Hungary. King Mathias (1458–1490) married the daughter of the King of Naples, ran an Italian-style Renaissance court, and had one of the greatest libraries in Europe.

All this was destroyed by the Ottoman Turks, whose capital was Istanbul. In 1541 they conquered Buda and occupied Hungary for a hundred and fifty years. Hungary was divided in three: the large central portion was under direct Turkish rule. The Principality of Transylvania in the east accepted Turkish rule but negotiated internal independence. Hungarian culture flourished there. A strip to the north and west was the refuge of those who fled from the Turkish occupation. They were allied to the Hapsburgs of Vienna. The Turks were expelled about 1700 by a joint Hapsburg-Hungarian army.

That left Austria in control of Hungary. The Turks had devastated the country. They destroyed buildings and art. They treated Hungary as a colony and despoiled the country for its natural resources. The area was depopulated. Austria was less draconian but was still an overlord. They populated the empty areas with speakers of foreign languages: Germans and Slavs. The Austrian Empire was an old-fashioned polyglot and polyethnic realm ruled from Vienna. No one asked for uniformity of language, religion and custom in those days.

In the spring of 1848, there were rebellions in many European cities, starting with France, that were contagious. The many issues included the end or lessening of aristocratic and feudal rule; greater democratic participation of the public in government, and the independence and self-rule of nationalities. Most of these rebellions were shortly put down. On March 15, 1848, the Hungarians rebelled against Austria and wanted to have self rule in line with their traditional history. The Austrians called in the czar of Russia, who sent a large army to put down the rebellion. For Hungarians, March 15 is their day of would-be independence, the birth of the modern country.

In time, relations with Austria improved. In 1867 there was a reorganization of the empire known as the Compromise, when the lands were renamed the Austro-Hungarian Empire, and Hungary itself was called the Kingdom of Hungary. The Austro-Hungarian Empire lasted from 1867 to 1918. The Kingdom of Hungary had most of what had been Greater Hungary, including Transylvania. Hungary had full control of its internal affairs and had much in common with Austria; they had a shared culture. This was the second time since the Middle Ages that Hungary knew prosperity, cultivated the arts, and came into its own. It was the age of operetta. The price for this was that Hungary was on the side of Austria in the First World War. Hungary was on the losing side in both World War I and World War II.

With the peace treaty after World War I, known as the Treaty of Trianon, in 1920 (Trianon is a palace at Versailles, where the treaty was signed), Hungary was dismembered. Two-thirds of its territory was lost, and over three million Hungarians became minorities in other countries. Transylvania went to Romania. Most of the large, secondary cities and the railroad that connected them were lost. In Greater Hungary, Hungarians had been the overlords, but in many of the outlying areas Slavic- and Romanian-speaking peoples outnumbered them.

This part of the world had been ethnically, religiously and linguistically mixed for many centuries and lived in relative peace together. Latin used to be the lingua franca. The new idea of nationalism required that a nation should speak one native language and belong to one ethnic group. The great Western nations, England and France, are pretty much homogeneous and fit this model. As overlords, the nineteenth-century Hungarians, now speaking exclusively Hungarian, wanted their subjects to be as Hungarian as possible, too. Some groups, like the Jews, assimilated willingly. Others hated the Hungarians for it and lobbied the great powers to give them a native country, too. Hence the many small Eastern European countries that have come to occupy the area between the Russians and Germans . . . After the Treaty of Trianon many Hungarians got to be the minorities in countries that used to be their subjects, which was not pretty. Because control of territory now depends on the ethnic affiliation of the majority of the population. Modern Eastern European governments move about and resettle ethnic populations at will to bring about the ethnic majorities they want.

Hungary was reluctant to enter World War II until Hitler promised the return of the territory taken at Trianon. And in fact, for a short time in 1939 and 1940, Transylvania and Upper Hungary were returned. (My mother and father met on one of the first trains that went from Budapest to reattached Transylvania in 1940.) In the end, of course, no matter how much the Hungarians complained, the Treaty of Trianon was reestablished after World War II. While Hungarians are still nostalgic over greater Hungary, most have learned to live with what they call "crippled Hungary." One advantage they see is that this smaller Hungary is homogeneous and has no disaffected minority problem. In the days of electronic media, there is less need for a people to be physically together to communicate.

The major issue of the Second World War was not Trianon but the Holocaust. Hungary stood with Germany and Austria and also persecuted Jews. Not willingly and ideologically but out of its own circumstances to be "whole" again. In the 1930s, Hungary's ruler was a "regent" of what was still called the Kingdom of Hungary but had no kings. Admiral Horthy was an authoritarian, conservative dictator. In 1919 there was a brief communist coup that was put down by the military led by Horthy.

He was very reluctant to enter the war on the side of the Germans but eventually did on the orders of Hitler. Horthy was more worried about the Russians than the Germans. He saw the Germans as the lesser evil. When Hitler threatened to invade Hungary, Horthy obeyed him. Eventually he was ordered to give up many hundreds of thousands of Jews to be taken to Auschwitz. The Germans did occupy Hungary towards the end of the war. Because of his consistent attempts at mitigation, Horthy was not considered a war criminal at the Nuremberg trials. He lived out his days in Portugal, supported by wealthy Hungarians, including Jews. He lived long enough to see the 1956 Hungarian uprising against the Russians and said to whoever would listen, "I told you so."

Hitler made the big mistake of attacking Soviet Russia. Like Napoleon's foray before him, the Russian winter destroyed his troops. This allied Stalin with the forces of England and the US. The German occupation of Budapest ended in the "liberation" of Hungary by the Soviets. In fact of course, the Russians were in charge of all of Eastern Europe, which they then occupied as their colonies. They installed native puppet governments. They instituted a communist economic and political system. At the same time, uranium was found in Hungary and was taken by the Russians to help build the bomb. Like the Turks, they robbed the countries of all their industrial, agricultural and natural resources. They nationalized all the factories and collectivized all the farms with a lot of bloodshed. They did not allow travel to the West, as they created the Iron Curtain.

In 1953 Stalin died, and there was a little thaw in Soviet communism. Khrushchev enumerated Stalin's crimes. Polish workers demonstrated for better conditions but the movement was immediately put down. Hungarian students planned a demonstration in solidarity with the Poles. This resulted in a general spontaneous uprising of students, workers, people in the street. On October 23, 1956, Hungarians all over the country rebelled against the puppet ruler and the Russian occupation forces. Welders dragged down the colossal Stalin statue.

The Hungarians hoped that western countries would come to their aid. Radio Free Europe, an arm of the US government broadcasting clandestinely, had been inciting revolt and implying help. This help never came. The US was not eager to attack the Soviet Union and start WWIII. Soon after October 23, there was a new crisis about the Suez Canal. Egyptians nationalized it, and French and English military forces were immediately sent to wrest it back. It took international interest away from Hungary. The Russians hesitated for a few days, perhaps also thinking of WWIII. But then they attacked on November 4 with superior military power and crushed the revolution. In those few days of liberty, two hundred thousand people left the country. The revolution lasted only twelve days. But it was the beginning of the collapse of the Soviet empire.

The next Russian puppet ruler, Kadar, liberalized somewhat the communist rule. The Soviets still occupied the country, but some private businesses were allowed. Western styles and rock music were permitted. The standard of life improved. Some travel abroad was allowed. This was known as "goulash communism." The Hungarian revolutionary "hot heads" had won this much.

In 1989 communism collapsed in the Soviet Union by going bankrupt. Many of its conquered provinces, like Ukraine and Georgia, the Baltic States, broke away from Russia. Eastern Europe was liberated from Russian domination. The Berlin Wall separating East and West Germany was dismantled. Hungary became a democratic republic.

The revolution of 1956 is now a national holiday on October 23. However, it has become politicized. Hungarians don't agree on what it was and what it meant. The parties on the right claim it as their own nationalistic uprising, while the parties on the left attack it as an opportunistic elite event. But on the whole, both sides are proud of the fact that little Hungary stood up to giant Soviet Russia.

☙ ❧

II

STONE AGE CIVILIZATION IN THE NEW WORLD

In the Stone Age cultures of the New World, sophisticated social engineering likely took the place of technological advances.

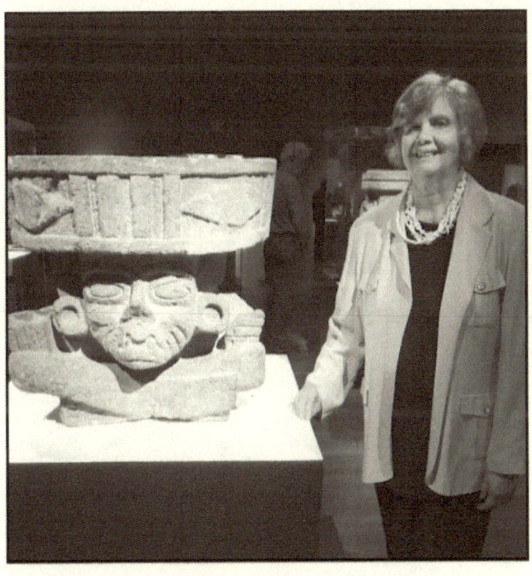

Author with stone brazier from Teotihuacán, known as the Old Fire God.

For Richard

ଓ ଓ

1. BACKGROUND

THIS ESSAY IS A RESPONSE to my interview with the BBC in preparation for their *Civilizations* series in 2016. I was supposed to talk about the colossal Olmec heads and their realism. And I did; I said this and that to the questions I was asked. After I left, I realized that I left out the important point that the Olmec heads were carved with stone tools. We specialists often leave that out because we take it for granted. I kept thinking of all the things I should have said about ancient America and did not. Clearly, the otherwise highly intelligent BBC personnel I dealt with did not know much on the subject.

When I came home, I made a short list of what I could have said or should have said, and I realized that it was the beginning of a study. Not a culture-by-culture history, of which there is a lot, but one examining briefly the special features of the Stone Age Civilizations of the New World—a somewhat personal thematic approach intended for the BBC's imaginary future programs and all those interested in such ideas.

It is not uncommon to look back on one's field in retirement and to see something new in it that the current scientific establishment might see as odd or heretical. One writes as much for future generations as for one's current colleagues and their trendy approaches. I am aware that such an endeavor might be solipsistic, but it might also be challenging and constructive. Hoping that this is the latter and that what is currently inappropriate is forgiven, even if patronizingly, I put a lifetime of ideas and hunches in front of the reader.

My focus, although changing with time, has always been—or come back to—Teotihuacán. I once thought that Teotihuacán was unique in Mesoamerica; later I tried to work it into the global evolution of art and culture—as a state, until now. I see it now more as a quintessential part of ancient American civilization. Depending on the context, each of these views make sense. I have played with Teotihuacán for a lifetime and new scholars will too. I think that understanding Teotihuacán is the key to understanding ancient America.

2. INDIANS

I HAVEN'T REALLY KNOWN ANY American Indians personally. I met a few, casually, at lectures or openings. Most Indian men had long hair in pony tails and had evocative names like Creepingbear or Echosomething. My only closer encounter was with a graduate student named Marcia Redcorn. In every way, she was just like the other graduate students. But, in the forty years I taught at Columbia University, she was the only American Indian student who applied and we accepted. We all tried not to make her feel unusual. Marcia was a beautiful young woman with long hair and a quick intelligence.

She was from the Kiowa tribe and came from a reservation in Oklahoma. The Kiowa were famous as a nomadic Plains tribe, who took to horses early in the nineteenth century and became fierce warriors. They were a practical people, who lived in teepees with floors cozy with furs. That was appealing. Women painted scenes on the buffalo-skin teepee covers. When they moved, they converted the long teepee poles into a dragging device called a travois and piled all household belongings on top. I remember seeing maps of the US in my student days in which every inch of the Americas was covered with the names of tribes now extinct or on reservations. A Kiowa student so far east was special.

Marcia Redcorn took all the basic introductory courses about art history, ancient Americans, American Indians, as well as the required method-and-theory courses, and did well. She could go into any field she chose—she could study Michelangelo or Japanese prints. But, not surprisingly, she was most interested in the works of George Catlin. Catlin was an early-nineteenth-century American explorer, who went among the Plains Indians, including the Kiowa, doing portraits and scenes of daily and ceremonial life among them. His paintings are accurate and beautiful. That was her world. In that, there was perhaps an appropriate scholarly field in which she could make a reputation and a contribution.

It did not work out that way. Marcia's private life intervened—a marriage, illness and a pregnancy, and she went back to Oklahoma. As far as I knew, she went back to work at the Kiowa Tribal Museum, where she probably did not need a PhD from Columbia University, but her training was of use nevertheless. The Kiowa Tribal Museum has a collection of traditional objects as well as famous artworks from Kiowa artists of the first half of the twentieth century. We were particularly sorry to lose Marcia because she had been special, but in fact her story is common. A number of students drop out for reasons of illness or private problems. That is just life. And, in fact, few land in as good a place as the Kiowa Tribal Museum.

Marcia Redcorn was a modern American Indian. She probably grew up on the heroic stories of the past and made that past come to life in the local museum. At the same time, she was living in the US and the modern world and had to fit in there. Much of her life consisted in negotiating the Indian past and the modern present. Knowing her did not give any insight into what American Indians had been like before American control; it gave insight into the dilemmas of modern American Indians. Successful contemporary Indian artists, such as Fritz Scholder (part Luiseño), mine the complex emotional territory between the Indian and the modern in their work.

This part of the book is about Indians, without the benefit of knowing Indians personally. It is based on what ancient Indians did, what they left behind, what they did not do. There is useful information in the accounts and chronicles of the sixteenth-century Spanish. There is also a lot of bias. If we can but read them, the most useful information is in what the Indians did with their own hands and thought up with their own minds. The most abundant surviving material is in Mexico, Central and South America. Hundreds of spectacular ruins exist in this area conquered and abandoned in the sixteenth century. Most of the surviving Indians there have long ago sunk into the abject poverty of peasantry and do not apply to Columbia University.

Although there were many differences between the Kiowa and ancient American Indians, there were also similarities. Ultimately they all came from northern Siberia, about twenty thousand years ago; their languages were once related; they used similar tools and valued some of the same things. Sometimes North American Indian information reinforces ancient American ideas, as we try to reconstruct them. There were and are many different American

Indians, but there is also an American Indian, just as there is a European or an American.

3. STARTING PLACE

THERE HAS BEEN A LOT of talk recently about intelligent life in the galaxies outside the earth. We have even sent messages indicating the location of earth for these alien beings, so they can visit us. Nevertheless, until now we have not encountered an alien civilization in outer space. The closest we can come to see what intelligent beings have accomplished somewhere else is to look at the Indians of the New World. They developed mostly outside the Old World. Europe, Asia and Africa have been interconnected for thousands of years, and we tend to assume that they are the norm for cultural development.. For better or for worse, the Americas were almost totally isolated until 1492, when Columbus landed in the Caribbean. From the predominate point of view, they are the other human experiment, and it is worth knowing what that is and why it is as it is.

A lot of confusion has been created by the fact that Columbus and the following Europeans thought that the land they discovered was Japan or East Asia or even India. They called the inhabitants "Indians." Originally, they were looking for spices and the Spice Islands, which were in Indonesia. Only gradually did they realize that this was a new continent they knew nothing about. By then they discovered that the Natives had some gold and immediately decided to conquer its most populous lands. In less than fifty years, they destroyed all the flourishing cultures they found. The two most important ones were the Aztecs in today's Mexico and the Inca in Peru.

Missionaries and chroniclers tried to reconstruct in pictures and writing what the Native worlds were like before the conquest. Depending on their interest and understanding, we have quite a lot of written information on the New World from the sixteenth century. Bur many cities of the New World were destroyed in the conquest, and some were abandoned in ancient times. Sometimes a Spanish city was built on top of the ruins. Mexico City was built on top of the ruins of the Aztec capital, and Cuzco was built on top of the Inca capital.

In the eighteenth century, Europeans became very interested in ancient ruins and explored the Americas to find them. They discovered that there were ruins older than the sixteenth-century Aztec and Inca, in jungles and mountains. Many of these belonged to earlier Native civilizations. In the late nineteenth century, professional archaeologists began to map and date all areas for sculptures and architecture. It became evident that people were living in villages from at least between 5000 and 4000 BC and that they were building complex architecture and erecting major monuments since between about 3000 and 2000 BC. We now have dozens of major ruins, visited by tourists, and hundreds of lesser ones still overgrown by vegetation.

The European conquerors had a rather low opinion of the Natives of the New World. The Native armies came at them with simple weapons with stone points. They had no horses or metal armor. For gifts, they tried to pacify them with trinkets and feathers. Nevertheless, the Europeans were impressed by the cities, temples, and assorted architecture. Many people in modern times feel the same way—they are very impressed by the ruined cities with their pyramids, palaces and observatories, but they are not impressed by what they learn of the Natives. It is not surprising that Westerners have often concluded that someone else must have built the monuments. For many centuries after the conquest, people thought that the builders of the New World wonders were the Lost Tribes of Israel—people from the Old World. Most recently, some people think that they were built by extraterrestrials who came to visit the earth with superior technology. But the wonders of ancient America make sense only as the work of the ill-understood American Indian, who was not like the European or American, because their circumstances were different.

4. OLD AND NEW WORLDS

The New World was a place of natural abundance and riches when the Europeans encountered it. Both in the east and west, there were huge trees like the California redwoods. The forests were teaming with deer, the plains with bison, the waters with fish. In southern regions, there was a hundred-foot-high tropical forest with its legendary variety of colorful birds and animals. The most populous cities were in the western half of the continent, from the American Southwest to Chile. Generally mountainous, the western half of the continent was the most suitable for agriculture and irrigation. Maize was domesticated by between 5000 and 4000 BC in the Mexico area and spread from there north and south. Wherever it spread, people came to live in settled villages. In the forests and prairies of the more lowland North and South America, people often did well by hunting and gathering and did not have to bother with intensive agriculture, or maybe just have supplementary gardens. If they did not get along with their neighbors or got to be too many for a region, they could move to another part of the land and start again. Relatively egalitarian, they did not have to kowtow to kings and aristocrats.

It was harder for the agriculturalists in the American West to move, because they were tied to their field. And their way was barred geographically by high, sometimes-snow-covered mountains, intermittently active volcanoes, and stretches of forbidding desert. Whatever the situation there, moving away was not an easy option. As the population increased, some became poorer than others and had to accept lower status in society. The ones who did well became elites. The elites eventually selected rulers or a ruling family, whose descendants were kings. Legitimizing their power and giving identity to the community, these chiefdoms and kingdoms built temples, plazas, palaces, and other stone buildings for their rituals and processions, using the labor of the poorer population. If recompensed adequately, people were perhaps willing to toil for their own center or city.

Despite all the natural richness of the New World, compared to Eurasia it lacked some of the basic resources that led Eurasia to earlier and more complex civilization. The New World did not have animals suitable for domestication. There were no sheep, goats, cattle, or pigs. Thus there was very little meat in the diet. There were mainly the turkey and the guinea pig, which were domesticated. There were dogs, some for eating purposes, some as pets. By necessity, therefore, the diet of the New World civilizations was largely vegetarian augmented by hunting deer, rabbit, etc.

Sheep, goats, and cattle, were domesticated in the Old World prior to the Neolithic (Stone Age) Period of Europe, before BC 7000. The presence of domesticated animals in proximity to Europeans also affected health. Animals and Europeans shared illnesses which resulted in human immunity to many diseases. These were not shared by American Indians, and as a result they died by the tens of thousands from European diseases that had little effect on Europeans. In many places, diseases spread before actual contact with Europeans. Disease conquered America as much as or even more than warfare.

Europeans also had a very special domesticated animal in the horse. Coming from Central Asia, people only learned to ride horses rather late, about 2000 BC, but then horses became a necessity in travel, war, and later agriculture. Columbus brought horses to the New World on his second voyage and so did all the conquistadors. As powerful, big, fast animals, they inevitably terrified all the Natives not used to them. (Some years later, North American Indians captured horses and became excellent riders.)

Not having horses and cattle, the ancient Americans also lacked an animal suitable to pull carts. Europeans wondered—and still wonder—why the Americans lacked the wheel. The explanation is that not having an animal to pull it, the cart with a wheel was of no use in the Americas. (Oddly enough, the wheelbarrow, which to us seems useful, was not an obvious invention anywhere and was first found late in Chinese history.) In the ancient Mexico, all objects and people were carried by human porters. In the Andes, there was a domesticated pack animal, the llama. The llama could carry a weight up to fifty pounds on its back but could not be ridden. Llama herds carried many goods. Actually, the ancient Americans did discover the wheel—wheeled toys have been found in some burials in Mexico. But no practical invention came from it. It didn't relate to anything ancient Americans found useful.

Europe-Asia-Africa is a huge landmass and has had many ancient civilizations that rose and fell. Besides having some natural advantages in fauna, one major advantage was in the human proximity to one another. By being close, civilizations could exchange inventions and ideas, from politics to religion. For example, ancient Egypt, Mesopotamia and the Near East were close enough to learn from each other, and even far-away civilizations like ancient China and the Indus Valley were a part of the trade of things and ideas, especially along what was later called the Silk Road.

In the New World, there were only two areas of complex civilization: Mesoamerica (Mexico, Guatemala and Honduras) and the Andes (Peru and Bolivia). By complex civilization we mean large kingdoms and empires, populous cities, elites and commoners, much stone architecture, and the development of writing and record keeping. These two regions were particularly suited with large areas available for agriculture and a favorable climate. Other areas, such as the American Southwest and Southeast, Central America and Colombia and Ecuador, had some but not all of the favorable aspects, so we think of them as intermediate, interesting but secondary, on the scale of civilizations in the Americas.

These two advanced regions, Mesoamerica and the Andes, were separated from each other by the rugged mountains of Central America and the Northern Andes. Foot or sedan-chair traffic across them was slow. Boat traffic, via raft and canoe, seems to have existed between Peru and western Mexico, but its effects on interaction were limited. (Seafaring was not a great American skill or desire.) As these two areas—Mesoamerica and the Andes—were very different, they could have learned a great deal from each other. However, they did not come into close enough contact to exchange information about things like writing and record keeping. Such exchange was crucial in the development of Old World complex civilizations. Distance and isolation was then a natural disadvantage for the development of American civilizations.

The story of the ancient civilizations of the Americas is usually written with reference to what they lacked from the point of view of the Old World and how thus why they were so easily conquered. But we could look at them in terms of what they had and what they valued that might have been different from the Old World. While it would not have saved them from European conquest, it might help to validate them in retrospect, in history. It might also throw an explanatory light on the special civilizations of the Old World. Can we can turn this around to see what the Old World lacked that the New had.

5. ESSENTIAL HISTORY OF ANCIENT AMERICA

The Complex Civilizations of Mesoamerica and the Andes

Mesoamerica, more specifically, consists of modern southern Mexico, Guatemala and Honduras. In ancient times the prominent cultures were the Olmec, the Maya, Monte Albán, Teotihuacán, Chichén Itzá, and the Aztec. The region is unified by a common lifeway: religion, calendar, trade, wars, intermarriages, among others. Trade with currency was usual. Politically, the region consists of separate states or city states, separate languages, and separate art styles. It was only partially unified by the Aztecs at a late date. The northern area is mountainous with volcanoes, the southern area is flat with tropical forest.

The Andes consist of mostly modern Peru and Bolivia. The prominent cultures of ancient times were Chavín, Moche, Paracas, Nazca, Tiwanaku, Wari, Chimú and Inca. The region is unified by common traditions in politics, religion and trade but separated by language, customs, and styles. Instead of currency, the Andeans had a barter-exchange system based ostensibly on kin. The Inca, and before them the Wari and Tiwanaku, unified much of the area in large empires. The Andes have rich fishing resources near a desert coastline punctuated by small river valleys. Mountains, some snow capped, rise to the east of the desert. From there, a tropical forest slopes in the direction of the Amazon.

Between Mesoamerica and the Andes, the intervening area of Central America, Ecuador and Colombia, is rugged and mountainous. The local cultures have some of the features of Mesoamerica and the Andes but smaller polities. Ecuador has been important in ceramics, Colombia in gold. Various inventions from Mesoamerica and the Andes diffused through these areas from one another. However, the diffusion was slow, and this in-between area was as much a divider as a connector.

Detailed history of New World civilizations begins with the development or introduction of pottery making. Where it began and who began it is a matter of controversy. (The earliest pottery in the world is now found in China, c. 20,000 BC.) The earliest pottery in the New World now comes from Santarem, Brazil, near the mouth of the

Amazon, c. 7000 BC. Other early potteries have been found in Ecuador, Colombia, and western Mexico. Pottery seems to have come from one source, since not only techniques but also some forms are similar. New finds may change that. Their importance is not just that they were a practical replacement for gourds and wooden containers, but that even when broken, their quantity, their materials and designs, can indicate the time and place of manufacture. They are thus indispensable for archaeologists. The history of ancient America has been reconstructed largely through the broken sherds.

Mesoamerica

Complex civilizations erecting monuments began in Mesoamerica about 3000 to 2000 BC, in what is called the Formative Period. Prior to this time, agriculture, pottery and settled villages had come together for a lifeway. The most spectacular of these early Mesoamerican civilizations was the Olmec located in the Isthmus of Tehuantepec near the Gulf Coast in Mexico. The two largest Olmec centers, San Lorenzo and La Venta, were not cities but places for ritual. Stone was not available in the area, so large boulders weighing more than 15 tons were found in mountains 80 km (50 miles) away. They would have had to be moved down to the coast, floated on rafts to the rivers near the sites. These sculptures represent human figures we cannot as yet identify with certainty. Olmec representations are at the basis of later Mesoamerican developments.

Mesoamerica underwent a particular florescence between 1 AD and 900 AD. The Classic Period is usually dated 300 to 900 AD. There were then two major civilizations: One was the huge city of Teotihuacán in the northern highlands, less than an hour from Mexico City. The other were the small Maya cities in the tropical forest of Guatemala, Honduras, and southern Mexico. Between them on the west was the major city of Monte Albán and on the east El Tajín. Dozens of these various city-states had spectacular centers with pyramids, plazas, administrative and palace buildings, as well as ball courts in stone.

Teotihuacán is noteworthy because it has the largest pyramids in the New World, although the less restored pyramids of Cholula and the Aztec capital were similar.

Teotihuacán's population of more than a hundred thousand lived at one time in 2,500 multifamily apartment compounds in the city.. Specialists argue whether it was a despotic monarchy or something of a republic.

The Maya cities are special because of their development of hieroglyphic writing. Writing was related to dynastic rulership. The Maya region is in limestone territory, which is softer to carve than the basalt of the highlands. Maya artists used it to make elegant portraits of the Maya rulers and their courts. These reliefs remind Westerners of Greek art, and many consider the Maya the apex of ancient American Indian civilization. However, the military power in the Classic Period was that of Teotihuacán, and for a time they even conquered the largest Maya city at Tikal.

The demise of the Classic Maya in about 900 AD and the earlier collapse of Teotihuacán ushered in a period known as Postclassic. Although there were spectacular cities such as Chichén Itzá, these centers looked back nostalgically to the Classic Period. The Aztecs came to power after 1400 AD and had only about a century to create a distinctive culture before the Spanish conquest in 1521. While many of the other centers imitated the Classic, the Aztecs turned to their own mythology to create new colossal images. Their capital city, Tenochtitlán, surpassed in population Teotihuacán whose ruins were only a short distance away. Tenochtitlán was an engineering marvel built with canals in the middle of a lake, like Venice. No one culture ever unified all of Mesoamerica. The Aztec Empire controlled less than two-thirds of the area, and it did not control it territorially—they just demanded periodic tribute in the form of goods.

The Andes

From the Old World point of view, the history of the Andes is more unusual than that of Mesoamerica. Because of the rich marine resources next to the desert coast, Andean people began to live in settled villages as a result of fishing, without the use of pottery and agriculture. That is, they had agriculture but mainly to grow gourds and cotton. Cotton was needed to make nets and lines for fishing. This period is known as the Preceramic. No other major civilization in the world began in a fishing culture.

The big surprise of the archaeology of the 1990s was that many ruins of the area were been re-dated to 2000 and even 3000 BC. All architectural remains are stone and impressively large and complex. There are large mounds, room complexes and circular plazas, but no figurative representations. Aspero, El Paraíso and Caral are a few. There is some current controversy whether food agriculture was there early or not. Because there are no rich burials, society may have been egalitarian.

Somewhat coeval with the Olmec was a remarkable oracle in the northern highlands of Peru, in a place called Chavín de Huántar. The Chavín culture was represented with shells and carnivorous animals (felines, condors, caymans) and fanged human beings. Most remarkably, these creatures came from all the ecological zones of Peru—the sea, the desert, the highlands and the tropical forest and were perhaps a first attempt at the ideological unification of the area. Later, more practical military attempts were made by the Wari, c. 1000 AD, and the Inca, 1400 AD.

From 500 BC to about 600 AD, there were regional cultures in the Andes, of which the Moche on the north coast and Paracas followed by Nazca on the south coast were the most noteworthy. Coastal architecture was largely adobe or earth. The site of Moche has the largest adobe structure in the New World, more than 1,100 feet long by 500 wide. Most of Moche images were ceramics intended for burial.

Textile preservation is greater in the burials of the south coast than anywhere else in the Andes because of the dryness of the desert. One find alone on the Paracas Peninsula consisted of over 400 mummy bundles, some wrapped in hundreds of textiles. Made of cotton and wool, expertly dyed with various dyes including cochineal, these are among the most complex textiles in the world. The south coast is also the area where the famous Nazca lines are located. Visible mainly from the air, they were discovered in the 1920s by early aviators.

Tiwanaku in Bolivia was a great building center with the finest stonework in ancient Peru, dated 500–1000 AD. The buildings consisted of small, coursed masonry linked up to oversize monolithic stone doorways, windows, niches, and other architectural elements. Soon after its collapse, the small stones were looted for Inca, Colonial and Modern constructions, so now only the very impressive large pieces remain. Most famous of these is the ten-foot-high monolithic Gate of the Sun (Spanish name) with a carved image of a deity and attendants. At Tiwanaku the cuts on figures and architectural stones are so precise, vertical and deep, that it is thought that metal tools—bronze—may have been used. Centuries later, the Inca ruler Pachacuti admired the ruins of Tiwanaku so much that he wanted imperial Cuzco to be built the same way. Inca masonry is very fine in its own way, but there appears to have been no continuation of metal tools, if indeed they existed.

After 1000 AD, Andean cultures such as the Chimú and Inca deemphasized the human figure in representation. By the time of the Inca, any figures were small and rare. Figures were not forbidden, only unimportant. Emphasis was on architecture, such as the great Inca estate of Machu Picchu. The Inca empire included most of the Andean area. Gold and silver, which go back to 2000 BC in the Andes, were more abundant then, and pottery appears to have been devalued. Even buildings had gold revetment over the masonry. Nothing could have been more different from the figurative, surreal, and mythic monuments of the contemporary Aztec than the abstract representations of the Inca.

6. HORTICULTURE

Everyone is familiar with the many plants and vegetables that were domesticated by ancient Americans that are a part of our diet. The long list includes maize, potato, many beans, squashes, peppers, tomatoes, avocadoes, chili peppers, cacao-chocolate, vanilla, just mentioning the ones that have been incorporated into our food culture. Many other exotic ones exist, such as amaranth, quinoa, various tropical fruits. If they could not domesticate animals, they would domesticate plants. The domestication of plants was one of the great achievements of ancient American Indians. As great if not greater than any achievement of other ancient peoples.

Domesticating plants required infinite patience over hundreds or thousands of years. The Indian approach was to work plants by cuttings and seed-by-seed planting. While the European farmer cast seeds by the handful, the American planter selected seeds individually to be the best possible for what he or she wanted. Without knowing the laws of Mendel and genetics, they refined each of the plants they were growing. Besides selection, they were aware of the need for fertilizer, placing fish or bird feces (guano) or whatever was available next to the growing plant, an innovation before any other farmers in the world. They were well aware of insects and bugs and kept plants that would distract pests away from the desired plants.

The point is that by giving such minute attention to plants, they created a rich and varied vegetarian diet for themselves, which eventually supported great populations. Corn, beans, squash together are a perfectly adequate vegetarian diet with all the necessary amino acids, without meat. With the addition of chili pepper or even chocolate, it is delicious. Cacao can be used as a sauce or as a drink seasoned by vanilla. A hybrid Mexican cooking is now world famous.

Corn (maize) was domesticated in Mexico nearly 10,000 years ago, and its many varieties were adapted in ancient times, from cool northern Canada to hot, tropical forest lands. Although many Europeans prefer wheat and Asians prefer rice, everybody feeds corn nowadays to their domestic animals and thus eats corn indirectly. It is the world's largest crop.

Potatoes were domesticated in the Andes about 8,000 years ago, where there are still over 3,000 varieties. It is a highland crop and thrives in cold regions where nothing much else grows. The few hundred varieties grown in the West have been responsible for one quarter of the world's population increase in the last few centuries. In fact, just the corn and potato have made possible the population increase needed for the Industrial Revolution in the eighteenth century. (The Irish Potato Famine of 1845 to 1849 indicates how reliant some places became on the potato.) American Indian crops have fed the world since the sixteenth century. They added spice, too. Where would Italian cooking and pizza be without tomatoes, Hungarian goulash without paprika (chili), and anybody without chocolate and vanilla?

Despite periodic difficulties like drought, ancient American Indians had an adequate, perhaps even good diet in comparison with the rest of the world. The Aztec and Inca had storehouses of foodstuffs for lean years. Recent excavations of the very early Preceramic Period in the Casma Valley in the Andes (1800–900 BC) reveal a structure with sixty rooms that seems to have been a food storehouse, indicating complex community organization very early. Inca storehouses were usually arranged on hillsides, with the contents needing the colder temperatures high up on the hill. Foodstuffs as well as many other things were stored in them.

7. STONE

WITH SOME POSSIBLE MINOR EXCEPTIONS in the southern Andes, all of the people of the Americas, be they hunting nomads or sophisticated city dwellers, used stone tools and weapons for all their tasks. In the terminology of the West, that makes them Stone Age or Neolithic.

Europe and the Old World had a Neolithic Period about 7000 BC, when people lived in simple farming villages with their domestic animals. By about 4000 BC, copper was developed for tools and shortly morphed into bronze. Copper is a soft metal and not ideally suited for weapons but it is very attractive. With the addition of tin or arsenic, it becomes hard and can be made sharp. It then has the name of "bronze." Bronze tools and weapons spread fast in the Old World, giving rise to spectacular civilizations like Egypt and Mesopotamia. We talk about the Bronze Age.

Old World invention, however, did not stop there. By about 2000 BC, iron ore was separated from its impurities and smelted into iron. Not as attractive as bronze, iron is much harder and can be made very much sharper. It is a practical tool and weapon and was the basis of the great monuments of Greek civilization. (In Sub-Saharan Africa, iron supplanted stone mostly without a Bronze Age.) We thus speak of an Iron Age. In most of the Old World, the Stone Age was swiftly followed by the Bronze Age and then the Iron Age. Next came steel. This may very well have been because so many civilizations existed in the Old World, cheek by jowl, and there was technological competition and exchange among them.

The ancient Americans seem to have been generally satisfied with stone tools. Bronze of tin and arsenic were developed in the southern Andes, but with a few possible exceptions were not made into useful tools. Or, in other words, stone tools were deemed as—or more—efficient, and there was not a wholesale changeover and refinement into metal tools. This seemed bizarre to the conquistadors and even to modern scholars. It's like the invention of the wheel—ancient

Americans were not following the model of Old World cultural development. They were dubbed "primitive" or "savages."

So what was this ancient American stone toolkit like? There were large, hard stones, like basalt, which were used as hammers or for pounding purposes. There were various-sized choppers and chisels, whose one edge was sharpened by knapping pieces off the whole. Some of those pieces could also be used as cutting implements themselves. Most important were implements made out of flint. Flint and chert are very hard stones that usually occur as a nodule in limestone. They are well suited for large cutting stones like knives. Polishing and abrading stone with sand finished many carvings.

Much desired through the Americas was obsidian or "volcanic glass" that occurs near certain lava flows. Obsidian is sharp and brittle and was used for all the things we use knives for. In the Americas, it was traded as far as four hundred miles from a source. One of the deadliest weapons of the Aztecs was a club studded with obsidian. Recently obsidian is of interest to some surgeons who find it better than steel scalpels in operations.

We don't know the details of working with stone tools, but a few points had to have been a part of it. The sharp edges of various tools must have worn off quickly and needed to be re-knapped frequently. Completely vertical-sided cuts were almost impossible to make, and many carvings therefore have slightly rounded edges. And stone workers must have had great patience to carve all the stones to cover pyramids or carve colossal figures. Enormous patience and time. They had patience with plants, and they had patience with stonework. Though stonework was arduous and time-consuming, ancient American Indians did not idealize shortcuts.

The Inca are famous for their beautifully cut "pillowy" masonry put together without mortar—so tight that a knife does not fit anywhere between the blocks. (This line has now been modernized to say that a credit card does not fit between them.) This was done by rubbing the stones against each other. Uniform rectangular stones would have made this work easier—and some walls have been constructed in this way. Many walls are, however, made of polygonal masonry, in which irregular pieces of stone had to be rubbed against each other like a giant jigsaw puzzle. The most famous of these is the so-called twelve-cornered stone in Cuzco, where variously shaped little stones embed the large stone into the masonry wall. While stonework was already work, ancient American Indians admired even extra work.

Perhaps an aspect of being satisfied with their stone tools was the fact that the ancient American Indians seem to have liked stone in general. The most precious objects in Mesoamerica were green stones—large enough for sculptures or small enough for beads. To Mesoamericans the green color was the color of vegetation and therefore of life. A proud Aztec father called his daughter his "little green stone" as an endearment. When Hernán Cortés and his men were being gifted by Montezuma, he tried to give them necklaces of green stone. The Europeans would have none of them or threw them away.

Obsidian and flint were seen as particularly beautiful and valuable stones. Obsidian was often cut into human and animal figures for offerings. The Maya in particular made flamboyant flint, chert, and obsidian carvings, nearly translucent in thinness in places, known as "eccentrics."

Something about the affection for stone is expressed in a drawing by Guaman Poma (Felipe Guaman Poma de Ayala). He was an indigenous nobleman who worked in the Spanish administration in Peru. He wrote a letter of about 1,200 pages with over 300 illustrations. He was partly self-taught and combined European drawing style with native elements. The book was about Spanish misconduct and meant as a complaint to King Philip III of Spain in 1615. This huge "letter" was never received, and the manuscript was lost for centuries. It turned up in a Copenhagen library in 1908, entitled, *The First New Chronicle and Good Government.* The book contrasts the orderly Inca empire to the chaos created by the Spanish. Examples of Inca order are pictures of officials in charge of roads, bridges, rest stops, etc., and stonemasons. In the stonemason picture, the masons are unique in cradling their stones as if they were their babies. To be sure, this is a colonial picture, since Guaman Poma was born after the conquest, but he still knew the Inca ways and may still have shared the indigenous feeling for stone.

In their own world, a stone technology did not hamper the ancient American Indians.

8. THE COLOSSAL

If stone tools were so awkward and laborious, why did ancient American Indians build such colossal architecture and carve such colossal sculptures? The very earliest Mesoamerican monuments are the Olmec colossal heads, six to ten feet in height, followed by dozens of Mesoamerican pyramids of which the largest at Teotihuacán—738 feet at base, 213 at height—is close in size to the largest pyramid of Egypt, and some sites like Tikal in Guatemala had five pyramids, the tallest of which is over 200 feet. Aztec architecture was also huge, and several sculptures, like the famous Calendar Stone, were three meters in diameter. Why were the Mesoamericans not satisfied with smaller works?

The answer I will come to, partly, is, "because they could." And "because they could" was because they had the necessary labor and labor organization. I will come back to Mesoamerica after a detour to ancient Egypt and the Andean region, where the available information is better. The fact is, none of the great preindustrial monuments of the world were built by slaves, including those of ancient America or those most noteworthy examples, the pyramids of Egypt. Large-scale-work slavery began in later times.

In the fifth century BC, the Greek traveler Herodotus started the idea that the Egyptian pyramids were built by slaves, a notion widely promulgated since in popular Hollywood films. Large-scale slavery was not practiced by the Egyptians nor by the ancient Americans. (There were individual slaves in many places in the ancient world.) Recent excavations near the Egyptian pyramids show that the builders of the pyramids were the Egyptian people themselves, in the slack agricultural season. They were fed, housed, and buried if they died on the job, at the expense of the state. In other words, they were paid for their work.

In the Andean area, the big undertaking of the Inca was not a pyramid but a road system. It was extensive in space rather than tall at a point. The Inca road system was colossal in itself—it went 3,000 miles from Ecuador to Chile. It consisted of two parts—a coastal route and a highland route, with periodic crossovers. On the desert coast, it was mostly adobe or earth; in the highlands it was stone, and it went up and down mountains, often on steps. As Inca rule was only about a hundred years before the conquest, the Inca did not build all of it. There were some preexisting road segments, and the Inca connected them in one huge system. Every twenty-five miles there were rest stops and periodically places to stay over. The Inca ruler himself was often on the road, carried in a palanquin.

From the sixteenth-century chroniclers and native writers, we know how labor was organized among the Inca. Although perhaps excessively idealized, the essential features are clear. The basic principle was "reciprocity." Land was not individually owned but belonged to the state. An individual plot of land was given for a family's use at the time of marriage or the birth of children. In return, everyone owed labor service to the state. This was called *Mita.* Women might spin and weave; men might do construction work, besides what they did for their own needs. At death, the land reverted to the state. In this way, the state took care of all the population, and it was said no one ever starved. (Nineteenth-century writers like William Prescott criticized the system for not allowing individuals to "better themselves" by accumulating capital.)

It is obvious that in this Andean system of reciprocity, the lord, ruler, king or state was bound to siphon off a portion of the goods or services to finance projects, and a large pool of workers was available for building. In the case of the completion of larger projects, the patron had to provide a major feast for the workmen. In other words, the Andean population was put to work and recompensed if not lavishly at least adequately depending on the situation.

That this was a common practice in the Andes is evident from the building of the Pyramid of the Sun at Moche. (It was named the Pyramid of the Sun by the Spanish.) The Spanish found or expected to find great treasure in this mound, and to make their work faster they diverted the river Moche to cut across the whole structure. The river ate away more than two-thirds of the original building. Even what remains is impressive.

In some ruinous areas of this huge adobe construction, one can see the brick interior. The whole mass was evidently built in vertical segments of adobe bricks only partially bonded to one another. In each segment, the adobe bricks were marked with a symbol—different from the symbols in the other segments. Research has suggested that the symbols signify a place or particular group who built that segment. The enormous monument was built of the labor service of many groups of people who insisted on their separate group identity by marking it in the bricks.

We do not have equally specific information about labor practices in Mesoamerica in textual sources. We know that most ordinary people lived in perishable, thatched houses. The houses were often built on a stone and/or gravel foundation, and when the house decayed these foundations often remained. They are often found and mapped by archaeologists, who call them "house mounds." These modest remains contrast with the pyramids, palaces, ball courts, and plazas of the elite. We know little of the labor arrangements between them.

In Mesoamerica, only at Teotihuacán can we see something of the social arrangement built into the city structure. Surrounding the two huge pyramids—also dubbed the Pyramids of the Sun and Moon by the Spanish and perhaps before them by the Aztecs—are masonry apartment compounds. "Apartment compound" is an archaeological designation for a walled masonry structure of rooms arranged around inner patios. Assuming that a patio and its rooms belonged to a family, these were multifamily dwellings with 60 to 100 people in each apartment compound. Only a few of these apartment compounds have been excavated and restored, but over 2,500 of them have been mapped. This is unique in the New World. They were on a grid plan with narrow streets between them. This is where most of the Teotihuacán population lived in later times of the city's history.

The apartment compounds were remarkably high-class and expensive in Mesoamerican terms. In another words, more resources and labor were spent on the dwellings of the population than anywhere else in Mesoamerica, suggesting that this population had correspondingly greater power. While they varied in room size, some looking slummy, many of them were embellished with high-quality mural paintings. Most apartment compounds have an important burial under the floor, often attributed to the "founder" of the compound. Inside the apartment compound, the people were ranked, judging from the fact that the rooms vary in size and quality. The compound probably had a headman or chief, and the patio groups varied in importance. Bone analysis indicates that the men were closer in kin than the women. The apartment compound was therefore inhabited by a lineage or clan with members of unequal importance.

How does this sociological picture relate to the building of the two colossal pyramids, the only-somewhat-less-large Ciudadela, and the ceremonial avenue that was more than three-quarters of a mile long and often 40 meters wide? We now know that the apartment compounds just described were built after the time of the huge ceremonial constructions. When the ceremonial buildings were built, the population was still living in perishable constructions later erased by the apartment compounds. Nevertheless, the apartment compounds are likely to be codifications or intensifications of the previous, perishable housing and social system.

Assuming that there was a reasonable correlation between the earlier perishable housing and the apartment compounds, many of the people of Teotihuacán may have been important enough to have had some voice in the city. Headmen numbering 2,500 are too many for a council or even for an assembly, but with intermediate statuses they could have represented levels in the social pyramid. Those on the top are likely to have been the labor organizers, those below the laborers.

Who were the rulers of Teotihuacán? Current Western archaeological theory has it that only a very powerful and despotic ruler could have carried out such building projects. In this view, a few designated areas may possibly be the ruins of a royal palace, but a palace is not obvious. To me, Teotihuacán has always "smelled" like a "collective place." There are no images of rulers, no images of great conquests. No, maybe one or two images of great gods. On the murals, people are shown in groups and processions.

There is an interesting parallel with the Roman Empire. The Roman Empire went through several forms of government—a kingdom, followed by a republic, followed by an empire. Teotihuacán lasted at least 800 years and could have had different governmental forms at different times as well. The era of the apartment compounds could have been something of a republic. Other times it might have been a kingdom or even empire.

The point of this roundabout discussion of Teotihuacán's social structure as reflected in the ruined remains, is that people seem to have been divided into clans or lineages and ranked in graduated stages. The people who built the civic-religious structures came from this complex social situation. They were embedded in a social matrix that ensured that they could identify with the various construction projects they were called upon to work.

Despite such varied statuses evident in the architecture, Teotihuacán things suggested egalitarianism. There is no division between aristocratic and popular art at Teotihuacán. Everyone had the same type of figurines, pottery, incense burners and even murals. This combination of the egalitarian and the ranked gives Teotihuacán its special character. We will be puzzling over the sociopolitical structure of Teotihuacán manifested in the ruined city for a long time to come, but it is there. Other Mesoamerican centers, especially the Maya, seem to have a greater division between the aristocratic and the popular.

We have some indications of the labor arrangements of Mesoamerica and Peru that made the erection of colossal works possible. In a way, that also suggests a reason for their building. The very process of building brought sometimes-diverse people together with the goal of creating something superhuman and not possible for a single individual. Whether that colossal work was for a ruler, deity, or both, it represented the community and the greatness of that community. Anyone who worked on it and partook of the concluding feast must have felt a part of it. Colossal structures, therefore, were literally state and community creators.

Other Neolithic cultures also erected some colossal works. In Neolithic Europe and in many parts of the Old World, huge, mostly un-worked stones were erected in small or large groups. Stonehenge is a complex example, but there are many smaller ones of menhirs and dolmens. (As a type, they are termed "megaliths.") All of these stones required great communal effort to move and set up and probably served the same purpose as the ancient American colossal works. However, generally, these stones are un-worked and the amount of labor that went into them is much less. The ancient American colossal constructions are more like the enterprises of the Bronze Age, such as in ancient Egypt and Mesopotamia, to which they are routinely compared. Those cultures had much more efficient bronze tools and weapons.

How and why did ancient America create a Bronze Age-level world with a Neolithic, stone technology? That question still remains to be answered.

9. FIBERS

Ancient American Indians may seem to be technologically backward, but they were technique-oriented when a material interested them. For some reason, they were particularly interested in fibers. As mentioned, cotton was grown in the Andes in the Preceramic Period, both to make nets for fishing and for carrying stones for building, as early as 3000 BC. How early textiles were woven for clothing, we do not know, but certainly by 2000 BC cloth was being woven. By the time of the conquest, Peruvian weavers had invented every preindustrial method known in the world and then a few unique to Peru. Maybe because it was ancient or for other reasons, but Peruvians liked things made out of fibers and related things like ropes. The Inca ruler did not wear a gold crown as a symbol of rulership on his head, but a yarn "fringe." This crimson yarn fillet was the symbol of Inca rulership, which perhaps says it all.

Suspension bridges crossing over rivers and gorges in the Inca road system were made out of fiber—in fact, grass—cables. These may have been the first suspension bridges in the world and were longer than the masonry bridges in Europe at the time. Over mats laid down along the bridge, people and llamas walked across. The Spanish had a hard time to coax their horses to get across, too. Bridges were renewed once a year and were part of the labor service of the surrounding communities.

Ropes and textiles require many of the same techniques. Similarly, boats in the Andes were made of reeds bunched together. Mostly they were used on Lake Titicaca and along the shoreline but not for open ocean travel. (However, in 1969–70 Thor Heyerdahl, the Norwegian ethnographer and sailing adventurer, built such reed boats modeled on ancient American and African designs from Lake Chad and proved they could be sailed across the Atlantic.)

Cotton was not unique to the New World, but it was superior to Old World cotton, which had short strands and was not suitable for weaving much of anything. The Roman senators sweltered in woolen togas. The Egyptians made cooler linen out of the flax plant. (And of course, the Chinese had silk.) New World cotton had double the length of Old World cotton strands and was therefore suitable for a variety of purposes. (Therefore it was the basis of the later development of cotton plantations in the US and the cotton mills of the Industrial Revolution in England, which were based on American cotton.)

At various times, both men and women wove in the Andes. They generally used a "backstrap loom," with one end attached to a roof or pole, and the back of the weaver holding the yarns taut at the other end. The cloths were narrow, and if necessary several were sewn together. In many cloths, the warp yarns were made out of sturdier cotton, while the weft cloths creating the design across it were often made out of camel or alpaca wool. Wool takes color better than cotton. Andeans had a rich variety of dyes and mordants and surviving ancient textiles are still brightly colored. A vivid red was created by cochineal, a dye made from insects. (Cochineal became very popular as a dye in Europe for everything from Cardinal's robes to English military uniforms known as "redcoats.")

Most Andean textiles were garments—loincloths, tunics, mantles, headgear. Andeans wove them as garments, including sleeves. They had no scissors and did not weave cloth to be cut up. They wove to size. Weaving necessitated counting—counting the warps and wefts—and basic mathematics was highly developed as a result.

Andean textiles were labor-intensive, like the stonework, and admired not just for their appearance but for the ingenious work that went into them. They had a few of their own unique techniques. "Discontinuous warp," as the name implies, is a technique in which there are no warp threads going all around the weaver's body, so that in each part of the cloth the warp and weft are separately woven. This was only possible by what has been called "scaffolding"—another set of warp yarns was set up for the duration of the weaving process and then removed. In effect, the weaver wove two cloths simultaneously. Such a cloth often had sort of a patchwork design.

What could have been the reason for such a complicated technique? Because in each woven area warp and weft could be the same color, perhaps the desire was for very saturated color. Because each woven area was woven of the same color, it did not have to be very dense and could have been light to the touch. Other textiles seem to have been made to be very light, and lightness may have been an Andean value. Some discontinuous-warp textiles have figurative designs that required exceptional virtuosity. Descriptions of textile techniques put Westerners to sleep, because we are used to machine-made cloths. Andeans enjoyed the complexities of weaving techniques—if for no other reason than everyone could weave at least a little and could appreciate refinements.

We know less about Mesoamerican textiles, because due to the wetter weather none have survived in tombs. Maya reliefs, especially in the city state of Yaxchilán, show queens in gorgeous garments. The Aztec tribute books show that the Aztecs demanded from their subjects great quantities of textiles. Some of these were not of cotton, but of a cheaper substitute made of maguey cactus fiber. In Mesoamerica, textiles in uniform sizes functioned as currency in the marketplace. (Cacao functioned as small change.)

While not of primary interest to the Spanish, textiles must have been interesting enough, because hundreds of Mesoamerican examples were sent to Europe as curiosities in the sixteenth century. They are mentioned in the boat lists. It is also recorded that they were given to individuals and institutions like convents, as gifts. Nevertheless, no Mesoamerican textiles exist in European collections. Being perishable they would have to have had careful handling and storage to survive. We have some old textiles that survive from the Middle Ages, such as the Bayeux tapestry, but no one treasured the ancient American fabrics sufficiently to take such care of them over the years.

An indication of the style and importance of ancient American cloths is their survival as a hybrid folk costume in many parts of Latin America well into the twentieth century. Despite five hundred years of Spanish colonial influence and cheap, modern garments.

10. METALS

THE CONQUISTADORS WERE ONLY INTERESTED in gold. In Europe, gold was the most sought-after material, and there was too little of it. It was acquired in small quantities and at great expense from the West African "Gold Coast," Ivory Coast, Ghana, Nigeria. Muslim middlemen brought it through the Sahara. In the medieval Church, gold was associated with light and even heaven. It has been a currency since Classical times. When Columbus saw a small piece of gold on a native in the Caribbean, the initial search for spices was put on hold.

Every adventurer with no significant livelihood in Europe flocked to the New World to find the source of the gold.

The Aztec and Inca were amazed by this hunger for gold. For them, gold was only one of several valuable materials. The Aztec father who called his daughter his "precious greenstone," would not have called his daughter his "precious excrement of the gods," *teocuitlatl*, gold, which means literally "excrement of the gods." Gold was valuable but not preeminent. The Inca referred to gold as the "sweat of the sun" and silver as the "tears of the moon." Apparently metals were seen as bodily discharges.

In the Andes, the Inca Atahuallpa was on the throne when Pizarro took him prisoner by stratagem. It was the ruler who noticed the conquistador's enormous desire for gold. Wanting to ransom himself, he offered to fill one large room with gold and two with silver in the city of Cajamarca. Runners went all through the Inca empire collecting gold and silver to fill the rooms. Of course, Pizarro did not let Atahuallpa go and executed him on some pretext.

All the gold and silver amassed in the Americas was melted down into uniform bars by the very goldsmiths who had made the pieces. One fifth went to the Spanish crown; the rest was divided proportionately between the conquering leaders and the men. A few huge Aztec gold pieces were sent back to the court of Charles V as curiosities, but eventually they too were melted down. As a result, only a few small Aztec or Inca gold and silver objects survive. (Out of his share, Cortés had a gold dining service made immediately.)

The oldest gold from the New World comes from the Andes and dates to about 2000 BC. From there gold and gold-making techniques spread very slowly and gradually to the north, to Colombia, Ecuador, and Central America. Mesoamerica did not acquire the precious metals until about 800–900 AD. The skill arrived from Central America, and Central American gold objects have been found in the great sinkhole offering known as the "cenote at Chichén Itzá" in the Maya area, dated about 1000 AD. Sometimes Mesoamericans melted these down and refashioned things to their taste. As gold-working was relatively new in Mesoamerica, Cortés could not have found huge quantities. The vast amounts of gold and silver came from the Andean region, ten years later in his conquest.

Andeans both cast gold and fashioned it by hammering over a wooden form. In casting, a model of the thing to be gold was made in wax, encased in a clay form, the wax melted out by heating, and gold poured in its place. Although the Peruvians knew this "lost-wax" technique, their preference was for hammering. Even three-dimensional objects, easier to make by casting, were made by hammering.

Although hammering sounds simple, it could be quite complicated. There are several three-dimensional figures from Chavín times, 600–200 BC, such as a jaguar or a seated figure blowing a conch shell, whose rounded bodies are made of hammered pieces. Each piece—head, arm, leg, tail—was hammered in pieces and had to be soldered together. Soldering requires great control over heat—the piece to be added to the original had to be heated to bond, but not heated so much that the original piece would melt or be damaged. Hammering may have been chosen because it used less gold, but the Peruvians also seemed to like the slightly uneven texture that caught the light in its appearance. In order to use less gold, metalsmiths usually worked an alloy of gold, silver and copper, known as tumbaga. An acid was added to the surface to remove the silver and copper and make it look completely gold. This process is known as depletion gilding.

Ancient Peruvians used gold for jewelry and prestige objects, and if there was much for vessels imitating pottery shapes. One of the most common objects were beakers made in pairs for ritual drinking at feasts. Much gold was available in later times for the Chimú, Lambayeque and Inca cultures. The Inca actually used gold as building revetment, inside and outside. The Coricancha, the Inca Temple of the Sun in Cuzco, was covered in gold. These pieces were the first to be taken down to ransom Atahuallpa.

Despite all the looting for gold—in colonial times mining companies looted the Chimú capital Chan Chan—gold has been found recently in tombs by archaeologists, especially in the Lambayeque region (north of Chimú). Besides umpteen drinking beakers, there were some great gold masks almost half a meter wide. The strange thing about these masks is that many were painted red, and other painted gold objects come from earlier cultures. This is very strange for any Westerner, for whom the point of gold is its shiny golden surface. For Andeans it was evidently enough to know that the object was gold in its interior "essence," and color could be added for symbolic or other purposes.

Casting was the preferred method of Central Americans and the skill that was learned by Mesoamericans. Aztecs and their contemporaries the Mixtecs were distinguished by fine filigree casting with pieces of wax so small they could barely be touched by hands. Two guilds made metal objects in the Aztec capital—one specialized in hammering, one in casting. Both areas inlaid gold with semiprecious stones like turquoise and colorful red shell. The Aztec ruler wore a turquoise diadem for a crown. Like jade, blue turquoise was an auspicious symbol of water.

Although some ancient Americans found stones we consider gems, in particular emeralds in Colombia, they were not interested in gems. In the Old World, gems surpassed the value of gold. When Marco Polo returned from his trading trip to China, he converted all his currencies to gems—great value, taking up little space. Turquoise was the favorite gemstone in the Americas.

Finding all this gold in Mesoamerica and the Andes, the conquistadors were hoping to discover other sources of gold in the Americas. There were rumors of a man covered in gold, El Dorado, in Colombia; they went in search of him. As time went on, the story got bigger and bigger, and El Dorado referred to a city or even a country of gold. The actual story was based on the initiation of a Colombian Muisca ruler, who was covered in gold dust he washed off in Lake Guatavita, while people threw gold trinkets into the lake. The story has had such power over the imagination of Westerners that they have tried to drain the lake a number of times since the sixteenth century. Most notably, once in the nineteenth century, when the lake was thoroughly drained, but its bottom turned out to be all deep mud. When the mud dried, it became something like concrete. Only a very small amount of gold was ever found in that enterprise. Nevertheless, thousands of gold objects have found their way into the Bogota Museum of Gold to astonish modern tourists.

The idea of El Dorado did not die. Conquistadors searched for it all over South America and the Amazon and then in Florida and the Southeast and the Pueblo areas of the Southwest in the sixteenth and seventeenth centuries. No such golden lands were found, but much of the Americas was mapped in the process.

What did Europe do with all the gold? According to Weatherford, most of the gold was made into elaborate ecclesiastical objects for churches—crosses, monstrances, and into royal ceremonial objects and some into expensive coins. In general, it may have had little impact on life in Europe, although it was its reserve wealth and might have caused long-term economic imbalances in Spain. But silver transformed Europe. It wasn't just the looted silver, but the find of the silver mines worked by Indians immediately after the conquest, mostly in Bolivia but also in Mexico. Silver was used for coinage in Europe on a large scale for commercial purposes at every level of society. What little was available before, was often adulterated and hampered commerce.

American silver accumulated in many European hands and ultimately formed the "capital" of the capitalistic system. Money began to supersede land as the major source of wealth and caused great social changes. There was so much silver, in fact, that in the sixteenth century it caused worldwide inflation and contributed to the decline of Spain. The new silver economy became global, drawing the Chinese and the Ottoman empire into one monetary system of related currencies. For Europe it meant superiority, and the capital eventually financed the Industrial Revolution.

Ancient Americans experimented with copper and bronze—both tin and arsenic bronze—at various times, especially in the Andes. In particular, the aforementioned Tiwanaku in Bolivia. Tiwanaku seems to have been a great oracle in its time, with an architecture of beautifully cut and precisely joined masonry. Most of the smaller stones have been looted, but big stones, including windows, niches and gateways still survive. Among them are stones that have been joined together with copper clamps. A channel was cut in each stone and lined up so molten copper poured into the channels would hold the stones together. A novel idea. This can still be seen at the site. The fineness of the masonry and the sharpness of the cutting of both the architecture and the figural sculpture suggest metal tools, although we don't have positive evidence of it.

Pachacuti, the Inca king who conquered the Tiwanaku area hundreds of years later and who marveled at the ruins, ordered that Cuzco be built the same way. And, although Inca masonry is spectacular in its own way, it lacks the geometric precision of Tiwanaku, nor is there any suggestion that the Inca used metal tools. If Tiwanaku had bronze tools, they did not spread into the rest of ancient America as a great, new innovation. Andeans and Mesoamericans continued to explore the use of bronze for a variety of limited purposes—little bells with pebbles for clappers, a unit of currency in the form of axes, now known as "axe money"—in an apparent attempt to get some use out of this material, but it did not amount to a anything significant. No Bronze Age. (It has been suggested that metalworking in quantity did not evolve in the Americas because they did not have adequate heat to melt the metals. European metalwork was more advanced because of the invention of bellows to provide more air in smelting. The New World blow tubes were adequate for the purposes of the New World.

11. FEATHERS

BESIDES REFERRING TO HIS DAUGHTER AS "green stone," the Aztec father might have added that she was also a "precious feather." Feathers were precious to all American Indians, from North America to the Amazon. The Plains Indians distinguished their leaders with "feather bonnets" made mostly out of eagle feathers and familiar in Hollywood Westerns. While the eagle is now a protected bird, American Indians still have rights to some eagle feathers for their ceremonial headgear.

Europeans devalued feathers as something cheap and perishable, perhaps because Old World birds were relatively drab in color and had been of little interest to them. They did however use exotic plumes on ladies' and men's hats for centuries. Many of these came from the Americas. Much of America is covered by tropical forest and is filled with the most fantastic and colorful birds, whose feathers were eagerly imported by both Mesoamerican and Andean civilizations. Amazonian Indians still make various grand headdresses and ritual objects out of them. The conquistadors threw away all the feathers they had been given as worthless.

Many Aztec feathered objects were sent back to Europe as curiosities, but as impermanent objects like the textiles, most did not survive. Less than ten examples now exist. In the nineteenth century a few turned up in a trunk in the attic of Ambras Castle in Austria. They were labeled "Moorish." The Duke of Bavaria sometimes took a feather out of it for his tsako and his horse.

Feathers were used by the Aztecs to adorn people, architecture, palanquins, much to the amazement of eye witnesses like Bernal Diaz. Perhaps most unusual from a European point of view was the use of feathers in war. The Aztec tribute book *(Matricula de Tributos)* indicates that what the Aztec rulers wanted most from their subject territories was feathered overalls—one-piece cotton trousers and sleeved top completely covered in feathers as warrior outfits as well as round warrior shields. Areas close to the tropics were to send bunches of red, green, and blue feathers. Even the costumes that looked like jaguar pelts were actually made of feathers. The warrior had a feather headdress, but if he was a leader he also had a large feathered standard stuck in the back at the waist that towered above his head.

This was not exactly a practical outfit, it was awkward to move in—imagine a little rain on all these feathers attached to cloth. Aztec warfare was in many ways a ceremonial activity, perhaps like medieval jousting. The aim of the war was to capture a victim and take him alive for later sacrifice. Not easy. The greatest coup was to capture the leaders, very visible because of their overhead back-standards. Men got killed on the battlefield but not necessarily a great number, because that was not the aim.

One of the feather-work pieces in the Ambras Castle trunk is a shield with the image of a coyote or possibly a mythological creature in red feathers outlined in gold, indicating the sumptuousness of this military finery. The other is a headdress or back-standard—scholars can't decide which—popularly known as "Montezuma's headdress," probably having nothing to do with Montezuma. It consists of an impressive quantity of green quetzal feathers, blue cotinga feathers, and some gold. The quetzal bird's habitat is the tropical area near the Guatemala highlands, and the more than 500 feathers, each more than a foot long, in the headdress had to be imported from there. Only the male quetzal has two, long tail feathers, so the headdress has the feathers of 250 birds. Quetzal feathers were by far the most valued feathers in Mesoamerica, next to iridescent hummingbird feathers.

The Feathered Serpent—Quetzalcoatl—is one of the oldest and most confusing deities of Mesoamerica, going back at least to Teotihuacán. Unlike the evil nature of the biblical serpent, the Mesoamerican serpent was a benign creature, sort of like the Chinese dragon. Because it sheds its skin, the serpent was a symbol of eternal life. Covered in green quetzal feathers, the reference was to green vegetation, the rainy season, and life itself. Shown in contexts of water and growing things, it was a symbol of fertility. In time, other ideas were attached to this symbol, for example the planet Venus. In the 260-day calendar, the birth date of Quetzalcoatl was "1 Reed."

Cortés happened to reach Mexico in the year 1 Reed. Montezuma and his councilors searched their books to find out who this visitor was—who was godlike. They came up with a legend about Quetzalcoatl that was not comforting. According to that legend, the ruler of a defunct city named Tollan, long before their time, had the name or title of the deity Quetzalcoatl. He was in conflict with another Tollan faction that was led by Tezcatlipoca. Some of this story is mythic—Quetzalcoatl was a creative spirit, while Tezcatlipoca was destructive, and their alternation explained the world. Some of the story may have been historical. Quetzalcoatl had to leave Tollan and went to the seashore. According to some stories he built a bonfire and jumped in, to become the planet Venus. According to other sources, he sailed off on a raft of serpents and vowed to return.

His return was bad news, in that Quetzalcoatl had a more legitimate dynastic right to rule than Montezuma. So Montezuma vacillated between the idea that Cortés was the returning Quetzalcoatl claiming his kingdom and the sense that he was just an unscrupulous foreign invader. He made the mistake of inviting Cortés in, and put him up in his father's palace. Right away, the Spanish broke down a wall in the palace and found gold treasure. It was the quetzal feathers that made the Feathered Serpent a powerful mythical creature and the accident of history that made him the most memorable Aztec deity.

The sixteenth-century Andean feather-work that was sent back to Europe did not survive, and all subsequent searches were for gold—feathers, if found, were of no interest. Recently, accidental finds and looting have unearthed hundreds of well-preserved examples of feather-work found in the coastal deserts of Peru; these have been of great fascination in our current culture. Private collectors, interested in transgressive postmodern art, have picked up these unusual and colorful creations. In 2008 the Metropolitan Museum of Art was one of the first to exhibit about seventy examples. The feathers were attached to a cotton cloth backing, starting from the bottom and overlapping like shingling.

Most Andean feather-work consists of headdresses and garments, but large hangings also exist. The designs are simple geometric forms or figures of birds and humans. A dramatic garment type is the tabard—sort of a large tunic with the sides left open. It's the feathers that are spectacular. The most common color is yellow from parrots and macaws, but there are bright reds and a brilliant turquoise from tanagers. Most date to the Chimú, c. 1000–1400 AD or a few hundred years before. The birds were acquired from the Amazon and perhaps bred in captivity as well. The most sensational objects are great hangings, eighty inches long, with alternating plain blue and yellow areas. A hundred of these exist and perhaps were hangings in a great hall. They were found rolled up in big pottery jars.

The Metropolitan Museum exhibition was protested by bird-lovers, who complained that the Museum condoned the killing of birds and that some of the birds are on the endangered list. While that may not have been true in ancient times, some birds, like the Guatemalan quetzal, are now nearly extinct. In the Western view, feathers are barbaric. Westerners do not consider animal pelts to be barbaric. In the North American fur trade of the seventeenth and eighteenth centuries, millions of animal pelts were sent to Europe for great profit with little investment. Indians were hired to do the actual hunting. The highly sought-after beaver, bear, otter and other animals were depleted by American traders overhunting them for an insatiable European market. Within fifty years, most of these rich animal resources were gone.

Many people now think that the wearing of feathers and pelts is symbolic of the destruction of our natural habitat made precarious by industrialization and human sprawl. Ancient Americans lived with a natural abundance of flora and fauna and saw its bounty as the same as precious stones and shells.

12. CODES

Writing and recording systems are generally seen as signs of civilization, and they are present in the Americas. Nothing proves more the separation of Mesoamerican and Andean civilizations from each other than their recording systems. The Mesoamerican system was a picture-writing hieroglyphic system similar to that of the ancient Old World, while the Andean system was a mnemonic one, based not surprisingly, on yarn. They seem to have been unaware of each other's system.

The Spanish conquerors had no admiration for the Inca yarn khipu (or quipu) which to them seemed as simpleminded as a rosary. Others had described it as looking like a string mop. Only from the second half of the twentieth century has the khipu yielded its secrets, and that, because of the computer. Not because of data fed into the computer, but because of the recognition that the khipu itself was structured like a computer. Much of Andean symbolism was based on a dualistic principle such as upper and lower divisions in cities and families or male and female complementary divisions in representations. The decipherment of the khipu began with the recognition that all the information in it was binary—like the computer.

Gary Urton showed that every part of khipu making requires a binary decision. Should it be made of cotton or wool? The primary cord may determine its overall meaning or category. Pendant cords with knots are added to the primary cord. Those yarns could be spun to the right (S) or to the left (Z). They could be pale or dark in color. The knots could also be S or Z. The pendants cord could be attached over or under the primary cord.. There could be secondary cords on the pendant cord. Altogether, the khipu maker had to make seven binary decisions expressing his material through the structure of the khipu. From this analysis we don't know what the khipu was about; we only know that it was laid out in a complex accounting system that the khipu keeper used as a way to remember perhaps vast amounts of data.

What kind of data was on the khipu? On a number of khipus, the knots are arranged in a decimal system and are clearly mathematical. Such khipus could have been census data, storage information, calendrical and other numerical data necessary for running the Inca empire. Sixteenth-century texts mention khipus referring to histories, genealogies, songs, and other literary forms. With the absence of the khipu keeper, these are more difficult to reconstruct.

As far as we know, the khipu goes back only to about 1000 AD, and the most numerous examples date to the Inca. As perishable objects, they have survived best in dry tombs. We now have about six hundred examples, and the more their structure is studied the closer we get to understanding their content. The khipu emerged out of the native Andean interest in yarn, the mathematical interest in weaving, and the dualistic practice of social divisions. It was totally embedded in Andean culture.

It is generally believed that writing in the Old World was invented in ancient Sumer, and like the khipu, its early content was economic and accounting oriented. Other Old World writing systems were influenced directly or indirectly by Sumerian writing. There is some question about early Chinese character writing, which in some views is of Sumerian inspiration, while in others an independent invention. Its content is religious and deals with contact with royal ancestors.

Mesoamerican writing is believed to be only the second or third independent invention of writing in the world. It is mostly dynastic, calendrical, and religious. Its purpose seems to have been to legitimize authority. Derived from pictures and sometimes parts of pictures, it is often called "picture-writing." At the high end, it is also phonetic and hieroglyphic. Because it may have begun as early as 1000 BC and was used one way or another by a dozen cultures until the conquest, it is quite varied. Although we know it mostly from nonperishable media—stone carvings, murals, ceramics—it is evident that books of native paper or deer hide were made very early. In the sixteenth century, the Spanish burned all these books as works of the devil, but sent some back to Europe as curiosities. Currently, thirteen ancient Mesoamerican books survive, mostly in various European libraries: three Maya and the rest contemporary with the Aztecs. All of them are either historical or religious.

Because it was so early, the origin of Mesoamerican writing is not clear. There are half a dozen early inscriptions in different styles and locations, all seemingly variants of one another, suggesting one ultimate source. Most confusingly, a greenstone block with writing-like incisions has recently been found in Olmec contexts. The signs on this Cascajal Block are quite different from the other known inscriptions. The origins point to the Olmec and quite early, 1000–500 BC.

Mesoamerican writing consists of signs or glyphs that are stylized pictures or word symbols. Associated with images, it is clear that the majority are names (of persons, gods) and places. Action signs are rarer, sometimes indicated by the picture (actions include things like capture, accession). So-and-so did such-and-such in such a place at such a time. An important part of the inscription is the date—when the event occurred. In fact, the date is so important that many inscriptions are largely dates.

Calendars were a Mesoamerican obsession. There was a basic 365-day agricultural calendar—similar to the one the Andeans had. But in Mesoamerica, on that was grafted and ran concurrently a 260-day calendar that worked something like a horoscope. The 260 days were the result of the concurrent run of cycles of 20 "day-signs" and 13 numbers, which came out to a 260-day cycle. This 260-day cycle has no obvious astronomical significance and was very ancient. It could have been a lunar cycle. Dates in this calendar, such as 1 Rabbit or 2 Jaguar, are more common on inscriptions than dates in the solar-year calendar. (Nowadays the 260-day cycle is thought to be the time for the gestation of a baby, which doesn't help explain anything.)

It took 52 years for the 365-day cycle and the 260-day cycle running concurrently to come back to the same starting point. For Mesoamericans, that 52-year time was the equivalent of our century. Every 104 years (52 x 2), the Venus cycles matched up with the 52-year human cycle. These time cycles determined the life of people and even the gods. The purpose of the 260-day cycle was divinatory: numbers and days signs were associated with supernaturals and had good or bad fortunes. These were calibrated by a specialist priest. These were also the subject of a number of the books used by the priests, some of which the Spanish took to Europe. For Mesoamericans, these time cycles were the order of the universe.

Mesoamericans imagined their calendrical cycles as a great circle or, more properly, interconnected circles, which is how we illustrate this in our books to explain it. Their concept of the universe was that time is cyclical. This was represented particularly by the Aztecs late in Mesoamerican history in the famous Calendar Stone monument. This almost-twelve-foot disc of basalt is somewhat unfinished and was found in 1790 in the rubble of the cathedral area of Mexico City. It would have been intended for one of the major Aztec temples. The 20 individual day-signs of the 260-day calendar are in a circle around a central diagram. The diagram shows the four previous creations and destructions of the world with the fifth world, the present, in the center. The four previous worlds had all been destroyed by natural calamities, and the present day would also be destroyed by the earth, through the calamity of earthquake. This cosmic picture was the belief of most Mesoamericans. The universe was not static but lived and died like humans.

There are a few dates in the 52-year cycle on the monument and a few glyphs, one of which is the name glyph of Montezuma. (The glyph consists of the turquoise diadem of rulership and a nose ornament.) While some of the glyphs are undeciphered, the monument seems to proclaim that time itself is Aztec or that the Aztec empire was a new era or that the Aztecs helped support the present era from calamities to come. The Aztecs did this not through a portrait of their ruler but in glorifying and codifying and perhaps appropriating time itself, which was usually an unrepresented idea that existed from time immemorial.

The Maya had yet a third calendar. The 52-year calendar had no fixed point in the past and thus was relative and hard to interpret. (It was called the "Short Count.") The Maya also had a linear calendar, known as the "Long Count," that enumerated days that have passed from a fixed point in the past, much like our 1 AD. (The Maya fixed point was 3104 BC, a mythical date, in that it is prior to all Mesoamerican civilization as far as we know it.) The Maya made long calculations into the past and even the future. We now know that the Long Count, in a more abbreviated form, existed prior to the Maya, closer in time to the origins of writing.

The recently deciphered portions of Maya hieroglyphic writing indicate that in a lengthy and elaborate form the texts refer to the lives and doings of dynastic rulers of the city-states. Basically, they elaborate on the name, place, and action—as do non-Maya inscriptions. They deal with birth, accession, war, marriage and death, the patronage of the gods. The actual glyphs are sometimes pictures, some are word signs, but also many phonetic elements. The language of the Maya appears to have been Ch'ol, and that has helped to decipher hundreds of phonetic signs. Maya writing is somewhat akin to Egyptian and Chinese writing in structure. Some Maya monuments consist mostly of text and date. The three surviving Maya books and examples of painting on vases indicate that there was a cursive Maya writing style and that there was a great deal of writing.

It is obvious to anyone from the Old World that Long-Count dating and Maya hieroglyphic writing are great advances in record keeping. Nevertheless, most Mesoamerican cultures did not borrow and use them, then or later. They stayed with the 52-year cycle and the few basic signs. Why? It's not that they were not acquainted with it. Teotihuacán conquered and temporarily ruled the Maya city of Tikal. The Maya traded with everybody. Teotihuacán possibly had a Maya barrio. Yet Teotihuacán had hardly a writing system worth its name, at least on nonperishable media.

One suggestion is that the hieroglyphics were based on the Maya Ch'ol language and did not fit a variety of other languages spoken in Mesoamerica. Another is that other Mesoamerican centers were polyglot and could read signs in a variety of languages, whereas phoneticism would restrict them to one language. Yet another theory is that Maya writing was associated with dynastic rulership and history, and other places might not have had dynastic rulers. Whatever the reason, and perhaps all of these, the rest of Mesoamerica did not find hieroglyphic writing and dating practical or necessary. It survived in a vestigial form until the sixteenth century, but in complete form it disappeared after 1000 AD, with the collapse of the Maya city states. The Aztecs had a system of signs and were on the way to develop a different, simple, phoneticism of their own.

Judging from their writing system, writing in Mesoamerica was not invented for a practical task, unless we consider propaganda practical. In a strange way, we can consider Maya writing practical, in that it helped buttress the power of dynastic rulership and support the political system. Presumably, few people could read most of the inscriptions except for a few signs. Writing of any sort was the esoteric knowledge of the elite.

The 260-day calendar, on the other hand, was basic to Mesoamerican thought and organized the unseen powers of the universe. It negotiated the forces of order with those of chance. It was important to all Mesoamericans. Without the component of writing, it has survived in a number of Native communities to the present day.

13. MIND GAMES

Precisely because writing was not highly developed or was nonexistent, ancient Americans created intellectual games and puzzles in other ways. A clear example of this are the Wari designs on tunics in the Andes, c. 600–1000 AD. Wari was the capital of the first conquest state in Peru, located in the southern highlands. Its culture, religion, and image system were similar to and perhaps borrowed from Tiwanaku in Bolivia. However, Wari did not erect great stone monuments. Most of its representations that survive are textiles and pottery from coastal burials. The tunics found on mummy bundles are believed to have been those of Wari officialdom.

Wari tunics had long been known for their jazzy, abstract, geometric motifs woven in bright colors. In the 1960s, Alan Sawyer took a long look at them and discovered that most were distortions of a single specific recognizable subject. This subject was found at Tiwanaku and consisted of a human or animal-headed figure holding a staff in each hand. At Tiwanaku this looked like a "deity" flanked by attendants best known from the Gate of the Sun. Patient analysis of the Wari textiles showed that they too represented a figure holding staffs; it is just that the design on one side had been greatly expanded, while on the other it was so compressed that hand and staff were just vertical lines. The design was further complicated in that woven in vertical strips, the designs on top and beneath faced in different direction. Moreover, the colors of each section of the body were different in each figure. No wonder it looked like a jazzy, syncopated abstraction and not a figure.

Most Wari textiles turned out to be variants on such a figure. The compression and expansion was more extreme in some than in others. But even stranger, some textiles just showed abbreviated versions of the figure—a diagonal line cut through the image showing just an eye and mouth in one half and a fret (tail) in the other. After compression and expansion, this truncated design seemed the most remote from the original, yet once it was explained, it made total logical sense. Every part of the design makes sense as a part of the figure. How can one explain a highly logical complicated system of images that presumably made sense only to insiders?

As an archaeological culture, we do not have information on the Wari to explain this. We presume that for reasons of state or religion, certain Wari persons had to wear a tunic with the Gate of the Sun design on it. Wanting to vary the design, the weavers abstracted it by compression and expansion, alternation of form and color and even dissection. Without losing any of the meaning of the original. Evidently the wearers of the tunic enjoyed the cerebral game, while the weavers competed on new variants of this limited form. These textiles were examples of Andean intellectual puzzles.

This particular mind game was not limited to one culture in Peru. Paracas embroideries played similar games in positioning and color, but with a great number of spirit beings. In fact, there are close to ninety on a textile in the Brooklyn Museum in New York, called by some a "codex in cloth."

In Mesoamerica, there was a mind game in which it seems everyone participated. It has no name, and it is not restricted to any medium. I will call it "Sign Association." (Those who study it now call it "iconography.") It is said that Chinese has 6,000 characters, all of which have to be memorized. I don't know how many symbols or signs Mesoamerica had, but it was certainly in the hundreds. Starting with the 20 day-signs, almost anything could be a symbol: flower, maize, bird, feather, arrow, blood, water, heart, skull, elements of costume, headdress, facial painting, various drops, scrolls, footprints, jaguar pelts, for a start. Some of these elements were combined in a figure or emblem to convey some particular or general meaning. This is especially prevalent at Teotihuacán and in the Mixteca-Puebla codices a few centuries later.

Reading these combined visual signs, however, is not a simple matter. Sometimes it isn't even easy to determine if a figure is male or female, since the signs in it may be mixed. This is true in myths too; in some Aztec myths the moon is female, in others male. Moreover, the signs themselves are often ambivalent. Should a skull and flowers signify fertility or death? A death sign can indicate the end or beginning of something. One of the ways in which scholars try to marshal the signs is by deciding whether the preponderance of the signs relate to water and fertility or to war and sacrifice. But in fact, these categories are not mutually exclusive.

From the iconographer's point of view, this is a headache. The rain god Tlaloc is one of the most recognizable images in Mesoamerica because of his goggle eyes and mustache-like upper lip. As a young scholar looking for meaning, I once divided the Teotihuacán Tlaloc forms into two types—based on the facial features. Many years later, I found that there were various intermediate forms, and my division into two types was meaningless. There were just variants on a theme.

From the Mesoamerican point of view, I imagine this open variation was a richer way of communicating than the specificity of writing, or our attempts to pin things down iconographically. There were endless possibilities and reinterpretations in the ambiguous sign system. Scholars debate whether the central face in the Calendar Stone is the Sun God, the Earth God, or more cleverly, the Sun-in-the-Earth. Had the carver made it clear which—which he could have—it would be easy. But those carvers and painters did not. And they did not, because in their universe everything was interrelated, and perhaps different things meant different things at different times or for different people.

Deities were not anthropomorphic entities with human personalities, but more-or-less stable constellations of signs and qualities, which they shared not just with similar deities but even with their opposites.

The intellectual game was to navigate this system as a communication device and as a way of philosophical exegesis and understanding.

Interestingly enough, the Maya played this game too, but with a difference. Because they developed hieroglyphic writing, much of the information elsewhere in Mesoamerica in the signs was now in the Maya glyphs, in themselves also ambiguous. Because the glyphs told their story in a more compact fashion, the figures began to tell a different story. That story was about naturalistic depiction. But the focus on the figures was not just on such depiction but on idealization, such as the elegance of line, the development of aristocratic beauty. Some Maya centers like Copán in Honduras still covered their figures with signs, but many, such as Palenque and Yaxchilán, tucked signs into headdress or costume details that did not interfere with the sinuous lines of figures. They seem to have invented visual effects for their own sake, for pure aesthetic delectation. We like it, because it is our definition of "art."

The complicated cerebral games in the representations of Mesoamerica and the Andes developed precisely because there was no or little writing there. They reveal the same processes of reason, logic, and mental ability that is in writing or, as we think, in persons of more "advanced" cultures. They indicate joy in the creation and reception of puzzles. They also indicate a concept of time that is not concerned with speed and efficiency but enjoys ambiguity and multiplicity of interpretations. Why the Maya developed hieroglyphic writing and self-conscious aesthetics is still an enigma. I think cutthroat competition in the tropical forest is behind it, but I do not know.

14. THE INVISIBLE

Most Mesoamerican monuments were meant to be seen. They proclaimed the power of rulers, people, and gods on great stone carvings They were meant to evoke awe, fear, recognition, sometimes even delight. They were meant to persuade a large or intimate public, but they were meant to affect them through the senses and emotions. The lowland Maya even had superstructures that we call "roof combs" on top of their buildings. (I think the term derives from the comb that holds a Spanish woman's mantilla on top of her head.) The function of roof combs was entirely visual—no one ever went into one except for construction purposes. It was a billboard, usually for stucco sculptures, once brightly colored. Although most are in fragmentary condition, enough remains that one can discover the images of oversize kings and gods in a complex iconographic scheme. Mesoamericans thought and ruled through images, backdrops and theatrical settings.

With the possible exceptions of Chavín de Huántar and Tiwanaku, both of which are now considered to be oracles and hence perhaps advertising their powers in stone images, many Andean representations were less visible and less emotion-oriented. Chavín is something of an exception in that its powers were advertised in stone reliefs outside, while the sacred image, the Lanzón, was hidden deep within dark galleries, visible only by flickering torchlight to a few. Plenty of emotion here.

Instead of hundreds of stone placards at sites, Andeans buried most of their things with the dead. Hundreds of thousands of finely made pottery vessels, textiles, and precious metals were buried with the dead. Much of this material has been excavated, legally and illegally, and filled our museums, because of preservation in the desert sands. Highlanders buried the dead in mortuary towers, the bones and artifacts less well preserved but some still there.

All of these things, sometimes unfinished at the death, were meant to be seen once, during the funeral ceremonies, sometimes at anniversaries, and then perhaps never again. Similar things were presumably used by the people in their everyday lives, but little of that has survived. Nor does there appear to be a concern with the spectacular appearance of the things buried. A number of gold heads and masks of the Moche and Lambayeque cultures were covered with paint hiding the gold surface. Whatever symbolic meaning the paint had, it was known that the gold was there, even though it could not be seen. Knowing that something was there without being able to see it was one of the ways in which Andeans approached representation. They were comfortable with the invisible. They seem more involved with their mind's eye than with their real eyes.

The now-famous Nazca lines were invisible until aviation revealed them in the 1920s. In the 1940s, some American fliers learned about them from the Peruvians and publicized the existence of these lines that can only be seen from the air or slightly from nearby hills.

The Western world has been fascinated by this phenomenon. Since then, innumerable tourists and scientists have flocked to the area to experience or solve its mysteries. In the 1970s, von Däniken, a Swiss restaurateur and amateur writer, proposed a daring and instantly popular theory, that the lines were created by extraterrestrials who used the site as a great airport. He was one of many who think that ancient civilizations had some kind of arcane knowledge superior to our own. In some ways they did, but not in the way von Däniken imagined. Almost everyone has now heard of the Nazca lines—they are one of the wonders of the world.

The basic facts are these. The lines are located on a barren plateau between the Ingenio and Palpa rivers in southern Peru.. There are no habitations or buildings nearby. The surface of the plateau is covered with small rocks, like gravel, oxidized dark on top. The lines were created by piling up the surface rocks on the sides of the lines and revealing a lighter color underneath. The "lines" are actually a foot or two wide. The find of Nazca-style pottery sherds near the lines dates them to between 1 and 700 AD. There are about 300 straight lines, some going for miles, 70 plant and animal figures and a number of shapes, such as trapezoids (von Däniken's landing fields). The lines crisscross each other and in some instances radiate from a center.

Some of the figures are very large. The great bird is close to 500 feet long. Standing on the ground, one cannot see the image at all. How did the Nazca create an image they could not see? The various life forms, such as the tree, monkey, spider, consist of a continuous line from the beginning of the design to the end. It has been suggested that they were laid out with ropes—another instance of thinking with fibers. Even with the ropes, it must have required great ingenuity and/or expertise to lay out straight lines and monkeys with spiral tails. So we marvel.

What was the purpose of the lines—now called "geoglyphs"? At first they were considered to be astronomical, but extensive research has shown that not to be the case. More recently, they were considered to be related to water and point to aquifers. More social explanations suggested that they were ritual pathways for processions for certain families or lineages. The answer is that we don't know. The best comparison is with the *ceque* system of the Inca, another partly "invisible" creation. While not the same, they share certain features in common that characterize them as Andean.

The Inca ceque system was a way of mentally organizing the shrines in the countryside around the capital, Cuzco. A shrine could be anything—a building, a spring or fountain, a tree, a rock. It could be big or small. Each shrine was imagined to lie on a straight line that emanated from a point in the Temple of the Sun in Cuzco, going in all directions. The shrines were placed along the imaginary lines like the knots of the khipu. There were approximately 41 lines. Each shrine was cared for, belonged to, a particular family and/or lineage, and each shrine had its special day in the calendar. Altogether there were approximately 300–365 shrines. The numbers are not exact, because changes in families and politics made for periodic adjustments. Nevertheless, the ceque system related geography to the calendar, to social structure and to sacred objects, without any visible actual lines to connect them. Some shrines were not even objects—"The Last View of Cuzco" was a shrine on several imaginary lines, and surely reveals a subtlety of mind. Although the best known ceque system, described by the sixteenth-century chroniclers, was around Cuzco, we now know that other Inca cities had their own.

If the Nazca lines were something like the ceque system, the geographic, perhaps calendrical, and social dimensions will remain obscure. However, the idea that crucial features in a landscape should be invisible is definitely shared. Andeans found no difficulty in imaginary forms, something that is alien to the West. Western artists first explored this imaginary dimension in the conceptual art of the 1970s. These artists came to the Nazca lines for inspiration and validation. Evidently Andeans were more interested in mental constructs than in visible monuments.

After this discussion, it is easy to see how the 3000-mile long Andean road system was as much an imaginary creation as a real one. It is unlikely that anyone went through on foot and saw all of it from Ecuador to Chile. (Although Inca rulers were sometimes carried from Cuzco to Quito.) But it is entirely imaginable that an Inca ruler and his engineers should have been planning it in concepts and in some material form of aid. For the Inca ruler it has to have been a great source of mental satisfaction that he had such a partly invisible road system as the symbol of his empire.

The famous natural or slightly modified rock shrines outside of Cuzco are also in some ways "invisible." People, things and animals were seen in natural rock, which were often set up on beautiful Inca masonry like modern statues. Sometimes their appearance and power were emphasized by casual architectural details carved into them, like steps, plazas, and rooms. The Inca did not erect conquest monuments—they governed in the name of Nature itself. Their power, personality, history were all invisible. This kind of sophistication has been found in Western Europe only in the twentieth century, after a long period of abandoning figurative art.

15. REALISM

Realism is the favorite artistic rendering of Westerners. Art history was "founded" in the eighteenth century by Joachim Winckelmann who demonstrated how Greek realistic depiction derived from Egyptian conventionalized stylization, step by step, generation by generation. According to him, realistic depiction was hard to achieve, required the development of special manual and visual skills, and was first achieved by the Classical Greeks. By the early twentieth century, the naturalism of Greek art was related to their rational philosophy, democratic government, and anthropocentrism, "man is the measure of all things." It made sense to them that realism should be the style of advanced civilizations. It was seen as something rare, "islands" in a "vast ocean" of conceptual or abstract non-Western styles.

The realistic Olmec colossal heads began to appear with frequency in scholarly literature, especially in the second half of the twentieth century. At first it was thought that they had to be "late" in date because no one "early" could have made them. All current evidence indicates, however, that they are the earliest Mesoamerican representations and date to about 1000 BC. There are now seventeen of them, ranging in size from twelve feet to half that size. The stones are boulders brought from many miles away. And, yes, they are amazingly realistic. In fact, at such a great size, their gaze is distinctly unnerving.

The many questions they raise include: How and why was realism created at the beginning of representation in Mesoamerica; what does it say about "realism" theoretically; and, of course, who were portrayed so realistically?

The realism question is easiest to answer. While realism is rare in world art outside Europe, it does occur occasionally quite suddenly. The two other most famous examples are the Moche of Peru and the Ife of Nigeria. Along with the Olmec, they demonstrate that realism does not require hundreds of years to develop, but can be created quite suddenly. It therefore did not require special manual and intellectual skills as suggested in the case of the Classical Greeks. It is available to any people at any time. So the question is, why didn't more people choose it and why did the ones who did choose it.

The illusion of realism in an object is relatively easy to create. A face with the eyes, nose, and mouth can be read as a "face" even if they are simple geometric forms. The realistic effect is created by developing the intermediate areas between them: modeling the cheeks, the eye-cavity, the chin and embedding the facial features in them. A second trick in creating the illusion of the real, is avoiding strict symmetry in the shape of eyes and lips. These are the ways in which the Olmec colossal heads created realism. If you understand these two principles, any good artist can create a realistic face. Ancient American Indians were good and patient observers, as their horticulture indicates.

Of the Olmec heads, the most realistic is San Lorenzo 1, where the face seems to speak in that the lips are slightly parted, too. The other Olmec heads are less realistic, and one can arrange them in a series from the most realistic to the conventionalized. The conventionalized ones are later, and it would appear that carvers imitated the earlier heads rather than creating new ones from new faces. That is also indicated by the fact that the faces and their helmets are all basically similar. Therefore, it would seem that there was one original colossal head copied in a number of other examples. San Lorenzo had ten heads, La Venta four.

The original head may have been San Lorenzo 1 or a head we have not found. How was it made? Clearly, it was modeled from life, perhaps in clay. The Olmec had quite a tradition of pottery, figurine and effigy pot making. The clay model could have been transferred to the stone boulder by carvers using stone hammers to chip the shape of the features and grinding stones to smooth them down. The real decision was that of the patron, who wanted something lifelike. Once this desire was made manifest, the artist seems to have had no trouble carrying it through. It did not require centuries of trial and error.

People in most cultures around the world find something very lifelike to be uncanny—as in the old days when non-Western people found photographs of themselves scary because it looked as though a part of their soul had been stolen. This does not apply to Europeans who, after centuries of realistic art, find realism generally pleasing and nonthreatening. Still, we have stories like *The Picture of Dorian Gray*, by Oscar Wilde, in which a painting of a man and his actual self are mystically interconnected, and the painting is more real than the man himself. There is something supernatural in realism. Therefore, most cultures around the world avoid what they see as excessive realism, as something potentially dangerous. The question is not why so many cultures do not have realism but why the few who do, do?

From the beginning, it was noted that the features of the colossal heads look "African"—flat noses, thick lips. Moreover, the rest of the physiognomy, heavy cheeks and a generally bulbous face, make them look like a specific individual, as in a portrait. Though fitted into differently shaped boulders, all the heads have a family likeness. Who were they? The general consensus is that they were the rulers of the Olmec, who transfixed their subjects with their eerie gaze. Ten such heads at San Lorenzo—in a row or in a group—must have been awesome. Interestingly enough, the rest of Olmec sculpture is not quite as realistic. As though what was demanded from the heads was not demanded of everything else.

There has been a flurry of theorizing that the Olmec came from Africa and represent Africans. However, a number of other works seem to represent Asians with epicanthic eye folds. The idea of Africans and Asians founding the Olmec together strains credibility. Most anthropologists point out that the various Olmec facial features can be found among the present-day inhabitants of the Olmec area. Still, this question of the facial features remains something of a mystery.

Nearly as amazing as the Olmec colossal heads are the Moche portrait vessels in clay from the Andes. Most Andean representation is conventionalized, if not downright abstract. The one exception is the Moche, who flourished on the north coast about 200 BC to 600 AD. Although there is some very impressive Moche adobe architecture, like the Pyramid of the Sun mentioned before, we know most objects from burials. Hundreds of thousands of Moche vessel have been found, most from illegal digging. Moche vessels, either molded or painted, represented seemingly all aspects of life: supernatural, elite rituals, warfare, hunting, sex, flora and fauna, curing. Just about the only thing not represented is agriculture.

Moche pottery has been divided into five phases: the first one or two handmade, the rest mold-made. Mold-making accounts partly for the large quantity of ceramics. Heads are occasionally found in phases two and three, quite stylized, with geometrically shaped features and large, staring eyes. Suddenly in phase four, the eyelids cover half the eyes, the mouths and noses are modeled, and the faces become realistic. Some heads look young, some mature, some wrinkled. At the same time that they become realistic, they are also idealized. Westerners think they represent rulers, and we like them very much. In phase five, the heads were no longer made. When the later Chimú culture revived some Moche ceramics, they did not revive the realistic "portrait" heads. Portrait heads were never made again in the Andes.

Moreover, recent research shows that the portrait heads were made in only five of the fourteen river valleys in all of Moche. Therefore, the time and space of these vessels was extremely limited. No one in the Andes seemed to think that this was an advance in representation to be imitated. It was part of a special, limited situation. We are not certain of the political situation of the Moche. We do not know if all river valleys formed one state or if there were several warring polities—perhaps at one time there were both.

The portrait heads were made in multiples, the same head found in various tombs along with other vessels. Royal tombs were excavated at Sipán, and they did not have these types of ceramics. Royal tombs had mainly gold and silver, some textiles and feather-work. Evidently ceramics were too lowly a medium for them. The large corpus of ceramics seems to come from middle to upper status burials and not royalty.

Who then did the heads represent? Christopher Donnan showed recently that some of the portrait heads represent captives, with ropes around their necks. He didn't extend this interpretation to all the portrait heads, but I suggest that might be the case. Most of the Moche vessels have lugs and a spout ("stirrup spouts") and once contained liquids, so one could drink from the heads. The portrait vessels could have been fancy trophy heads of particular conquered enemies. Trophy heads are a common theme in Andean representation, since local feuding and the taking of heads seem to have been an Andean practice. The naturalistic representation of the portraits could have been more of a humiliation than admiration.

It would appear that for a time and a limited space, conquered victims might have been commemorated in portrait vessels. The artists seem to have had no problems creating a realistic face when they were so commissioned, without a long developmental period. Nearly twenty years ago, Claude Baudez suggested that the Olmec heads represented captive victims, because they were so "ugly" in comparison to the Mesoamerican beauty ideal. Everyone laughed at him. The Moche example suggests that that might be a better interpretation than the ruler hypothesis.

Captives were frequently represented in Mesoamerica. In fact, dead captives were the first monumental representations at the site of Monte Albán in the so-called three hundred *danzantes*. And though rulers take precedence in Maya art, they often stand on top of captives, or the captives kneel in front of them. The Aztecs represented the captive victim in a dismembered female mythological guise in a colossal carving in front of their major temple.

Why represent the captive in such a prominent way rather than the conquering hero? It seems counterintuitive in our culture. For Mesoamericans, the captive was not an anonymous or nameless person but an individual. The Maya and Monte Albán victims are frequently associated with glyphs that signify their names. Who you conquered was sometimes more important than who conquered. Moreover, the Mesoamerican belief in fate, as decreed by the 260-day calendar, indicated that one day one might be the conqueror, the next day one might be the victim. The victim was another side of the self. An Aztec warrior, dispatching his conquest, first made him a speech calling him, "my son."

In emphasizing the victim, Mesoamericans also got to avoid glorifying excessively the conqueror and/or ruler, which might suit a particular prevailing political arrangement. Except the Maya, who glorified dynastic rulers in images, other rulers probably had allies, councilors, and other great lords to consider in keeping a lower profile. Focusing on the victim might have been a successful political move.

There is one detail that suggests to me the rightness of the victim interpretation for the realistic heads. There is one colossal head (La Venta) shown smiling or laughing, and one Moche portrait head shown smiling or laughing. It is very unlikely that a ruler would cast aside dignity and show himself in such a state of silly levity. In sum, while realistic depiction is always possible, it is emotionally disturbing and therefore rarely chosen unless desired for just such a specific emotional effect. And that effect seems to have been awe, fear and pride but not necessarily admiration.

16. SACRIFICE

In the popular mind, ancient American Indians are associated primarily with the violence of sacrifice. A number of (male) colleagues have asked me flirtatiously: "Why's a nice girl like you studying the Aztecs?" (Perhaps something kinky?) When it comes to violence, the Aztecs are beginners. Hitler exterminated 6 million Jews among the 11 million murdered by Nazis in the Holocaust; Stalin killed 50 million to 100 million Russians; the Turks killed 1.5 million Armenians; the Hutu of Rwanda killed 800,000 Tutsis; and our atom bombs at Hiroshima and Nagasaki were responsible for a mere 280,000—all in the twentieth century. Add to that the casualties of WWI and WWII and the Vietnam War, and the numbers become astronomical.

The term "genocide" was coined in 1944. Scholars disagree on whether the disappearance of the American Indian was genocide or a "clash of cultures." The scholarly population estimates of the American Indians before Columbus are hotly debated, because the evidence is so scanty. Somewhat at random, I took off the Web the number of 120 million Indians. According to that estimate, by 1650, 150 years later, there were only 6 million. In the conquest alone, 80 million may have died. According to other figures, 90 percent of the Indian population died out by the first hundred years after the conquest. The figures may not be correct, but the magnitudes are.

We put all such violence in context—we would not dream of boycotting German music, Russian literature, or American movies because of these reprehensible acts of violence, all of which were done in the name of something seen, at least by some parties, as "good" at the time. But with Mesoamerica and especially the Aztecs, their violence is considered unforgivable. There may be several reasons for this. One of these is the obvious; that Indians had to have been bad (even evil) so as to justify their extermination and taking their land away from them. The European settlers and conquerors were "good" and were the hands of fate (Providence or God) that punished the Indians who were "bad."

Except for Cortés and his soldiers, no one really saw Aztec sacrifice. Bernal Diaz, who mentions blood on the stairways of temples, knew about sacrifices, but it is unclear whether he witnessed any. He knew that captured Spaniards were sacrificed after a battle. The chroniclers didn't see sacrifices; they had the newly baptized Aztecs tell them about it in great detail, so they could write them down. They were inordinately interested in how people were ritually killed. Bernardino de Sahagún wrote down in detail the sacrifice that took place every month in the Aztec calendar. It is this grisly detail that condemns the Aztecs. Why were the Spanish so interested?

It must be remembered that these were the years of the Spanish Inquisition, which had also been instituted in Mexico a few decades after the conquest. There was a great deal of interest in the nitty-gritty details of the Inquisition's methods of torture—the rack, the wheel, the body-crusher, impalement—which were particularly nasty, and of course burning at the stake. These chroniclers were mostly churchmen, all too familiar with torture. This was their perspective they brought to Aztec sacrifice. The Spanish had cruder forms of torture, such as unleashing their mastiffs on the Indians and watching the dogs disembowel them.

All Mesoamericans, including the Aztecs, practiced human sacrifice. As did most ancient people—the Andeans, the Chinese, the Hindus. The Europeans/Middle Easterners talked about human sacrifice as taking place in their immediate past but not in their present. In the Iliad or Old Testament, the favored human sacrifice was someone close and dear—the child of the ruler or important man. (Iphigenia and Isaac come to mind.) A well-known ancient Eastern European ballad tells the story of a castle wall that always collapses until the wife of the master mason is walled up in it. The relevant question is WHY do so many other cultures practice or say that they once practiced human sacrifice? It is not simply an Aztec problem.

The chroniclers are mum on the subject—they attributed it to the Devil.

In fact, human sacrifice has been practiced primarily by cultures at a certain level of development, which are the larger, successful, Neolithic and Bronze Age eras.

In smaller, hunter-gatherer and subsistence agricultural societies, there is usually not much human sacrifice. The small kin groups do not "need" it. That does not mean that there is no violence—small groups feud among each other and often take trophy heads. The trophy-head taking is justified by a concept of limited energy in the universe, resulting in taking the energy (the head) from a neighboring group. Such captured energy brings fertility to nature and women. These practices indicate a literal view of the world. Such violence is based on individual or lineage volition.

Human sacrifices are usually given up by societies that are quite literate and have sacred books (Bible). Books encourage a more transcendent and metaphoric view of the world, in which sacrifice can be symbolic, as in the Christian Eucharist, and does not have to be messily real. One does not actually consume the blood and body of Christ in ritual. In those cultures violence continues, but it is usually in the form of punishment.

Sacrifice is most common in largish states, kingdoms and chiefdoms, with no or only a small amount of writing. Such places continue the literal thinking of early times. For example, if the sacrificed Aztec children cried a lot, it would create rain. Tears equal rain. At the same time, states or central powers remove violence from the hands of ordinary people and lineages and concentrate it in the state or whatever ruling body. The ruling body then makes the sacrifice a public affair to which many are invited, as it is done on their behalf. In some places, as in Mesoamerica, sacrifice is a theatrical affair. In less theatrically minded places like the Andes, it is less so. The concentration of sacrifice is therefore a centralizing project—like the building of pyramids.

What does this look like on the ground? When asked by the original twelve missionary friars about sacrifice in 1524, the Aztecs (priests, wise men) answered clearly:

> It was the doctrine of the elders
> That there is life because of the gods,
> With their sacrifice they gave us life.

At the core of sacrificial thought is the idea that the gods sacrifice themselves for humanity, and in return humanity has to sacrifice the most precious thing it has. Most precious to humans, is human life. That is the most basic logic of human sacrifice. It is the acme of literal thinking.

Ancient American Indian religion was based on nature. The sun, the moon, the earth, lightning, rain, corn itself, were gods. Sometimes these were seen in human or composite symbolic forms. But in fact, the gods were the phenomena themselves. The Storm God was literally the lightening, the Corn God was the corn you ate. They had to be thanked and compensated for giving themselves. Nor were the gods eternal—they could die with the end of the destruction of one world and had to be recreated in a new world through sacrifice.

A myth retold by the chronicler Sahagún explains it clearly.

> After the last destruction of the world, the remaining gods got together and built a big bonfire. Whichever god threw himself in it would become the new sun. A rich god sacrificed jades and quetzal feathers but could not bring himself to jump in. A poor, sick god who had nothing to offer came along and jumped straight into the fire and became the sun. Ashamed, the rich god jumped in too, but by then the fire was less hot, and he became the moon. The heavenly bodies did not move until everyone who was there had jumped into the fire.

Aztec sacrificial rituals were worked into the calendrical cycles on certain months and days. From the accounts, we do not know if they did the same cycle every year. Were the accounts a pastiche of rituals found in different places and times, structured into a "calendar year" by the orderly chroniclers? Were they so everywhere or only at Tenochtitlán? There are many questions about the organization of the sacrifices. Were the sacrifices of the salt-makers for everyone or just the salt-makers?

Contrary to popular belief, they did not sacrifice primarily "virgins." (That is a Western sexualized idea.) They did sacrifice some women, usually by beheading, but mostly they sacrificed men who were war captives, by cutting out the still-beating heart. Some victims were "bought" for that purpose from poorer people. Often the victims impersonated the gods, and the sacrifice was a reenactment of the god's original sacrifice, as the return gift. Sometimes the victims had to enact little scenes like mock battles. In the ball game, the loser was sacrificed by beheading. Increased fertility was to be the result.

The most famous of these scenes was the sacrifice of the impersonator of the god Tezcatlipoca, who was a complicated, dark but necessary force in the Aztec pantheon. He was impersonated by a young man, "perfect" in body, who was well treated for a year, given mistresses and taught how to play the flute. On the given day, he ascended the pyramid steps playing and breaking a flute at each of the four stages, until he reached the top and was sacrificed. Hallucinogenic drugs were given to victims, so they could play their roles more willingly.

A glorious afterlife awaited sacrificial victims. In Aztec belief, the afterlife was not based on how one had lived but on how one had died. Those who died in war or sacrifice or women who died in childbirth accompanied the sun on his journey across the sky. Those who died through the agency of water went to a verdant paradise; small children went to a place of nourishment, and everyone else went to a colorless but not bad underworld called Mictlan.

How many did the Aztecs sacrifice? This is impossible to calculate. The Aztecs augmented the numbers to prove how successful they were in war. The chroniclers augmented the number to prove how barbaric the Aztecs were. The Aztecs wanted to kill their victims in ritual afterwards and not on the battlefield. With warriors dressed in feather outfits, standards and headdresses, the battles themselves were unwieldy matches. But as mentioned above, the aim was to capture victims, with the major focus to capture the leader of the group and sacrifice him. So the Aztecs kept their violence mainly for sacrifice, not war.

The population of the basin area of Central Mexico has been estimated to have been about a million at the time; the capital Tenochtitlán, 200,000, with four or five other major cities making up the rest. Were the sacrifices in the hundreds? Thousands? It's not the numbers that appall the modern mind; it's the institutionalization of it.

Still, is it as bad as the Romans, who sacrificed similarly large numbers of victims in gladiatorial combat and wild animal shows purely for entertainment? They also fought extensive wars with heavy casualties. We do not think the less of them and do not find it inconsistent to go on admiring their Plutarch and Seneca.

Although most of our information on sacrifice comes from the chroniclers and therefore about the Aztecs, there are enough indications in the representations of other Mesoamerican cultures that they had similar practices of sacrifice. At the Maya site of Toniná, a relief was found representing a conquered Palenque ruler, tied up with ropes and ready to be sacrificed. Inscriptions tell us of the death of a Copán ruler at the hand of his Quiriguá neighbor.

Recent research on the Maya has emphasized the fact that the Mesoamerican elite—rulers, priests, and others, drew blood from various parts of their bodies—leg, ear, penis—as indications of personal piety. Aztec representations bear this out, too. These penitential acts performed in private, their aftereffects visible in public, probably demonstrated that the elite gave of themselves, too, and did not just send others under the sacrificial knife.

The chroniclers of the Andes did not obsess so about sacrifice, although they noted the practice. Often they merely referred to numbers—such as hundreds or, rarely, even five hundred—but did not detail the how and why. Andeans preferred to sacrifice women and children—who were, in their estimation, of lesser value than adult men. Much of our information comes from archaeology.

Humans were entombed with royalty in their burial. At the Chimú capital in Chan Chan, a large number of sacrificial victims were found, mostly youngish women, probably the harem of the lord. Only partially excavated, there were probably over 200 women. This particular burial was only one of the nine royal burials at the site. Extensively looted for gold, all burials did not have intact remains by modern times. Fewer sacrificial victims, male as well as female, were found in the Moche Period royal burial at Sipán. Andean human sacrifices seem to fall into the common category of "wives" and "servants," who accompany the dead in the afterworld. This pattern is the most common human-sacrifice type worldwide. The Andeans seem to have imagined the afterworld as a pleasant place where life continues as on earth and so provided the dead with every necessity.

We know from the sources that the Inca made human sacrifices to natural features such as high mountains. Icy and snowcapped mountains over 20,000 feet were worshipped as the origins of streams flowing downhill through the desert coast, and in themselves as sublime presences. They were essential to irrigate agricultural fields. In the last twenty years, a number of frozen child sacrifices have been found near the mountain summits in Chile and Argentina. Mostly girls but some boys as well, the children were drugged with coca and alcohol before being killed and/or exposed wearing their Andean garments and with ritual objects. They were from six to early teens in age.

Human sacrifice seems to be the price ancient human societies have paid for developing larger, more complex civilizations in which the population in general was more-or-less secure and at peace. It is a paradox. We object to but are inured to the numbers our societies kill, because of the impersonal or remote nature of numbers. What is a hundred thousand or a million or two? One can't take it in. But we are particularly appalled by the personal, even intimate nature of sacrifice performed in early state societies. Humans seem to be a violent species.

17. THE INEFFABLE: A MAYA HAND

So long ago, so far away, without clear descendants, through the impersonality of archaeology and the bias of old texts, in curious rites and bizarre preferences, the ancient American Indian does not really "live" for us or speak to us. We marvel, but we don't recognize ourselves in their mirrors. There are a few hints, here and there, that make us feel that they, or some of them, were sentient beings like us—or at least "us," as we flatter ourselves to be.

There is the delicate hand, with pinkie raised, holding a paintbrush between thumb and forefinger, engraved on a small, shovel-shaped piece of bone. The hand emerges from the open maw of a partially rendered reptilian monster. The focus is on the hand; the maw is really the frame. Nothing else, just a lively hand and a paintbrush.

The bone was found with other carved bones at the site of Tikal in Guatemala, inside Temple I, in the burial of a ruler once called Ruler A but now named Jasaw Chan K'awiil. Dated about 700 AD, all the other objects in the tomb are typically Maya, showing various identifiable deities.

In ancient American art, various deities or persons emerge from a monster maw, an image that is supposed to signify birth or rebirth. The monster is a divine being, such as the earth or the sky. The image is a positive one and suggests divine origins, for anyone familiar with Mesoamerican symbols. Therefore, in this unusual little bone, the hand, presumably of the artist or scribe, emerges from something divine. Perhaps the artist or his art is "divine."

But a Maya iconographic interpretation is not the point. The point is that lively hand with a brush that communicates with us so directly across time and space. We know that hand from our own experience. No one has to tell us what it means. Cultural differences disappear.

Only occasionally do we have moments like this from the ancient Americas.

18. AZTEC POETRY

Having shuddered through the monthly sacrifices described by Sahagún, my students were always amazed by the immediacy of Aztec poetry.

Will I have to go like the flowers that perish?
Will nothing remain of my name?
Nothing of my fame here on earth?
At least my flowers, at least my songs!
Earth is the region of the fleeting moment.
Is it also thus in the place
Where in some way one lives?
Is there joy there, is there friendship?
Or is it only here on earth
We come to know our faces?

Poems—or songs—were chanted to musical accompaniment at feasts among the Aztecs. The instruments were drums and flutes. Ancient Americans did not have string instruments. The singers were professional bards. Some poems were written down in the early Colonial Period in the Aztec language, Nahuatl, by the Spanish. They come to us in various translations from Nahuatl to Spanish, to English, sometimes directly Nahuatl to English. The translations vary in style and quality, but the thoughts are clear.

Remove trouble from your hearts, oh my friends.
As I know, so do others:
Only once do we live.

Let us in peace and pleasure spend our lives;
Come, let us enjoy ourselves!
Let not those who live in anger join us,
The earth is so vast,
Oh! that one could live forever!
Oh! That one never had to die!

Below is another version of the same idea. Evidently the composers don't show certainty in religion as we know it from the same early Colonial Spanish sources. They are full of doubt and questioning. As my students usually commented, anyone, anywhere could have written these lines.

What are you meditating?
What are you remembering, oh my friends?
Meditate no longer!
At our side the beautiful flowers bloom,
So does the Giver of Life concede pleasure to man.
All of us, if we meditate, if we remember,
Become sad here.

Ostensibly, the poems were composed by the rulers and other important men among the Aztecs. In some poems, their names were woven into the text: "I, Cacamatzin [or whoever], sing this." But the bards usually sang them, and sometimes wrote them. Nezahualcoyotl, (Hungry Coyote) was the Aztec ruler of Texcoco, a town near Tenochtitlán, and an ally. He was famous for his poetry, as a few lines attest.

Not forever on earth, only a little while.
Though jade, it may be broken;
Though gold, it may be crushed;
Though quetzal feather, it may be torn.
Not forever on earth, only a little while.

Aztec poetry is now recognized as one of the great poetry traditions of the world, and is often anthologized in books on world poetry. But that is not why it interests me. Because it gives a more human view of ancient American Indians to which I can relate. In the end, they were humans just like you and me. Not to mention that they also wrote humorous and bawdy poems, like the one about the old women and their young lovers—

19. INCA MUSIC

IN THE LATE 1960S, PAUL SIMON met a Peruvian folk band called Los Incas in Paris. Both were performing in the same theater. He was especially impressed by one song they played, known as *El Cóndor Pasa (The Flight of the Condor* or *The Condor Passes).* In 1970 Simon and Garfunkel put the song on their album, *Bridge Over Troubled Waters.* They wrote a new lyric *(If I could)* but had Los Incas play the music. In that form, it became a part of our tradition.

The chroniclers described the Inca musicians as versatile on panpipes, flues and drums. The wind instruments came in soprano, alto and tenor tonalities and harmonized in a pleasing way, also to the Spanish ear. They said that Inca musicians could imitate any kind of music. No actual preconquest Inca music has come down to us. But it continued to be played in the Colonial Period in poor peasant communities with nostalgic lyrics. In 1913, a Peruvian composer and ethnomusicologist, Daniel Alonia Robles, wrote a suite that contained *El Cóndor Pasa*, which popularized it.

The folk lyrics of *El Cóndor Pasa* encountered in Paris were in Quechua, the language of the Inca empire.

Oh, mighty condor, owner of the skies
Take me home, up into the Andes.
Oh mighty condor,
I want to go back to my native place,
To be with my Inca brothers, that is what I miss the most,
Oh mighty condor,
Wait for me in Cuzco, in the main plaza
We can take a walk in Machu Picchu and Huayna Picchu.

The condor is an awesome creature, the largest Peruvian bird of prey, with a wingspan of ten feet and symbolized the great Inca empire.

Simon and Garfunkel's lyrics were also about nature. "I'd rather be a forest than a street" is one line.

El Cóndor Pasa has become one of the most popular melodies in the world. More than four thousand versions of it exist with at least three hundred different lyric versions.

Here and there an image, a poem, a song has emerged out of ancient American antiquity to speak to us, to move us, to touch us, not as anthropologists and antiquarians but as people living at this moment, looking for solutions for the dilemmas of our own lives. Perhaps in time, there will be others.

20. STONE AGE CIVILIZATION: NO NORM

In order to assess ancient America, one has to look at Europe and the Old World that conquered it and with which it is compared. Eurasia is a huge continent close to Africa where humanity evolved. It has been the location of migrations and conflict since the beginning of human time. There is the well-known conflict between Neanderthals and *Homo sapiens* in the time of early man. There have been four major early civilizations, starting with Mesopotamia. Egypt, the Indus Valley, and China developed largely independently but inspired more or less by Mesopotamia. From time immemorial, there have been contacts between all four of them, later on through the famous Silk Road connecting East and West, Europe and China. Secondary cultures of different ethnic groups, languages, and races existed between the four. Techniques and ideas were exchanged over large distances. For example, many scholars think that the ideas of Jesus and Christianity were inspired by Buddhist monks.

One aspect that Eurasia has is diversity: more major civilizations and more secondary civilizations than the New World. A second feature it has is contact between civilizations, which cannot be emphasized enough—in the thirteenth century, the Venetian merchant Marco Polo went to China with his father and uncle and brought back new information, new inventions, including how to make noodles, movable type and printing. Others had been there before them, but Marco Polo cowrote a book about it (with Rustichello da Pisa, while they were in prison together). The third feature Eurasia has is almost constant war and conflict. There is a reason why there are ruins of fortifications and castles on every other hill in Europe.

Not only were the various people bellicose, after the domestication and riding of the horse, pastoral nomads in the large steppes between Europe and China specialized in raiding and killing the settled peoples in every direction. Many early hordes like the Goths and the Huns ravaged Europe in ancient times. The Chinese tried to keep them out with the Great Wall. Nevertheless, the nomadic Mongols created huge conquest empires East and West—when Marco Polo went to China, a Mongol ruler sat on the Chinese throne. Ancient Egypt was twice conquered by outsiders. The Europeans fought over religion, ethnicity, language, political systems, to say nothing of trying to create empires and dislodge peoples.

It is not surprising that the Old World and Europe set great store by practical and especially military inventions. That they went in such a short time from stone to bronze to iron and then to steel tools was a matter of sharing, borrowing ideas, and perfecting them to stay ahead of their neighbors and enemies. The right invention could be a matter of survival or getting ahead. The polymath Leonardo da Vinci painted Madonnas and also designed war machines. The cultures of the Old World were intensely competitive. Chinese Taoist alchemists developed gunpowder for medicine; it was used it for fireworks and eventually with simple weapons. In a few centuries, it was known all over the Old World, and Europeans invented the musket and cannon, with which the Conquistadors battled the stone tools of American Indians.

In conclusion, we cannot take the cultural development and timing of the Old World as a norm. The Old World was a special case of multiple civilizations, settled and nomadic people in conflict, continued *wars and migrations*, intense competition, and focus on inventions necessary—in their view—for survival. It was and in many ways still is a very tough world. We are blinded by the glories of Old World culture if we don't see it.

21. ISOLATION

The ancient Americans had it easy. As migrants from northern Asia, they came into a continent lush with flora and fauna and no human competition. They began by hunting the big Pleistocene fauna which could best be done by cooperation. With the demise of the larger animals and the lack of smaller ones suitable for domestication, they turned to the exploration of plant life, which was prodigious. Nevertheless, in comparison to Old World grains, maize was complicated to domesticate, and it took longer for the New World to settle down with successful agriculture. In the end, they created a nutritious diet. According to eyewitness accounts by Europeans, the people were well fed and healthy. There were many such reports. The Native American nutritional system greatly improved the European system after the conquest and still does.

The question that this essay has asked, "Why and how did the ancient American Indians remain a Stone Age people while creating a Bronze Age civilization?" can now be answered.

First and foremost, the Americas are smaller than Eurasia, and in only two areas could agricultural surpluses supporting complex civilization develop: Mesoamerica and the Andes. Moreover, these areas are separated from each other geographically, such that contacts and ideas did not frequently or speedily go from one to the other. In other words, the areas did not fertilize each other. They were isolated.

This is not totally true. Various inventions did go from one area to the other, not by individuals taking them but by diffusing very slowly through people to people. For example, maize was domesticated in Mesoamerica c. 5000 BC and spread south through Central America and the Northern Andes to Peru by farmers. It took several thousand years to get to Peru, c. 2000 BC, by which time the Andeans had begun their civilization without it. In Peru, maize became mainly an elite food.

There is a similar story with pottery, which began perhaps at the mouth of the Amazon in Santarem c. 7000 BC and moved to Ecuador and Colombia c. 3000 BC. From there it diffused quickly to Mexico in the north and then slowly to Peru in the south. It took several thousand more years to arrive in Peru, about the same time as maize. Later technical inventions in pottery, such as oxidation firing and mold-making, spread to Mesoamerica and the Andes slowly by way of Ecuador.

Diffusion went south to north as well. Metallurgy, in the form of gold, began in Peru about 2000 BC and spread north, slowly arriving in the Mexican Maya area around 800 AD. Bronze technology was explored to some extent in Peru about 500 AD, but in Mexico by the time of the conquest, the Aztecs found it curious but didn't quite know what to do with it.

Part of the lack of contact between Mesoamerica and Peru can be explained by the lack of shipping. The Conquistadors claimed that they saw large rafts and canoes carrying trade wares somewhere in northern South America, between Mesoamerica and Peru, but it seems to have been infrequent. Seafaring was not an ancient American skill or interest. (The closest seafaring culture was that of the Polynesians, and although they may have made contact with ancient Americans occasionally, they were not a part of that world.) Where should the ancient American seafarers have gone? Generally, they hugged the shores. The South American Moche went as far as the Guano Islands to get bird guano to fertilize their fields. They could have explored further, had they wanted to, but they did not.

Archaeology reveals further contacts, but they are very weak. Judging by ballgame paraphernalia in the Caribbean, Mesoamericans and Arawaks interacted for a while but were not incorporated in each other's cultures. Similarly, mounds and pottery in the US Southeast suggest some limited contact with Mesoamerica. Perhaps Mesoamericans went to the American Southwest in search of turquoise. Andeans may have had contacts with adventurous seafaring Polynesians. But on the whole, Mesoamericans and Andeans seemed to think that there was nothing of interest outside their boundaries and were turning inwards. There were no ancient peoples among them like the Vikings or the Phoenicians, who specialized in trading or raiding from boats and connecting people.

As isolation brought no cross-fertilization of new ideas, it also brought no threats to survival from the outside. That is important to emphasize and puts Cortés into context. American Indians did not expect threats from the sea. The ancient American Indian civilizations were one of the safest from invasion or migration in the world, or so they probably thought. Moreover, since they were not inspired from the outside, they turned for diversity within their own areas.

Although there was plenty of conflict and war within their own land, these were usually not world-changing events. The conflict that did exist actually resulted in a greater homogenization and unification of their cultural area, with fewer possible issues of dissension. The Maya, Teotihuacán and the Aztec in Mesoamerica shared a lot in common, as iconographers like to point out. (Despite the fact that I spent a lifetime teasing out the differences.) Similarly the Moche, Chimú and the Inca of the Andes share many features in common.

22. TIME

ONE OF THE BIGGEST DIFFERENCES between the Old World and ancient America is their concepts of time. Stone tools require extra time to make the same objects that metal tools can make faster. You have to have a great deal of patience, blocking out and grinding away. But the ancient Americans had time or seemed to feel that they had time. In not rushing into bronze and iron, in thousands of years they explored the potentialities of stone technology in dozens of cultures and monuments. They made the discovery that they could do almost anything. (Well, not land on the moon.) Massive piles, like the Pyramid of the Sun at Teotihuacán, or intricate mosaics, like on the House of the Governor at Uxmal. They showed that more was possible with stone technology than anyone would have imagined in the Old World.

They had time not only for individual monuments but for entire cultures. Different cultures explored different variants of sociopolitical systems, as well as art styles, in the course of several thousand years. We now have the remains of an amazing cornucopia of Stone Age possibilities that were once tried. Some lasted a short while, but many lasted hundreds of years.

In art styles, they explored everything from realism to abstraction and minimalism. Many European styles have parallels in ancient American styles, though not necessarily in the same order, thus scrambling our ideas of stylistic development based on Old World traditions. Ancient Americans demonstrate what can be done with stone tools, time and imagination. The time before and near writing is one of the most prolific for representations that we call "art." The ancient Americans communicated through what we call "art," and there is the richest quantity, quality, and variety of styles.

This sense of time is not just the actual time it took to make something but a more existential sense of time. No one and nothing was urging ancient Americans to hurry up into a new future. There were no serious migrants, invaders looking to conquer land and get rid of the population, nomadic horsemen raping and raiding, breathing down their necks. They did not have to search for new types of weapons in a hurry, something sharper, more lethal, more innovative against the foe. There was less of a premium on practical innovation. While they warred among themselves, they did not have to deal with wild and unexpected enemies, who seemed to come out of nowhere. They had the time and security to develop their world.

The Old World and Europe in particular rushed from one technology, one religion, one social arrangement to the next, measuring itself by the ticking of clocks that were invented in the thirteenth century. European art historians admire the rapid development of their art styles and find other parts of the world that have no such "development" lacking in proper art. In fact, this European artistic development is like the rush of a train through stations without stopping, as the culture moved from one societal form to another. In the rush, many possibilities were left behind. The ancient Americas tell us something about Europe, too.

Ancient Americans occasionally developed in new ways in their art, in time, but mostly they explored and elaborated on traditional forms. They were not all going to the same place, because they were already in the same place. They were not future oriented. For example, in Mesoamerica there were four architectural styles with stone mosaic decoration: Rio Bec, Chenes, Puuc, and Oaxacan. In the Andes, there were a number of ceramic figurine styles of more-or-less contemporaneity, prior to the Moche: Salinar, Gallinazo, Vicus, Recuay. One could say that ancient Americans developed horizontally rather than vertically.

This does not mean that the Americas did not develop in the usual sense of the term; they did, but very slowly. Starting between 3000 and 2000 BC—and it's a mystery why they began more or less together—the Andes and Mesoamerica went through similar overall stages. The early centuries are fascinating but in many ways enigmatic for us. Somewhere from 200 BC to about a 1000 AD both areas had a variety of flourishing cultures with well-defined art styles. Many think that this time was the height of ancient American cultures. After 1000 AD, attempts were made in both regions to create conquest empires, which were successful just about two hundred years before the conquest in the Aztec and Inca empires. Perhaps in another five hundred or a thousand years, an American Alexander would have conquered and united both Mesoamerica and the Andes. (An Andean, to be sure, since they were better at conquering.)

23. WAR AND PEACE

MOST FIGURATIVE REPRESENTATION IN ANCIENT America deals with the subject of war. That has led to the assumption that the cultures were warlike. This is on the principle that representation is an accurate mirror of reality. (On which bases we could argue that most Western women went naked because they are so represented in many images.) I will argue differently. Often you represent what you wish to see or present not what exists in reality. These American Indian cultures, numbering 10,000 to 100,000, people were large societies which were in fact mostly peaceful but bonded together through real and ritual warfare. A characteristic of representations of war in Mesoamerica is that the glorious winners are only sometimes represented. The focus is on the victims and prisoners. Maya titles sometimes even referred to the ruler-warrior as the conqueror of X, Y and Z, naming the prisoners exactly. The centralizing powers or rulers seem to find it better not to represent themselves. Or, warfare was represented in a mythological guise or through the substitute battle of the ballgame. All suggests a low profile for leadership.

The big problem for early states must have been internal cohesion and the fear that various warlords would segment and break up society. Organizing war against a common enemy—an enemy that had the same problem—would aim at consolidating the community in a common enterprise. How big were these wars? As mentioned, for the Aztecs these wars were partly ceremonial, with costly regalia worn. Supplies could last only for relatively small campaigns. They usually fought only in daylight hours. Only rarely did they go very far from home. Their aim was to get live captives, preferably the prestigious leaders—and booty. And at home they put up monuments to their successes and bravery; images of the captives they had acquired as victory monuments. It was also a way of saying: Don't mess with us; we are fierce warriors! Much seems to have been symbolic or propaganda.

The practical aim of warfare was the acquisition of wealth. Mesoamericans did not usually fight for territory. Wealth in Mesoamerica was foodstuffs, maize, chili peppers, textiles, feathered shields and warrior gear, jaguar pelts, greenstone necklaces, amber, gold, bunches of feathers, and turquoise. We know this from Aztec tribute books that detail which towns are to send what tribute to the Aztec capital. The Aztec empire was a tribute empire—when provinces were conquered, the rulers were left in place, but tribute from the above list was demanded of them. As the provinces periodically rebelled and stopped paying tribute, a military expedition would be sent to put them down. As such, there were small wars at various parts of the empire at most times. Cortés took advantage of this and got some of the subjects of the Aztecs to revolt and join him. Those who joined him had no idea that the Spanish were fighting not for tribute but for territory.

A telling detail about Aztec war is the story picked up by the chroniclers about "flowery war." Evidently, when the entire Aztec empire was pacified and there was peace, it was not possible to get captives for sacrifice. As a result, the Aztecs got together with their traditional enemies the Tlaxcaltecas and decided to have small encounters at certain times and places, so that their warriors could practice and so both sides could take victims for sacrifice. This was called the flowery war. To the Spanish, this was a story about sacrifice. To me, this is a story about peace. Much of the time the empire was also at peace.

The Inca in the Andes dealt with war and peace differently. Theirs was a territorial empire, and they did not have a Mesoamerican type of warrior and sacrifice cult. (Although there, too, as indicated by the Moche, war had supernatural, ritual and propagandistic aspects.) The Inca wanted peace and order, at all costs, in their large empire. They would get the goods later through labor service organized by their administrators. They resettled entire, solid Inca communities in those conquered provinces they deemed to be rebellious, in order to pacify them permanently. Those who were moved were not happy about going, but they went. Both the Inca and Aztecs succeeded in making their languages, Quechua and Nahuatl respectively, the basic idiom of their lands, a major step in pacifying and controlling the population.

There was a lot more peace in the ancient American world than the bellicose surface suggests. What did people do during peacetime? Of course, many were agriculturalists and tilled the fields. They built fantastic cities, buildings, and took part in time-consuming colossal projects. They wove thousands and millions of textiles, they hammered gold and silver, they developed all those distinctive and puzzling art styles. Mesoamericans exchanged their wares at markets; Andeans bartered with their designated kin groups in the desert, highlands, and tropical forest. They spent their time on festivals and feasts in fantastic costumes, with music, songs and dances, and sacrifices. Andeans toasted each other with fermented chicha in golden beakers and got royally drunk at feasts and parties, small and great. Mesoamericans were fond of oratory and gave speeches in and out of the home, and their clichés probably often bored their listeners to distraction.

24. WHO WAS IN CHARGE?

THIS IS A SILLY QUESTION—obviously there were powerful kings. Cortés dealt with the Aztec Montezuma, and Pizarro with the Inca Atahuallpa, according to histories the conquest. But is it as simple as that? Europeans were used to dynastic monarchs, who practiced primogeniture and had near-absolute powers, depending on their personality. To them, monarchy was an obvious and natural institution.

The Spanish, the Portuguese before them and the English after them traded with many non-Western groups in many parts of the world, including Africa, that were not all necessarily kingdoms or even chiefdoms. For obvious reasons, they always preferred dealing with one person rather than a group of contentious elders and assumed that one person was in charge. So if there was a king or chief, they dealt exclusively with him. Or if there was not, they selected a person as their primary contact, gifted him, especially economically, so he acquired prestige, and in fact they managed to change the group, sometimes inadvertently, into a chiefdom. Centralization sprang up wherever Europeans traded and in whatever they described.

For Cortés, the story of the conquest of the Aztecs was all about Montezuma. Montezuma was powerful, but his Aztec empire was, strictly speaking, an alliance between three cities—his Tenochtitlán and the nearby Texcoco and Tlacopan, whose rulers were his advisors and co-rulers. At his coronation, the ruler of Texcoco put the royal headdress on his head. Moreover, Montezuma was elected from the various members of his family and was not the son of the previous ruler. (This detail much pleased eighteenth-century thinkers in Europe, who wanted to do away with monarchy. The Aztecs were admired by them.)

The Inca case is more complex, too. Huayna Capac, the last creator of the vast Inca empire, divided it in two for two of his sons. Huascar received the southern half and the city of Cuzco. Atahuallpa received the northern half and resided at Quito, Ecuador. Of course, the two brothers started a war for supremacy. Atahuallpa met Pizarro first, coming down from Panama. Pizarro understood the advantages of the situation; his men captured Huascar and brought him to Atahuallpa in chains. Soon after, Atahuallpa was executed, too. The Inca emperor was supposed to marry his own sister but had many concubines and many sons. All the sons were potentially eligible to succeed him. Among the Aztec and Inca, there was no rule of primogeniture. Sometimes two or more individuals could be on the throne for various reasons.

Powerful monarchies play a major role in Western political theory, especially as they were dramatically toppled with difficulty in the American, French and Russian revolutions. In prerevolutionary Western theory, societies developed from egalitarian beginnings through various intermediate forms to monarchies. Ancient Egypt was supposed to be a good example of the early development of an absolute monarchy, putting up great pyramids and other architectural wonders, which were proof of its power.

At Teotihuacán Mesoamerica built pyramids close in size to those of Egypt, and large cities and other impressive buildings are scattered throughout Mexico and Guatemala. Surely these structures were built at the behest of powerful rulers similar to the pharaohs of Egypt and the monarchs of Europe— This has been the accepted interpretation for Mesoamerica. As discussed previously, at Teotihuacán in particular, the lack of royal imagery, the good quality popular housing, the impersonal symbol system, all suggest at least an ideology, if not the reality, of a more cooperative type of organization. Or if it was a monarchy, it suggests some structure of participation for at least part of the population.

This lack of ruler glorification is, with some exceptions, found in most of Mesoamerica. The number of sites that are now described by scholars as having "councilor" governments is growing. This means that most Mesoamerican societies may have had monarchical rulers, but their rule was limited and/or amplified by other powerful personages, with further consent lower down the social scale. The rulers had no professional police or standing armies to enforce their edicts. Participation in war, construction and so forth had to be largely willing.

"Willing" may mean no more than the similar willingness to perform necessary agricultural labor. Community work was likely inspired and planned by the elite but structurally carried out as a normal part of the life and activity of the people. It was likely supported materially, spiritually and sociopolitically by a sense of belonging and by some form of real or symbolic participation. I have argued that in a Stone Age society, social and political organization likely took the place of technological progress. In other words, the great skill of ancient American Indians was social engineering in tying the social fabric together through great enterprises. Much of the theatre and propaganda of ancient American Indian expression seems to have been the creation of a more-or-less coherent social body. While the subject of this expression was often conflict, its makers presented themselves as a unified, participating community and not a single individual. Outside of the Maya, ancient America has no tradition of monuments such as to an Augustus Caesar or to Pharaohs.

From the 1980s, I was very interested in the excavations of Peruvian architecture, dated as early as 3000 BC, in what is called the Preceramic Period; places like Aspero, Caral, El Paraíso, etc. Pyramids, large room complexes, and round courtyards were common at these places. No agriculture was evident except for cotton and gourds, no pottery. No figurative art has survived. No elite or royal burials were found. Subsistence was based mostly on fishing. I was fascinated by the impressive building complexes and the apparently more-or-less egalitarian context.

It reminded me of the impressive buildings of Chaco Canyon and Mesa Verde by the Anasazi of the American Southwest, at the other end of the settled, agricultural, ancient American world. Those, too, were more-or-less egalitarian cultures without kings. No monumental, figurative arts. No fancy burials. The ruins consist of room complexes and round communal ritual rooms called "kivas." Pueblo Bonito is just one of these spectacular places with four stories at one end, 350 rooms, and a central plaza. It has 32 kivas, of which three were extra large. Inhabited for only a short time, Pueblo Bonito is supposed to have had a population of no more than 3,000. Lived in for less than two centuries, these amazing constructions were abandoned in the thirteenth century due perhaps to drought. They are made of beautiful masonry and consist of several floors. The kivas were usually thought to be religious in function, on the model of modern Hopi culture, but recently they have been interpreted as rooms for governing councils.

The modern Hopi are believed to be the descendants of the Anasazi in Arizona. They are well known for their ideology of peaceful living. Nevertheless, research has shown that warlike activities had occurred both by them and their ancestors. There is such similarity in the architecture of ancient American Indians, from the American Southwest through Mesoamerica to the Andes, that it suggests a widespread building tradition by the communities of these Stone Age peoples at various levels of social development. Looked at this way, Teotihuacán could have been Pueblo Bonito "on steroids."

There was one region in Mesoamerica that had dynastic rulers for whom lineage and genealogy were important, the Classic Maya of the tropical forest of Mexico and Guatemala. Oddly enough, they had the smallest territories and actual power but some of the greatest theatrical pomp. Consisting of six large and many smaller centers, they were at war with one another and intermarried. Palenque, Yaxchilán, Piedras Negras, Tikal, Copán, Quiriguá, and Seibal were the major ones. A fine local limestone provided the material for handsome and idealized ruler portraits inside and outside temples and palaces. Elaborate inscriptions in hieroglyphic writing detailed their parentage and accomplishments. The entire Maya area shared the system of hieroglyphic writing and calendrical counting, proof of the extensive interactions between them. Handsomely idealized rulers are shown with royal regalia, with conquered prisoners, sometimes with a woman—a wife or mother. We think of these highly aestheticized figures as sophistications and refinements, but could they have been signs of artistic competition more intensive than anywhere else in Mesoamerica? Was "artistry" a weapon in a culture war?

It appears that Maya society was organized around the dynastic ruler and his court. This culture is considered by us to be the most beautiful and advanced in ancient America. They've been called the "Greeks of the New World." Besides art, there were advances in writing, astronomy and calendrical systems. This dynastic experiment came to an end between 800 and 1000 AD. The cities were abandoned; the area was depopulated. Only today is the area being gradually resettled. Did they compete themselves out of existence?

The Classic Maya we usually think of was a short-lived phenomenon. Classic Maya culture lasted from about 300 to 900 AD, although its roots go back at least to 1 AD in the Izapan tradition that followed late Olmec. Ultimately, it has Olmec antecedents. But in fact the height of the phenomenon was only the three hundred years from 600 to 900 AD. The unique elements of the Maya—the royal portraiture and dynastic cult, the hieroglyphic writing with its associated special dating system—disappeared with the Maya themselves. It had been a fascinating experiment, but not in the mainstream of Mesoamerican life. The mainstream of Mesoamerican life glorified the community and not an individual.

25. A GOOD LIFE?

BERNAL DIAZ DEL CASTILLO WAS one of Cortés's soldiers who wrote the best eyewitness account of the conquest of Mexico, *The Conquest of New Spain* (1565). He wrote it at the age of eighty, looking back. One of his most famous statements is: "We came to serve God and to get rich," which puts the conquest and the European point of view in a nutshell. Bernal Diaz looked around more than most and was impressed by the throngs of well-dressed people, all the goods in the market, the feather-decorated palanquins of the elite. A much-quoted passage describes his view of Tenochtitlán, the Aztec capital.

> And when we saw all those cities and villages built in the water, and other great towns on dry land, and that straight and level causeway leading to Mexico rising from the water, all made of stone it seemed like an enchanted vision from the tale of

> Amadís . . . the sight of the palaces in which they lodged us! They were very spacious and well built of magnificent stone, cedar wood, and the wood of other sweet-smelling trees, with great rooms and courts, which were a wonderful sight, and all covered with awnings of cotton . . . I say again that I stood looking at it, and thought that no land like it would ever be discovered . . . But today, all that I then saw is overthrown and destroyed; nothing is left standing.

Bernal Diaz did not question his heritage or the nature of life in the New World. The Indians were heathens, practicing human sacrifice. The Spanish had recently expelled Jews and Muslims in a religious frenzy; they now turned on the Indians, who were dubbed "savages." Europeans saw the New World civilizations in negatives, what they did not have: guns, metal, horses, the wheel. The Indian cultures collapsed so quickly, the Christian conversions were so fast, Spanish rule was so chaotic, so many died from disease—that most chroniclers on whom we rely for information did not see the functioning cultures. They saw misery and heard nostalgia.

Modern archaeology and, alas, looting have revealed a different picture. The ancient Americans did not know that they were isolated and flourished in their isolation. All we have to do is walk through the ruined cities. We can see the beauty, the imagination, the care, the skill they lavished on their universe. They took their time with everything they did. Within their own terms, they made clever and intelligent things we are still trying to figure out and stuff our museums with. It has been estimated that there are 100,000 Moche vessels in museums around the world, and that is not counting the broken or "uninteresting" pieces left behind. The thousands and tens of thousands of pottery, textile, stone, and metal objects found in tombs indicate that many more than the top elite had a high standard of living.

Though proving it is circuitous, generally the ancient Americans seem to have been as much interested in cooperation as in competition. It is worth restating that a Stone Age technology, lacking a professional police and army, encouraged various ways of inspiring and rewarding the population—either materially, sociopolitically or spiritually—in community endeavors. Violence was restricted to certain times and places, leaving safe and peaceful times in between. Besides an abundance of nourishing foods of their own creation, they had three other things in abundance: time, lack of competition, and relative peace.

Within these Stone Age cultures, as we have discovered, two very different and in their own ways intellectually and practically interesting civilizations were created: Mesoamerica and the Andes. This relative peace, time, and space were both a gift and a curse. It allowed them to explore in detail what was possible for a patient, Stone Age civilization—and indeed they achieved as much as the Old World did in the Bronze Age, proving that technology is not everything. But it turned out to have been a fool's paradise.

At the hands of steel swords, crossbows, muskets, cannon, metal armor, horses, epidemic diseases, and European competitiveness for gold, the ancient American civilizations collapsed like a house of cards. The moral is all too simple: however splendid your world is, in its own terms, if it does not have weapons against technologically superior invaders bent on conquest, and if you do not understand their mindset, there is nothing you can do.

* * *

What is evident from this essay is that there is no norm for cultural development. The Old World and Europe developed as they did because of their particular historical and geographic circumstances. Similarly, the ancient Americas developed as they did because of their historical and geographic circumstances. The people of both regions were clever, talented, and sophisticated in their own terms and even in one another's terms. Which would have been a better time to live in? It is not a simple answer. In some ways, surprisingly, ancient America before the conquest might not have been a bad time to live.

26. EPILOGUE

Ancient America was unique in the world to have had a geographically favorable place for development, with a simple toolkit, and the absence of serious competition. Other Stone Age people surviving into later centuries were in marginal locations and never materially developed beyond basic subsistence. Was or is there another place in the world that had somewhat similar circumstances that could be compared?

Oddly enough, the US came to my mind. As the Indians became dispossessed, the land emerged as the greatest treasure in the conquest. The American continent was experienced as an abundant "wilderness" of rich soils, colossal timber, innumerable flora and fauna available for Europeans, whose own lands had been despoiled for centuries. For many years, the fur trade alone provided great wealth with very little investment. The masts of the nineteenth-century ships were cut from the great American trees. Besides, the US is neither too cold nor too hot for settlement. Behind every subsequent accomplishment in the United States were the natural riches of the land.

Although this was true of the rest of the Americas, too, the US was special in that it was not, with some notable exceptions, founded on great landholdings and plantations worked by slaves and peons. Much of it was occupied by immigrants with small plots of land and/or shops and therefore was relatively egalitarian and ambitious to make good—in a situation without much competition.

Independence and a non-monarchic constitution established certain democratic rights derived from eighteenth-century political philosophy relatively early. Some of these ideas were also inspired by the semi-egalitarian Indian tribes the new Americans came to know and who were, at first, their guides in the New World. For better or for worse, independence from England fostered a sense of uniqueness. As a result, the US individual got to participate more fully in this society and cooperated in its ventures more wholeheartedly than anyone in the Old World or Latin America.

In general, the US has had very few wars on its soil compared to the Old World, which had been warring almost incessantly throughout the centuries. Although there were some border wars with the English in Canada and with Mexico, they were not of great magnitude for the rest of the country. The biggest war in the US was internal: between the plantation-and-slavery-owning South and the more industrialized North. This war ended with a more complete unification of the country, to its benefit. The long Indian wars hurt primarily the Indians. Generally, the US population is used to peace in its own land, and even in modern times wars have been intentionally concentrated outside the country. This peace has been conducive to great economic development and a great sense of wellbeing.

The US is in many ways physically isolated from the Old World, partly because it is so big and oceans separate it from Europe and Asia. Also because it has in the past cut itself off from the Old World. And, because it seemed "backward" to Old World cultures until the twentieth century, they paid it little attention and it went on its own way. Americans like being isolated and are often isolationist; many think they can exist on their own. Generally, they do not speak foreign languages and only a small percentage travel abroad. Unfortunately, as a result, Americans have little understanding of the motivations of foreigners. They tend to think that everyone is like them.

Old World intellectuals are mystified by and look down on the "average American" as provincial, uneducated, simpleminded, uncritical, and smug (savage?). But most of the world knows that America is a good place to live, precisely because it is safe, wealthy, and in fact not that critical. America is the goal of immigrants around the world. Despite the fact that violence is also a significant part of American culture. Americans think of solving all too many conflicts with private and official guns.

The ancient American Indian world was, in its time, perhaps also a good place to live with a rich natural land, relatively good standard of living, and adequate incorporation in social and political life, relative peace, and the isolation from people wishing to destroy it. There is a parallel, but here the parallel seems to end.

Of course, the US was always different in having advanced technology, grand projects like the transcontinental railway and going to the moon. By the twentieth century, the East and West Coasts have become sophisticated centers of wealth and learning. An unexpected new advantage to the US was that the Old World centers warred themselves into near collapse, so that after World War II the US emerged as a world superpower without conquering anybody. It was imitated, though not understood, by most everyone else. At the same time, it still remained unique and tried to spread its ideas and institutions wherever it could, with no great intentional success.

Competitiveness is in the blood of Old World civilizations, since perhaps even Neanderthal times, and in the twenty-first century, as I write, the rest of the world—in the form of China, Russia, Iran, North Korea, and who knows who else—are challenging and/or ganging up on US supremacy. It is hard to imagine that the United States could be suddenly conquered like ancient America had been, but it could be weakened. Its wealth and intellectual secrets could be exploited by unscrupulous powers, and the US, with its delicate balance of the integration of its peoples, could be thrust into the background. Divisiveness could harm it from the inside. So much for crystal-ball gazing. Just as likely, of course, competitive outside powers may destroy each other again and need the US to save "civilization," in some sense of the word.

And, then there are those extraterrestrial adventurers with their superior technology—perhaps not even life forms but robots—that people the movies and the fantasies of all of us: not much good can be expected from them.

27. AFTERWORD

At the risk of calling down the ire of the scientific establishment on my head and encouraging the nutty amateurs, I will mention the forbidden subject of transpacific contacts. A historian is a historian and follows the leads where they go. This study suggested to me that IF—and I am not convinced that there have been—but IF there had been transpacific contact what, where, and when might it have been?

This study of ancient, Stone Age Americas has made the differences between Mesoamerica and the Andes very clear to me. The Andes seem truly unusual and idiosyncratic from a European point of view. At the same time, all of its cultures seem very consistent and coherent. It all makes sense.

Mesoamerica seems more comprehensible from a European point of view, with its large figurative sculptures, calendars, and writing. Because it seems to make more sense to a Westerner, there has been more research on and appreciation of Mesoamerican representations and culture. But in some ways, it makes less sense as a whole.

Take the writing system. As I reviewed the writing system, I was bothered by several features. First of all, if Sumerian was the first writing system in the world, Mesoamerican writing was the only second independent system in the world. That's pretty special and unique.

Could that be true? There must have been some powerful reason for it. What would have been the reason for this invention in Mesoamerica? (The khipu makes complete sense in the Andes as a numerical device and is relatively late.)

Certainly, the Mesoamerican recording system was not economic; it dealt with gods, ancestors, rulership. And it appeared very early—c. 1000 BC on the Olmec level. Why? Not only did writing appear early, calendrical counting was associated with it. No one knows the origin of the 260-day "horoscope" calendar, but it is believed to go back to the earliest times in Mesoamerica. What was going on then that accounts for it?

The appearance of all these intellectual inventions on such an early level, for a reason I could not explain, raised in my mind the idea of potential outside influence, particularly that of China. As it has long been noted, the veneration of jade and greenstone in both China and Mesoamerica is an unusual coincidence. But perhaps only a coincidence.

Early Chinese writing was on "oracle bones" and consisted of references to contacts with the ancestors. This writing was either independently invented in China or the idea was stimulated by Sumerian writing. In either case, it could have been not a model, but a stimulus for Olmec writing. If that is the case, then writing might only have been invented once in the world, an interesting question to ascertain in itself.

The earliest counting in China was by "rods," by which is meant little sticks in the requisite number, laid out on the ground. They could be arranged decimally, like Mesoamerican numbers. They are very similar to the "bar-and-dot" numeration on the earliest Mesoamerican monuments.

The 260-day calendar in Mesoamerica is curious, too. Generations of scholars have compared it to cyclical Chinese calendars, such as the Heavenly Mansions or "lunar series," with sequences of animals similar to those of the Mesoamerican 20 day-signs. Both the Chinese and Mesoamerican calendars are illustrated in circular form, as in the Aztec Calendar Stone. (Our explanation of the 260-day cycle in Mesoamerica is still quite inadequate.)

If there is any merit to these observations, then around 1000 BC, at the very beginning of Mesoamerican civilization, four new ideas might have been introduced without any specific objects: the idea of writing, the idea of recording counting, the idea of a ritual calendar, and the idea of the value of jade. They presuppose a Mesoamerican cultural context with developing elite organization that could recognize and benefit from such ideas.

All could have come from China, where adequate boats, the desire for exploration, and the accounts of new worlds discovered are found at various times in Chinese history. If these were all ideas, it is useless to look for material parallels.

Arguments against transpacific contact abound—one of which is the deprivation of the American Indians of their intellectual talents, creativity and heritage. After all, they have been deprived of almost everything else. So it is unfair to attribute their recording systems to the Chinese— Still, history is history. Suppose such an early injection of Old World ideas was made in Olmec times, their reinterpretation and development would have still been entirely local, creative and Mesoamerican in spirit. Maya writing would still be Maya writing. Pre-Olmec archaeology might throw more light on these issues, and the context of writing and dating might, in time, be more coherently understood.

Much lies ahead.

REFERENCE GUIDE

This essay was written with the experience of forty years of teaching ancient American art history at Columbia University. Hundreds of books and articles, conferences and talks, lie behind it that cannot be quoted. Here I just list a few that have been particularly important to me. One of the authors that got me started was Miguel León-Portilla, and I quote from him in the book. Miguel León-Portilla:

Aztec Thought and Culture: A Study of the Ancient Nahuatl Mind, University of Oklahoma Press, Norman, 1963.

Pre-Columbian Literature of Mexico, University of Oklahoma Press, Norman, 1969.

Most recently, I have been reading books by Jack Weatherford that have been a source of great inspiration and plenty of needed data. I recommend them highly. Jack Weatherford:

Indian Givers: How the Indians of the Americas Transformed the World, Fawcett, New York, 1988.

Native Roots: How the Indians Enriched America, Fawcett, New York, 1991.

The Internet has been an invaluable source of facts, dates, ideas and distractions, some illuminating, some contradictory and totally confusing. I relied on it all too much and apologize for any errors or inconsistencies. Below I list those of my works that are related to this project and hope that their bibliographies are helpful for future reading. Esther Pasztory:

"The Iconography of the Teotihuacán Tlaloc," Studies, Dumbarton Oaks No. 15, Washington D.C., 1974.

Aztec Art, Abrams, then University of Oklahoma Press, Norman, 1983.

Teotihuacán: An Experiment in Living, University of Oklahoma Press, Norman, 1997.

Pre-Columbian Art, Cambridge University Press, 1998.

Thinking With Things: Toward a New Vision of Art, University of Texas Press, Austin, 2005.

"A Civilization Going Mad—The Aztecs in Western Thought," in

Arqueología e historia del Centro de México: homenaje a Eduardo Matos Moctezuma, ed. Leonardo López Luján, David Carrasco, and Lourdes Cué, INAH, Mexico, 2006, pp 637–644.

Inka Cubism: Reflections on Andean Art, http://www.columbia.edu/~ep9/Inka-Cubism.pdf, 2010.

Aliens and Fakes: Popular Theories About the Origins of Ancient Americans, Polar Bear & Company, Solon, Maine, 2015.

ଔ ଓ

III

THE MAYA VASE

a Novel

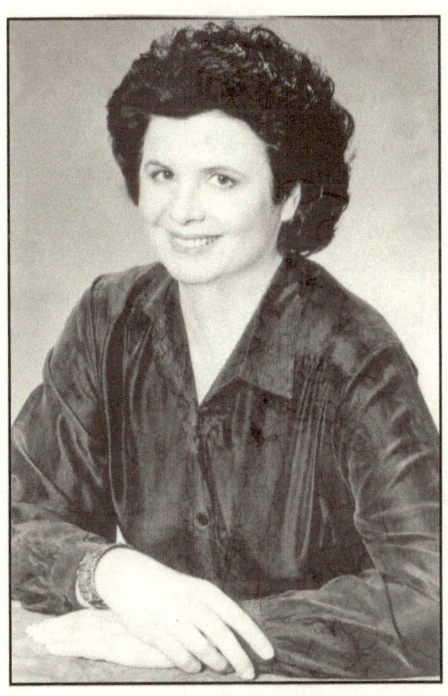

Prof. Esther Pasztory, 1995

For Wayne

☙ ❧

1.

Naomi woke from a vivid and frightening dream of Professor Brown sprawled dead at the bottom of his staircase, blood beneath his head. His glassy blue eyes seemed still to follow and beseech her. She could not get them out of her mind. She remembered him as a muscular and bearded man in his fifties, who had the most amazing stories about his adventures in the rainforest of Guatemala, excavating Maya ruins.

It is true that for a very brief time they were more than teacher and student, but Professor Brown was known for his interest in attractive female students. Naomi was just one of many, and she was now slightly embarrassed by her former infatuation. She had admired, even hero-worshipped Professor Brown, and he had made her feel special as his PhD candidate.

Sleepily she calculated that five years must have passed since she last saw Tim Brown. She herself had had some extraordinary adventures: In the midst of writing a romance about a girl in Indian times before Columbus, she had disappeared into ancient America, incarnating as her own heroine—and of course married a Maya lord. She knew more about the ancient Maya now than Professor Brown, as she lay on soft, thick hand-woven rugs in a thatched cottage on the outskirts of the Maya city of Tikal.

As on every morning, waking, she listened to the parrots and birds up in the trees, before the serving maid brought her a cup of sapote fruit juice for breakfast. Naomi was known there as Marigold. Her husband, the Tikal lord Night Sky, had died a year before from snake bite. They'd had an idyllic relationship, and he was mourned by many. She could not imagine any man she had known in the modern world with whom she could have spent such happy years. The circumstances may have seemed primitive, but bathing in the cool waters of a cenote, one of the dramatic natural sinkholes, had been a delight of which she never tired.

Of course, being the widow of the ruler of Tikal still entitled her to maids and cooks and other servants who were eager to please her. Not that Marigold was anxious to lord it over others, but the fact that they took care of the practical necessities meant that her life was easy. She spent her time weaving cotton garments and throws. This morning she woke in one of the old cotton shifts she had woven in her first years there, now soft and discolored from washing and very comfortable.

Marrying Night Sky had been a conscious decision. She preferred the old Maya ways to the modern era of the Northeastern region of the United States, where she had grown up. Professor Brown had taught in the Morristown branch of the University of New Jersey and lived in a nice Victorian house. Marigold hadn't thought about him in a long time. Writing a dissertation on the Maya nowadays seemed absurd; it was strange that she should dream about him lying dead at the foot of the staircase, with those eyes staring at her, as if he wanted to speak.

Marigold knew something about dream interpretation among the Maya. They would have said he was communicating with her from the afterworld, because perhaps he had no one else. He had not seemed to be a spiritual person, not one to consult the local shamans with his troubles. Professor Brown was strictly scientific. He had been doing a computer analysis of the house mounds in the dispersed city of Tikal. He was not even particularly interested in the carvings of royalty that she was supposed to write about in her dissertation. Their affair had been based on physical magnetism rather than shared views of the Maya. Marigold found Night Sky's emotional romanticism much more fulfilling than anything she could have had with Brown—whom she'd called "Professor Brown" to the end. Still, there was something special about his intellectual energy, tropical knowhow, and a passion for living that endowed those blue eyes in the dream with compelling power.

Night Sky's death had coincided with the return of Sky Rain, the rightful ruler of Tikal, who had been living in exile since the armies of the city of Calakmul had conquered and burned Tikal, scattering its population.

Night Sky, who was an uncle of Sky Rain, had gathered the remaining people around him and became their unofficial ruler. Without a large population and many craftsmen, they erected no pyramid nor palace of stone. Theirs was a spacious, thatched village fronting a central square and dancing ground, away from the ruined city. Having survived wars and troubles, Night Sky wanted to live in peace and paid tribute to the ruler of Calakmul to be left alone.

The spies of Calakmul assured their lord that Night Sky was not a threat, so the uncle was allowed to rule over his little community. Occasionally, Night Sky was ordered to the Calakmul court as a subservient making obeisance in front of other notables, and he performed these as necessary duties. In the meantime, he organized song contests and story-telling contests at home, with feasts as lavish as they could muster. While not of a great military or political power, the era of Night Sky's Tikal was remembered as a cultural florescence, and his subjects had thought him a wise king. Marigold thought Night Sky the wisest and warmest human being she had ever met. She considered his strategy with Calakmul brilliant and that it had saved many lives. At a time of war and cruelty, they had lived in an enchanted world of play and art.

How Night Sky came to be bitten by a snake seemed something of a mystery. It could of course have been an accident, since occasionally snakes got into the village from the forest. But there were those who thought the snake was intentionally placed in his room, either by someone from Calakmul, after all, or by one of his disaffected subjects who wanted war rather than song contests. The culprit was never found, though several suspects were executed by the ruler of Calakmul.

When Night Sky's experiment ended, his son Dusk returned, having followed Sky Rain, and he prepared the village to participate in the ousting of Calakmul. When Sky Rain triumphed and restored the legitimate dynasty to Tikal, the once semi-royal village of Night Sky became just a village.

Sky Rain embarked on great public works, such as roads and exceedingly tall pyramids for himself and his wife on the main plaza of Tikal. All the earlier rulers had buried their dead in a traditional, small cemetery area, but Sky Rain took up some of the main plaza for his grandiose future burial temple. He became a great ruler who glorified Tikal with colossal architecture to celebrate its freedom from foreign occupation. Night Sky was buried on the edge of his village, and only a wooden carving marked its location. Marigold took orchids from the forest and laid them at its base.

Her life in the village was not immediately changed by Sky Rain's triumph. To be sure, many of the villagers had left to join in the war and construction. Remaining were the elderly, mothers with young children, those who had fields nearby, servants who preferred not to exchange their masters for new ones. The kind atmosphere created by Night Sky continued for a while. Marigold wove now as much for sale as for herself and thus paid for the services of her retainers. She had a certain fame in Tikal as the former dancing girl from Teotihuacán—sent once upon a time as a gift from that city to Night Sky, ruler of Tikal.

Sky Rain was busy these days, but he looked forward to meeting her. She was dieting to fit into some of her exotic old clothes, having put on a few pounds in easy married life. Sky Rain was probably just curious and had his own bevy of dancing girls. Still, she had been the wife of his uncle and wanted to make a good impression.

But now she had dreamt of Professor Brown, dead at the foot of the stairs in Morristown, New Jersey, signaling with his eyes.

2.

When Naomi left the modern world to be with Night Sky, she meant to stay with him among the Maya for the rest of her life. She took her choices seriously and was not interested in a brief adventure. Since Night Sky was older, there was always the chance that she would outlive him, and she thought about what her life would be like among the Maya without his sheltering presence. She was always considered the "foreign woman"—from the big city of Teotihuacán.

Marigold had black hair like an Indian. In externals she looked perfectly native, while her mind and soul still belonged to Naomi, although after five years it was hard to tell where Marigold ended and Naomi began.

Getting on in years, by Maya standards of the time, she would still be very young in Morristown. As a Maya widow, her options were not so bad for all that. Being something of a celebrity in her own right and having had a titled husband, she could hope to remarry at least as a second wife. Given her skills in weaving and basic medicine, old and new, she was an artist or shaman. Besides, in village Tikal, she was popular. She had a bright smile and a friendly word for everyone. Night Sky's death was a shock and cut him down in middle age. What Marigold had feared might happen down the line happened when she'd least expected it.

One great source of comfort for her in this time of pain was Night Sky's married daughter Green Parrot, who lived in the next cottage with her children. Because she had no children of her own, Marigold spoiled her nephews and nieces. Green Parrot was her best friend, and they often borrowed each other's clothes for the festivals and made up each other's faces. Marigold considered telling Green Parrot her dream and asking what it meant. She hadn't told her about Morristown and the modern world. Green Parrot might have understood but might have thought Marigold was ill. The main reason not to tell was that she didn't know what she meant to do about it, if anything at all.

And her first reaction was to go to Morristown. It had been a strong initial response on waking up. She was needed there. Then she looked around at the Maya world, and going to Morristown for any reason seemed absurd. She always assumed that she could go; she still had safely hidden the books that allowed her passage between times and places. She had not abused them, only used them twice: once to go back home and once to return to Tikal and marry Night Sky. The books were in the storeroom in a satchel. She had not opened them in the last five years.

After breakfast, she looked in and found the satchel, ominously damp and lumpy—her safety exit from the ancient Maya world. Testing gently its interior, Marigold found it crumbly. Evidently mice or little rodents had been there. Much of the middle of one book had been chewed away. The outer edges still remained, but the designs were unrecognizable. She felt a moment of panic. Why had she not put the books in safekeeping where she slept? Why hadn't she looked at them before this? Was she now stuck permanently in Tikal village? She hadn't finally decided to go to Morristown, but the fact that perhaps she could not go at all upset her. She went to visit Green Parrot and accepted a cup of leftover chocolate. She didn't tell her anything but was pensive.

That night, while the dancing continued around the bonfire, she sat slightly apart staring into the flames. The fire was past its great intensity, and billows of smoke were emerging, making her eyes water. While dabbing her eyes, Marigold remembered the page from the destroyed book that she had used on trips through time. Slowly, as if she were mentally drawing it, a circular area of grey smoke or clouds swirled before her eyes. From various points at its circumference, little spirit beings with red, pointed caps emerged, one foot still caught in the grey mass. It was all framed by a goddess, and in her middle there was an opening for the passage to another page of the book. But to enter a time tunnel Marigold needed only this one page. She sat there reconstructing the page in her mind. When it was all there, she was in a trance and saw the outlines of the tunnel emerge. She was both frightened and excited by its prospect and quickly lost her connection with the vision. But the message of the moment was clear—she did not need the actual book; memory was enough for her to meditate on it. She could go back to the modern world. That was reassuring, though she had not actually decided to go.

She had once thought that the Maya world she entered would remain long unchanged—the impression she had from her reading. The same ceremonies would be enacted, even if the principals changed. She knew about Sky Rain from books where he was presented as the great builder within a tradition. The reality would have been a shock. But with her more intimate inside knowledge, Marigold had not been surprised when he rearranged the life of Tikal so completely. After Night Sky, who was so fastidious and honest, Sky Rain turned out to be corrupt and grandiose. His lordly underlings managed to get tribute from the peasants like no one had ever done. The tasks of unskilled laborers were also increased. In return, Sky Rain presented lavish festivals with great feathered dancers and many sacrifices. The surrounding area's lords all came and impressed the populace. This was not a big surprise, but Marigold loved how things had been at the time of Night Sky. She had to remind herself that they had been vassals of Calakmul—not truly independent.

She prepared for her interview with Sky Rain very carefully, wearing her finest dyed cotton garments, a jade pendant, and a feathered headband. She carried two sprigs of orchids in her hands. An intricately woven shawl was thrown over her shoulders. She was accompanied by her maid Pebbles and an older servant, all in their best clean clothes. Thus they made a procession to the palace, where Sky Rain received them in his reception court.

Marigold had never seen so much jaguar skin. Sky Rain was dressed in a jaguar-skin vest and headdress and sat on a jaguar-skin pillow. There were other lords about, loaded with the weight of jade necklaces and earplugs. The lord of Uaxactún was trying to outdo everyone and had jaguar-skin sandals with jade ankle bracelets as well.

Sky Rain motioned Naomi into a private room, ceremoniously commiserated on the death of her husband, commended him on his stewardship of Tikal, and mentioned his fine manners and temper. The speech was rehearsed. Marigold thanked him graciously but was mostly quiet as befitted a woman of that time. Sky Rain then asked what she proposed to do, and she replied that she had no plans other than to applaud his impressive enterprises. Sky Rain appraised her as a woman. He liked them young and submissive; he was not interested in adding her to his wives or concubines. He wondered which of his lords might like to have her as a wife. As the widow of Night Sky, she had an illustrious pedigree. He couldn't think of one right off, but he would keep it in mind. It was no good having an important woman hanging around unmarried. Perhaps the ruler of Uaxactún might like such an alliance. He motioned for her to leave.

Marigold sensed that Sky Rain had not taken to her personally, that he was thinking of some other use for her, and that this use would involve some of the lords she saw in the reception court on her way out. She took an instant dislike to the lord of Uaxactún, who seemed to her an unbearable fop and social climber. She went back to her thatched cottage, went to bed, announced to her household that she was ill, and had herb tea brought to her. Under the covers and with the warm tea coursing in her veins, she became drowsy and saw in front of her mind's eye the grey smoke with the little figures in the book. She looked at it more intently, and the smoke began to dissolve. The outline of a tunnel was visible. For a moment Marigold hesitated—should she leave all her comforts and go back to the messy modern world she had left behind so long ago? Then she had a vision of Professor Brown at the foot of the Victorian staircase and thought she might be needed, after all. Should she take anything with her? She was still dressed in her court finery. She grabbed the rest of her jade jewelry. The maid had come in; Marigold told her she was ill, to take good care of her and of the house. She gave her a seed necklace.

Pebbles began to cry, thinking that Marigold was going to die. But Marigold reassured her, while saying that she might be ill for a long time.

Then Pebbles saw two Marigolds, as Naomi arose and stepped forward into something invisible and disappeared, leaving one Marigold very much alive on the bed, in her care. The maid went to tell the cook of the strange things she had witnessed; they both decided to tell no one what had happened so as not to lose their positions.

3.

When Naomi emerged from the tunnel and the mists vanished, she found herself at Professor Brown's house in the guest room where she had initially passed into the ancient Maya world. No one seemed to be staying there now, but there were voices outside the door. Naomi stepped into the adjoining bathroom to fix her hair and saw a blonde, blue-eyed woman looking back at her from the mirror—it wasn't Marigold. Five years since she had seen a glass mirror—she gave a little start at her own face. Her embroidered Maya outfit looked too exotic, but she had nothing else. Coming out of the door, she bumped into Brenda Brown, who seemed only slightly surprised to see her.

"Naomi dear, I guess you are back from the field, and you've come! What a wonderful outfit; you must have gotten it in Chichicastenango."

Naomi was embarrassed and murmured something indistinct. Evidently Brenda thought that she had been at Tikal doing research for her dissertation. Everyone in anthropology was supposed to do "fieldwork," and people went to and from the "field."

"Come, everyone is in the living room. We're trying to deal with the shock." Said Brenda, as she put an arm around Naomi and led her into the early American style living room with its sofas and wing chairs occupied by old friends as well as people she didn't know. They all had drinks in their hands, and there was a lot of food on the dining-room table. Ham, cheeses, vegetables, casseroles. *This must be the wake after the funeral*, thought Naomi as she accepted a glass of wine.

In the corner of one of the sofas a young woman was crying her eyes out, while another young woman was comforting her. Naomi tried to recall whether Professor Brown had a daughter, but she only remembered a son; in fact, the young man cutting a piece of ham—what was his name—Kyle. Brenda leaned over Naomi by way of explanation.

"She is making a spectacle of herself, carrying on like this." Brenda put up with Tim's momentary girlfriends, but she did not think they ought to make their relationships public.

Racked by sobs, Jennifer was out of line and not playing by the rules. Her friend Philippa was also calling attention to herself by all that comforting; Jennifer would pipe down if no one paid attention to her. Naomi noted that Brenda was dry eyed and, if anything, irritable.

At that point, Tom walked into the room with a short, dark-skinned man with Maya features, who was smoking a pipe. Tom stood transfixed at the door: "Could that be Naomi!" he said loudly, forgetting his anger at having been left by her five years ago. Naomi walked over with a smile and a hand outstretched to take his.

"You look terrific!" he said, although he thought the native garb was a bit much. "This is Professor Guillermo Villasanchez." He pointed to the Guatemalan, "He is our visiting professor this year."

"You can call me Bill," said Guillermo and shook her hand.

In similar fashion Naomi met other members of the archaeology department of the University of New Jersey at Morristown, including the eccentric Egyptologist, Sophie Parker. Having given up smoking at the age of fifty, she held onto an antique ivory cigarette holder for social occasions. She said cattily to Naomi, "Were you one of Tim's special friends too?"

Naomi did not answer that, but enquired, "How could such an agile, muscular man, fall down the staircase in his own home?"

"Maybe his *balance* was not very good." Sophie emphasized "balance," to mean several things, leaving Naomi with the feeling that she knew more.

While spearing a tomato, Naomi overheard Tom explaining about the fall. "It was after dinner, and Brenda was in the kitchen when she heard a loud crash. Kyle did not hear it, because he was in his room playing loud rock music. Professor Brown had a slide carousel in his hand, which had fallen with him. He must have tripped in the rug. Brenda had just had a rug installed on the stairway."

Sophie and another archaeology professor listened intently to this recital. They had heard it before; the details went like wildfire through the university the day after it happened. They also knew that there was a broken glass with the remains of whisky, which he likely had carried in his other hand. Professor Brown was not an alcoholic, but he liked a drink on a regular basis and held his liquor quite well. But carrying a slide tray and a glass of whisky on a stairway—

Naomi looked at the stairs. Indeed there was a rug on the steps matching the colors of the Persian rug in the living room. It muffled the sounds of those who walked on it—like Jennifer, who came catlike down in her ballet slippers. Naomi didn't know quite why she was there and why Professor Brown had called to her in her dream. It had obviously been an unfortunate accident—the slide tray, the drink, and the new rug, combined with a loss of balance. Why had she been so unsettled by this as to leave her home? And anyhow, where was she to spend the night? And what was she going to wear tomorrow? At the wake, everyone assumed that she had just come back from the field, but she could not go on wearing Maya clothes. Nor could she very well go back to the apartment of five years ago. She took a large chunk of pâté on a piece of dark bread, as this was going to be her main meal of the day. Brenda came towards her. "Naomi dear, as you are just back and may be unsettled, could you do me a favor? Could you housesit for a few days, since I have to go away on business. Feed the cat. In fact, I'd like to be on my way as soon as this, er, this wake is over with. I don't believe in wakes after funerals, but custom is the custom. I must get out of here. And, oh, if you need to borrow a t-shirt or something, go ahead and look in my closet. Maybe the girls will do the washing up."

Naomi murmured something very grateful, but her comments were interrupted by Tom clearing his throat and announcing that he had just conferred with his colleagues that there would be a memorial service in the fall, when distinguished speakers, friends and family would talk about the achievements of Tim Brown on a more formal occasion, and he hoped that everyone would be there. That was the note that ended the gathering, and people began to leave after pressing Brenda's hands and wishing her well.

Brenda was suitably serious, but Naomi knew that basically she just wanted to get away and wondered where she was going in such a hurry.

Sophie had an ironic smile as she said goodbye, and Guillermo "Bill," smoking a pipe in his tweeds, pretended to an Anglo-Saxon detachment.

Naomi saw, but did not understand. She agreed to have lunch with Tom the next day, and he said he'd pick her up at noon.

When she went into the kitchen, Jennifer and Philippa were washing up the platters and putting the leftovers in the refrigerator. Jennifer was still teary eyed and blowing her nose. Naomi caught the tail of a sentence before they realized that she was coming, ". . . she did it because she knew." That was followed by a fruit bowl that clattered out of Jennifer's hands.

Philippa said, "Oh, do be careful Jennifer! These are Brenda's best dishes." To which Jennifer put down her dishrag and ran out of the kitchen.

Naomi smoothly took Jennifer's place and asked how long Philippa had been in the program.

Philippa said, "Four years," and sighed. "I don't know what's going to happen to me now. Professor Villasanchez is only here for another year, and I can't very well switch to that bitch Sophie and Egyptology at this late date. They're unlikely to give Tom tenure at this early date. And besides—"

"Besides what," said Naomi quietly, not to stop the flow.

"There is no one like Professor Brown—was."

"Was what?"

"Well, you must have known. A real man."

"Hm," said Naomi repeating it, "'a real man.'" To herself she pondered, *What is a real man and what does Philippa consider a real man? Someone bearded and muscular? Someone with knowhow in the academic jungle? Someone with knowhow in the real jungle? A womanizer?* After some moments of silence stacking clean dishes, Naomi asked, "What do you think of Brenda?"

"She is a bitch."

"Oh."

"She made his life hell. That's why he—" And to Naomi's surprise Philippa dabbed at her eyes. "I wouldn't be surprised if she got that rug on purpose. And maybe," she added, "she crept up behind him and shoved him down the stairs."

"You're not serious—"

"Well, no, but I wish it were so, and the police would come and take her away."

4.

Naomi availed herself of Brenda's closet and got a t-shirt with a Tikal design, which fit her perfectly. Brenda was a little heavier in the middle, but a pair of drawstring pants pulled tighter did very well. She tried to feed the cat, but none was visible. She put down cat food and water in the kitchen and left the door half open so Ixchel could come in whenever she wanted. She was a little concerned about meeting Tom after all this time, as once they were almost engaged. He hadn't changed much, except he was less boyish and more manly. Was he married? Was he angry at her still? Was he still attracted to her? Was he still so devoted to his work? Evidently, he was teaching in Professor Brown's department. Did that have a future? In fact, did that have a future now that Professor Brown was dead? And beyond Tom, what was she going to do with herself without money and a car?

But then Tom was there in a grey Subaru, and she hopped in as if they had been in the habit of meeting like this since yesterday. He discoursed on the places they might have lunch, and they agreed on the old diner they used to frequent with its comfortable booths. Naomi wondered what explanation she would give for her five-year absence, while she waited for the cheeseburger to arrive. "Do you like teaching?" she asked, looking for a neutral topic.

"I Love it. I love to turn on the students to the marvels of ancient American archaeology."

"What do they like best?"

"Would you believe it, they love talking about human sacrifice. Their eyes shine at the mention of cruelties."

"Why do you think that is?"

"Because it's different from us, I guess. I don't really know."

"Do you think because it's something forbidden?"

"Trust you to psychoanalyze it," he said, taking a bite out of the burger. "I think they're too immature to know what they're doing. I just notice, that's all."

"They must think you're a very fine teacher," she said, cringing mentally at the flattery.

He smiled and shrugged. "Well, I guess so— See here, Naomi, it's one thing for you to turn up like this so suddenly. I understand that you've been in the field all this time working on your dissertation. Is it done?"

"Sort of—"

"You look splendid. Is that the latest Tikal t-shirt?"

"Um." Naomi looked at his hand which had no wedding ring.

"I have to admit that I've been seeing someone else in your absence. Maybe you remember Joyce. Anyway, it's pretty much over. She couldn't hold a candle to you. But you were gone a long time." Tom had an apologetic tone. Naomi smiled and said she understood and that there had been someone for her too in Tikal.

"Not that jerk Rod Rogers, who couldn't see a house mound if he fell on it?"

Naomi assured him that it was no one from the department. She was friendly but not eager, and that reassured him that she didn't expect to pick up automatically where they had left off. Slightly disappointed, he could feel his interest piqued.

"What do you think happened to Professor Brown?" she asked, with a crunch on a potato chip.

"He fell. He had an accident." Tom shrugged. "It's a tragedy."

"For whom is it a tragedy?"

"Well, for everyone. For Brenda. For the Department. For me. For archaeology."

"For Jennifer?"

"Oh, really, you know better than that. That was just a—you know what I mean."

"Aren't your chances for tenure better now?"

Tom blushed. "Now really—next you'll say I pushed him down the stairs." The alibi came fast: "I was in the library."

They sipped their cokes quietly.

"Are you trying to say that it was not an accident?" he asked incredulously.

Naomi was tempted to tell him about her dream but wasn't sure if it was a good idea. "I had a dream about Professor Brown as I was coming back," she said finally.

"You don't mean to say that you dreamt that he was murdered and you came back to investigate!—" he scoffed. "You've been reading too many mysteries."

"I did not come back to investigate, but it is a coincidence. And what d'ya think of Brenda leaving right after the wake?"

"She doesn't want to stay in the same house for a few nights. I can understand that." He added facetiously, "Maybe his ghost turns up and she doesn't want to meet him. But you might—" he said with a wink.

Well, Tom had been jealous of that incident, so she let that go.

"If you think someone wanted Professor Brown's job, you might look at Guillermo, alias Bill."

"Oh," said Naomi, quite surprised.

"You saw him trying desperately to be American. If he doesn't get another job here in a year, he has to go back to Guatemala. Just because he is half Maya—he can still be a suspect."

"You really think so?"

"No, but you started this conversation about suspects. Or try Sophie, for all that. She and Professor Brown did not get along at all. She was all for graphs, and he was all for the field. She wants to be head of department."

"All right! I get your point. Perhaps I'm being silly."

"Well, not silly, just out of it. You've been away, and you don't know the current situation. You're jumping to conclusions," he patronized. "Are you coming over to the department soon? I can give you a ride tomorrow on my way in, say about ten o'clock?"

Naomi thanked him for the lunch. Tom drove her back, and she accepted the peck on the cheek before she got out of the car, saying, "See you tomorrow."

She went back to the empty Victorian house and found the cat, a lovely calico, sprawled in Professor Brown's favorite armchair, fast asleep. Perhaps she had jumped to conclusions about Professor Brown's death, she wondered, and all those people never entertained the idea of murder, as Tom had said, even for a moment. In fact, why did she assume that Professor Brown had called her to find his murderer? The dream could have been something else, something entirely different, something that had to do with her, something unfinished from her previous life. It was something compelling to be sure, otherwise she would not have come. Tom's idea of the ghost of Professor Brown was facetious but could not be ruled out. Maybe not exactly a ghost, as in stories, but the spirit of the man. How well did she know Professor

Brown, after all? What more was there to know? She had a slight headache and rummaged around Brenda's medicine cabinet to find an aspirin. She was going to lie down and have a nap, and afterwards she would go into Professor Brown's study and look around, to see if she could find the real man.

5.

Naomi lay down on the guest bed, which wasn't all that comfortable. She had to remove a stuffed monkey and a stuffed elephant, remnants of Kyle's childhood. She could hear Kyle drumming from the garage. Brenda had instructed her to leave him sandwiches in the kitchen, and the sandwiches disappeared at a regular rate. The drumming ceased, so Kyle was probably going out. Quiet descended on the Morristown street in the middle of the afternoon. It was a cool May day, and Naomi pulled on a cover. She planned just on forty winks but sleep would not come. So she lay there letting her thoughts meander.

At first she was thinking of practicalities. Money. A car. More clothes. A place to live. She hadn't thought through all of this while she was at Tikal but had followed the impulse to come back to this world. She would have a few days at Brenda's, but beyond that she had to find some solution. How long did she plan to stay? Was she here for a short time to solve whatever it was about the death of Professor Brown, or was she planning to stay on longer? Clearly she couldn't "solve" anything in a matter of days. So even if she didn't stay for very long, she needed money. At this point the sleep that had been eluding her caught up. Not being able to solve her problems, she let herself go and slept.

She dreamed of Professor Brown's summer house in Milford, Pennsylvania, where he had taken her on that one memorable occasion. She was there alone trying to get to sleep on the queen-size bed. He wasn't in the house. It was night and the frogs were croaking in the pond. All of a sudden she heard anxious human voices outside and the sound of swooshing water, as if a dam had been released and flooded the little pond. The water kept rising—soon it was at the base of the house and would come in the doors and windows.

Naomi woke up not quite knowing where she was but with a clear sense that she had valuable jades in her satchel. She found it and the half-dozen gleaming green stones nestled inside. She saw the car and the new clothes. *At least I brought some treasure from Tikal.* She wondered at her state of mind, to have forgotten the jade! They wouldn't be easy to sell, as they were illegal antiquities, but she would worry about that later.

She went to the kitchen and made herself a cup of tea. Suppose she was wrong, and Professor Brown was not murdered? But suppose that he was and whoever nudged him down the stairs gets away with it? Shouldn't she first try to find out what happened and then eliminate the possibility of murder? Maybe it was best to go on the assumption that the situation was not clear, despite what Tom said. He was a nice guy, but he did not have the greatest insight into things. *Or, perhaps, as Philippa had said of Professor Brown, Tom was a real man—thus unintuitive.* She was thinking of Tom being useful just now but didn't want to give him any encouragement. And anyway, he had an affair with Joyce! Fat and short and with low self-esteem, Joyce was pathetic. Couldn't handsome Tom do any better? Naomi said to herself that she shouldn't take Tom for granted. He may not be the same Tom she had known. Everywhere she stepped, she saw a potential minefield—she was of them and yet not of them.

Low sounds of drumming could be heard, and Naomi decided to tackle the study. Professor Brown's study was next to the guestroom, which was sometimes Brenda's and sometimes the assistant's room. The study was a cheerful white-painted room with bookshelves and filing cabinets that smelled of pipe tobacco. There was a computer on the desk and piles of handwritten cards. Professor Brown was of the generation that had written information on cards and was now painstakingly entering them on the computer. Or his assistants were doing it for him. She didn't know what she was looking for; he didn't seem like the type who would keep a journal or love letters, but even a man who seemed so on the surface might have secrets or activities most people did not know about. She pulled out the drawers full of pens and university stationary in the desk and found his bills and taxes in the filing cabinet. The will was there, too, leaving everything to Brenda and Kyle. Interestingly it stipulated that he be cremated and his ashes scattered at Tikal, which obviously was not done. That was curious, Naomi thought, and wondered why. That request made Professor Brown more romantic than all the other mundane elements in his office. She hadn't found a secret, yet, but now the man had a potential for secrets.

She hadn't noticed that the drumming had ceased but was suddenly aware of muffled footsteps on the carpeted stairs. There was a closet in the room not used for clothes but for piles of quilts and blankets, and Naomi crept in, pulling the louvered door behind her.

Kyle came into the room after peering into the guest room to see that she wasn't there. He rummaged through the desk as Naomi had done, but he seemed to know what he was after. In the middle left-hand drawer he found what looked like bills and papers, and underneath them he brought out a set of little keys. There were actually two sets of keys, and he hesitated as to which one might be right. He selected one and again looking around to see if she was anywhere, he left the room.

When the drumming began, again, she came out of the closet, refolded the blankets, and looked at the middle left-hand drawer. How had she missed it? Of course, the bills on top were telephone bills. But underneath there were receipts and forms in Spanish, sometimes with a Guatemalan seal. And as far as Naomi could tell, they were giving Professor Brown permission to take research materials out of the country. All archaeologists do that; they get mostly potsherds or at best little figurines and arrowheads. Worthless, except to scholars. The keys were probably to a closet at the university where these were kept. What did Kyle want with them?

Under the papers, there was the small name card of one Clifford M. Turner, fine arts, with a New York City address on Madison Avenue at 79th Street. Naomi pulled it out and observed it carefully. Now what would a scientific archaeologist do with the card of a Madison avenue art dealer, besides spit on it? Naomi's first thought was, *Now I can sell my jades*. Her second thought was *What am I getting myself mixed up in?*

But she took the card and retreated to her room. Maybe Mr. Turner didn't buy Maya jades, but he surely knew someone who did. It was illegal to take Maya treasures out of Guatemala and bring them into the US. It was illegal to sell them in the US. It wasn't just a matter of being caught; it was the morality of the thing. Grave robbers destroyed ancient sites in order to find artworks to sell to collectors. In selling

Maya art, she was abetting the destruction of Tikal and other sites. On the other hand, that's all she had to sell. Her Maya clothes, being unknown, would fetch nothing. She was on a mission to help find a murderer—maybe—and she couldn't imagine that Professor Brown had anything to do with the illegal traffic of antiquities, regardless of that card. Maybe she could find some way of doing harm to the antiquities trade at some future time. And after all, those jades, so special here, were no big deal at Tikal. Night Sky only had modest treasures compared to Sky Rain and the lord of Uaxactún. These lesser jades she could surely sell.

While she was heating up one of Brenda's frozen lean cuisines, Kyle came in to get a sandwich. Naomi took a closer look at the gangly seventeen-year-old. She couldn't very well ask him what keys he had taken out of his father's drawer and why. He had only a little acne and perhaps looked good to a seventeen-year-old girl. He snatched the sandwich off the plate and disappeared. Naomi kept her eyes and ears open but could sense no indications of him moving about the house, opening cabinets, or in any way rummaging around. He seemed to be watching television.

She went to bed planning her next day. Calling Turner. Going to the university with Tom. She tried not to think of what she was doing here. Perhaps time would tell. One thing she did note: She had gotten very interested in these people since arriving among them so abruptly—something was waiting for her here.

6.

Tom was there on time and they drove the short distance to the university. He said he had to hurry to make his class, but he would pick her up in the student lounge at 4:00. Naomi wore her Maya huipil over Brenda's drawstring pants and walked into the office. The secretaries were all young and new, but the administrator had been there since her day. Annie oohed and aahed over Naomi's return and how well she looked and tried to fill her in on some of the gossip.

Most of it had to do with how wonderful Professor Brown had been as head of the department, since he had let her off every other Friday so she could work on her prints. She was devastated by his death and couldn't believe that his fall was accidental. She thought some woman was behind it, literally behind him, pushing him. Maybe one of his favorites, like "that sniveling Jennifer," or even "that tough bitch" his wife. Annie was never Professor Brown's mistress, to her knowledge, but her devotion was legendary. She said that she was keeping her ears open in case she heard anything incriminating about it.

Naomi changed the subject. She wanted to know if anyone in the department had a part-time job available for her, in the office, in the library, with one of the professors. A middle-aged man came into the office and was introduced as Michael Corbett who taught anthropological theory. He had been at the wake, but Naomi had not met him. "You're the one back from the field?" he said to her absentmindedly as he asked one of the secretaries to fax something to London. London was big in theory.

Annie looked through a clipboard and said to Naomi, "Sophie Parker needs an assistant, and it doesn't have to be an Egyptologist."

"Is it letters and books from the library and photocopies?" she asked hopefully.

"Yes, in fact she is quite desperate and wants somebody right away. She will even take an undergraduate." That was a sign of desperation. At least Naomi was a superannuated graduate student.

"Is she in her office now?"

Annie called and assured Sophie that a good assistant will be right over.

"Ah, the prodigal daughter back from the field," said Sophie, as Naomi entered the neat little office.

"Yes, Professor Parker, I understand that you need a helper."

"Yes, actually, you can be of help to me right now. I'm doing a book on Ramses II, and I have a lot of correspondence I need to get out to publishers and illustration sources. My last assistant had a nervous breakdown. I'll give you the information, and you can do them on the computer in the student computer room. Everything is due yesterday. Aren't you going to get that nice, ethnic top dirty if you wear it every day? Haven't you seen something nice in that boutique near the student center?" She was fishing for information.

Naomi mumbled that she just wanted to show it off in the

department. She would have to go back to Brenda's closet until Friday when her first check came through. Which reminded her about the dealer Turner and her need to call him. Perhaps Sophie knew something about him. But then she thought better of it; maybe it wasn't a good idea to mention Clifford M. Turner to Sophie; she was so curious and perceptive. As it was, she knew that something wasn't quite right about Naomi. Wait until Sophie went to lunch or to class and use the privacy of her office telephone. So she picked up her notes and materials and sat down at a computer, keeping one eye on the corridor to see Sophie's comings and goings. She consulted Annie about Sophie's classes; the next was at 2:00.

She snuck into the professor's office and dialed Turner's number. A secretary answered that Mr. Turner was in a meeting, but if it was important she could let him know. Naomi said that she had some very rare antiquities and needed his advice urgently. Thereupon the secretary went and fetched him.

"Miss Sedgwick, what is it that you have, exactly."

"Some pre-Columbian objects of rare value."

"Where did you acquire them?"

"I can't discuss that over the phone."

"How do I know that they are as special as all that and that they are not hot?"

Clifford Turner had great experience dealing with people who wanted to sell things. They all claimed their stuff was rare and special, and they turned out to be things like the ceramic copy of the Aztec Calendar Stone or tourist knickknacks. But then again, every now and then, he found a treasure. This woman didn't sound stupid; she seemed to know what she had.

"Where are you located, can you come in?"

"I am in Morristown, New Jersey, and I can't come in right away."

Turner consulted his calendar. "On Friday I will be in the vicinity consulting with an African art collector. Perhaps we can meet."

Naomi designated the student center cafeteria and told him she'd be wearing a Maya huipil.

So if all goes well, she thought, on Friday she'd get paid and sell the Maya jades. She was making a list of all the things she needed: a car, a computer, a place to live, some nice clothes. She hadn't thought of all this when she left Tikal so impulsively—it was one thing to go "native" in ancient America; that required leaving things behind and acquiring very little. Going "native" in the US required a great deal. Nor did she know whether this was just a temporary visit or a permanent stay.

So she had almost a week to manage without all those things and without money. To most people, including Tom, it seemed normal that after a long absence in the field she should have to start afresh, and they were willing to help. Tom ferried her back and forth to the university. She laundered Brenda's t-shirts she wore to her job and emptied Brenda's freezer to feed herself and Kyle—who often went out to McDonald's with friends, so that was not difficult. Life acquired a certain routine.

She watched the news with her microwave dinner. Then she sat down to think. She got a pad of lined paper and wrote at the top:

Tuesday

1. Professor Brown carried a slide tray and maybe a glass of whisky. He was preparing to give a talk, and he was not comfortable with PowerPoint and the computer, hence the slides. He was the last person in the department still to use slides. It's not clear whether he really carried the glass of whisky in the other hand or whether it was upset in the living room.

2. Who else was in the house? Brenda. Where was she? The kitchen or was it the bedroom? Jennifer had just come with the slide tray. Was she in the study? Was Kyle in the house? These three people were certain. Could anyone else have been there? Did these three people have a motive?

3. Brenda—she had installed the new carpet on the stairs. She didn't seem broken up at the wake. She left for parts unknown right afterwards. She seemed to see my arrival as useful to her purposes. She knew all about his womanizing. Several people think she did it, if anyone did.

4. Jennifer—she was on the right spot, the study, and had given him the slide carousel. But she was madly in love with him, so there was no motive. Unless they had a quarrel. She was awfully broken up at the wake.

5. Kyle—many teenage boys hate their father, but few murder them. He seemed such a stereotype of a teenager with his

loud music and McDonalds. But then he wanted those keys for some reason. Access to money to buy marijuana? How does he get along with Brenda?

6. Ixchel—did the calico cat get under foot and trip Professor Brown? Was the cat chased by someone human? A pretty unlikely possibility.

That left out the long shots, the colleagues who wanted jobs or chairmanships or whom he might have been blackmailing for who knows what. All that, however, was far fetched and Naomi had to admit that it must have been an accident. At this point, she had to admit that her trip seemed useless, and she might as well go back to Tikal. Meanwhile, Brenda was out, and it seemed reasonable to search her desk and space to find an answer to where she might have gone and what her motives might be. After all, if there was a likely suspect, it was she. Naomi reflected on wearing Brenda's clothes and living in her house. What did Kyle think about that? But after Friday she would have her own money, Brenda would be back—and there would not be another chance.

7.

"How about lunch," said Bill to Tom in the corridor of the department.

"I have a class in an hour and a half, but why not."

They went into the cafeteria at 11:30, before it was full and noisy.

"How is your course, The Maya: Ancient and Modern, going?" asked Tom politely.

"The students are more interested in the 'modern' than in the 'ancient,' Bill sighed. His English was softly accented by Spanish. As usual, he was dressed in a blazer and tie like a preppy American.

"I can't wait for exams next week and to be done with all this," said Tom, biting into a tuna-fish sandwich. He thought Guillermo's affectation of everything American was silly. They'd hired Guillermo

Villasanchez Ford (his mother was American, and in Latin American style her name was added to his father's name) because he was Latin American for the Latin American visiting professorship, and here he was calling himself Bill and looking like an Ivy League professor with a Maya face.

"You and Naomi were once engaged, were you not?" Bill said casually.

"Yes, that was a long time ago."

"And she's been in the field for five years?"

"I guess it's five."

Bill dressed his hamburger with ketchup and relish. "Don't you think that's something strange?"

"Why? some people take ten years to write a dissertation!"

"Yes, but they come and go in the ten years. They don't just disappear." He paused and then added, "And suddenly reappear."

"It seems to me it's the same old Naomi," said Tom with a mouthful of tuna fish.

"And that outfit she wore—I know the dress of Chichicastenango natives; each village has a different style outfit, and none are quite like that. It's too fine a cotton, almost gauze or lace."

"Maybe it was made for tourists. Naomi always liked clothes."

"So you don't think there is anything strange about Naomi?"

"Well, to tell you the truth, Naomi is not quite like you and me," said Tom."

"Why is that?"

"Well, because she was adopted. She doesn't talk about it much. But I know from experience that adopted people are different. They are sometimes unpredictable."

"How do you know?"

"I have an adopted cousin, and she has been through three marriages before the age of thirty."

"So you think Naomi went off and left you for five years because she is adopted?" Bill enquired.

"Yes, adopted people are a little crazy—you have to have patience with them. They're all right in the end. My cousin is happily married with number three. They have two children. You'd never know."

"All the same," Bill concluded, as Tom got up to leave, "something is strange."

* * *

Jennifer and Philippa were having coffee in the student lounge. Jennifer was studying for the exam for The Maya: Ancient and Modern. "Who was that strange woman?" she asked Philippa.

Philippa understood the question. "I've never seen her before."

"But everyone else seems to know her—they know her here."

"Not everyone."

"She works for Sophie Parker now," Jennifer reported."

"Yes, and you can be sure that if anything is strange, Sophie Parker will find out."

"She acted as if she belonged there, as if she and Professor Brown—and she came to his funeral . . ." Jennifer looked back to her studies.

"There is no use pretending that Professor Brown was all yours."

"He was mine now," Jennifer said stubbornly, pretending to read.

"Has it occurred to you that you might have been the last person to see him alive?"

"You're just saying that because your affair with him ended a year ago and you're sore." She looked up at Philippa.

"No, I'm not sore, I am philosophical. Professor Brown was a rite of passage, a stage in my life that is now completely over."

"Well," said Jennifer, "he was no 'rite of passage' for me. I loved him and he loved me. He even took me to his childhood getaway in Milford."

"He took me to Milford too. So what."

Jennifer began to cry quietly. Philippa gave her a Kleenex and continued, "Still, I don't like to see that woman in the department. I think she is snooping around, and I don't know what right she has. She acts like she owns the place."

"I tell you what, Jennifer, we will invite her to join us for coffee sometime and find out what she is all about."

* * *

"Annie, could you step into my office?"

"Yes, Professor Parker, in a minute." She hit the computer's save button and followed the professor. There was a moment while Sophie Parker resumed her place behind her desk and seemed to wait for an unspoken answer.

"Is Naomi working out OK?" asked Annie, finally.

"Yes, she is a fine assistant, although she knows nothing about Egyptology. There are some things about that young woman that are odd. Well, of course, she did just come back from the field, and then they're all a little out of it. But Naomi is more out of it than usual. She is very bright, and she does her work well, but where is her cell phone? Why is she living at Brenda Brown's house? Something doesn't add up."

"I'm sure I can't explain her. She was a very ordinary student."

"Was she one of Professor Brown's women?"

"Probably, weren't they all—God rest him. He won't have any more," Annie replied with a rueful smile.

"Isn't there anything you can remember about her background, her application, that would explain her bizarre reappearance at the wake?"

"I can't explain her behavior any more than that she has returned to resume her place and her life after years away, and we all welcome her back."

Professor Parker waved casually. "Of course we welcome her back. She is a worthwhile young woman, I am sure."

"I do remember one thing about her." Annie paused by the door. "Her parents died in some kind of an accident, a car accident, I think, when she was a teenager. I think that was in the application. She needed a fellowship. There was some sympathy for that."

"Well, it's not important, I was just curious, since she works for me. And that native gown of hers is spectacular!"

Annie was dismissed.

* * *

Michael Corbett was photocopying pages of the exam for Method and Theory in Archaeology, which he was finishing for the deceased Professor Brown, and he was watching Naomi come and go. He had only been in the department for two years and was on the fringes of its political and gossip life. In other words, he was out of it. He liked watching Naomi, because she was so self-possessed and as oblivious to all the goings on as he. Like everyone else, he had heard that she was just back from the field after a long absence, and that made her seem mysterious. He watched her blue eyes shaded by her blonde hair and seemed to see the knowledge of strange things, unusual experiences, unexpected thoughts. It did not occur to him to accost her. He wasn't thinking of possessing her; he just enjoyed watching her and fantasizing about her. Where was it that she was supposed to have been?—the Maya city of Tikal. How deeply did she go into that experience? It seemed to him that she must have come back from very, very far away. She was clearly acclimatizing, but he hoped she wouldn't become like the usual graduate student girls like Philippa and Jennifer, for whom he had nothing but contempt. It was best to keep Naomi as a visitor from another planet, whatever her planet was, and if he had the chance to shield her, he would.

8.

Naomi woke with a headache and called Annie that she wouldn't be in unless absolutely necessary. Professor Parker was spending the day in New York at the Public Library and did not need her. It was Wednesday, definitely a day to check out Brenda's things. She had a cup of tea and toasted some tasteless frozen waffles, having eaten all the cereal and saving the bread for Kyle's sandwiches. *Money on Friday*, she told herself.

Brenda's desk was in an alcove off the master bedroom. Unlike Professor Brown's, it was neat with very little on top except a clock and a picture of Kyle as a four-year-old. Probably she kept all her professional papers in the lab at the university's biology department. Naomi knew that Brenda had something to do with fish and was herself an accomplished scuba diver. Poking around in the drawers, she found nearly a dozen brochures for cruises, especially in tropical places like the Caribbean. The one on top had a date starting on the day of Professor Brown's funeral and ending this Saturday. She opened the flyer and saw a picture of Brenda with the text, "Along on the cruise is Professor Brenda Brown from the University of New Jersey, who will explain the coral reefs and their teeming life, off the coast of Belize." So Brenda's "business trip" was a cruise, and she was too embarrassed to talk about it. Despite the funeral and wake, she wanted to go and she went.

Naomi supposed that there could have been no great love lost between the Professors Brown. No wonder she put up with his womanizing. Naomi flipped through the other brochures. Evidently Brenda went on cruises often and, as a lecturer, for free. The boats were all lavish with names like *Sea Nymph* and *Sea Cloud* and had about as many staff as guests.

Naomi called Brenda's department and enquired after her. The secretary was prompt with the answer: Professor Brenda Brown was away on a research cruise for a few days. So it wasn't exactly a secret, *Except from me?*

Perhaps it was questionable to have gone at such a time, but otherwise everything was as it should be, as it had been planned. Was it imaginable for Professor Brenda Brown to have committed a murder and gone on a cruise the day of her husband's funeral? Naomi had a hard time thinking of Brenda as "Professor Brown."

She continued to examine the brochures and started to look at the other professors who went with Brenda. There were usually two lecturers on such cruises, one in antiquities and one in natural history. With Brenda, in most cases, the other person was a woman archaeologist from Stanford University, named Evelyn Forbes, who lectured on Tikal and Chichén Itzá. Guests would be flown into the sites for a day's tour.

Next to Brenda's photo, Evelyn looked anemic but evidently she liked cruising, too. There were two photos of men, also from Stanford, possibly substitutes for Evelyn. Tim Brown probably knew all of them.

Next Naomi tackled the closet and drawers. She'd looked in them before to find something to wear, but then she was thinking of herself, looking for t-shirts and not Brenda. Now what struck her was that the color scheme of Brenda's clothes was dark and neutral. Beiges, grays and black predominated with occasional whites for brightness. None of the reds, mauves, or purples middle-aged women like to dress in were there. Moreover, there were very few patterns, nothing cute like cats or animal pelt designs. No little embroidered flowers. Brenda's clothes were plain and simple. She must have spent a pretty penny on good-looking simplicity. In the bottom of the closet, there was a plastic bag, evidently for scuba gear, that was empty, and Naomi now understood the reason and didn't bother to unzip it. But there were also two big, open, plastic garbage bags full of clothes that were far more colorful and patterned than the things in the closet. They looked quite worn. Some of them looked old-fashioned, such as a full skirt with an eyelet-trimmed petticoat. These looked like discards to be given to the Salvation Army and forgotten. Naomi noticed after a while that there were no skirts and dresses in the closet, either, only pants. She shrugged her shoulders. Nowadays women did not want to bother with skirts and hose and preferred pants. Brenda was obviously athletic and liked trousers; it didn't mean anything. But the "Salvation Army bags" indicated that she hadn't always been like that. Brenda used to go in for a cute, "feminine" look.

The exploration of Brenda's things took only half a day, and Naomi went into the master bedroom to listen to the news at noon—Senate hearings and the weather—but with only half an ear, her mind still on Brenda and the cruises. Such cruises must be fun once or twice, but going dozens of times must be a bore, she thought. How many times could she enthuse over coral reefs to a group with drinks in their hands, disinterest in their minds, and credit cards? Was she fundraising for a cause? Thinking of the closet, Naomi saw mentally all the handbags—actually shoulder bags—that Brenda had on the top shelf and decided to take a look in them for whatever new information she might find.

The bags had all been neatly emptied, except for one that looked to have been in constant use but passed over for another bag temporarily—*maybe her travel bag*. Wallet and credit cards were missing, but there were crumpled supermarket and gas receipts, a chap stick, Kleenex, a small container of pills, and a pocket calendar. *Probably using the calendar on her iPhone.*

In the transparent back flap of the calendar, there was a small color photo showing two women. The bigger one was in scuba gear and had her arm across the shoulder of a smaller woman in a red bathing suit. Naomi jumped to the conclusion that it was Evelyn Forbes. Obviously the picture was taken on a cruise and the two women were friends. Or were they more than friends?

Naomi watched herself jump to the conclusion that there was a relationship, in order to give Brenda a motive for killing her husband. But was an affair with a woman, even if true, a reason for murder? She caught herself. Didn't that happen all the time nowadays? and wasn't divorce a lot less risky than murder? Besides, wouldn't Tim Brown have just laughed? *Such derision could have led to murder*, she finally thought with irony. Professor Brenda Brown took herself very seriously. That closet was a serious closet.

Naomi heard Kyle come in from school and retreated to her room. She had found out something about Brenda, but the person she knew little about was her own "Professor Brown." What was he really like? *He seems to have been a caricature of the avid archaeologist and lover of the good life.* Why had he signaled to her in his death? Had he signaled to her, or had she made it up? No, the blood stains were still on the floor where he had fallen, and no amount of cleaning could get them up. Why had she assumed that his look asked her to come back and find the murderer? Why had she come back? And what were they thinking in Tikal of Marigold lying in bed and sick for so many days? Does Sky Rain pay attention to Marigold's illness? Should she worry about what is happening back in Tikal?

Naomi decided that since she had not been gone for long, probably everything was all right at Tikal, and she wasn't going to worry about it for a while. Some other questions were bothering her, but she decided, for the moment, to concentrate on the present, on the issue of murder. She would assume she had come to find a murderer, and she would do her best to find him or her. Admittedly, it didn't look promising. *Certainly the police do not think it was murder, and all are agreed on the accident interpretation. Maybe this was not murder in the technical sense.* But that would have to wait until she knew more. Tomorrow she would try the university. And then she was to have dinner with Tom. Another Tikal t-shirt would not do. She would have to try Brenda's closet again. After her recent analysis, dressing as Brenda felt a little creepy. Maybe she'd get something out of the discard garbage bags.

9.

"Would you like to have coffee with us?" asked Philippa.

"I can't, just now," answered Naomi. "I have to photocopy this whole book from interlibrary loan. It has to be returned tomorrow."

"Jennifer and I just thought that you might have advice for us about fieldwork."

"Hm. I'll look for you a little later."

"She is making you work hard?" said Michael Corbett standing at the other copy machine.

"I was out yesterday, I have to make it up." Michael Corbett was not one of her suspects and didn't interest her.

"See ya," he said and left.

Later in the day, Naomi saw Jennifer and Philippa in conversation with Bill in the student lounge and went over to them. Bill was talking: "When Guatemalans talk about the 'colossus of the north,' they don't mean the US; they mean Mexico. We've had a very troubled history with Mexico. They're so much richer than we are. They can take care of their ruins, while we don't have the money for it. And we have some of the best Maya ruins, like Tikal and Seibal. Piedras Negras and Uaxactún are almost completely unexcavated, except by looters."

"Don't Guatemalan scholars speak up about this situation?" asked Philippa?

"They do, but in Guatemala no one listens to scholars." Bill emptied his pipe into a paper cup. The lounge was a smoke-free zone, but Bill was allowed his pipe. He had been in the process of coauthoring a paper with Professor Brown, but now the authors names might have to be reversed to "Villasanchez-Ford and Brown," which would be to his advantage.

"Do you really think that everything has to be dug up?" asked Naomi naïvely. "Shouldn't we just let the past be in peace. We know enough about it already."

Philippa and Jennifer protested that we hardly knew anything. "Besides," continued Jennifer, "we have to have our share of the glory of discovery. What would we do if we stopped digging?"

"Well, I just thought a time might come in the future when there would not be an interest in archaeology, and taking care of all this excavated material might be burdensome."

The three looked at each other as if Naomi had gone soft in the head. It was unanswerable. One could think of five, ten years ahead, but not eons ahead to when archaeology might be of no interest.

"You have spent too much time in the field," said Bill indulgently. "By the way, where did you acquire that Maya-style outfit you were wearing? It could not have been Chichicastenango, which I happen to know quite well."

"You're right, it was not from Chichicastenango. It was made for me by a Maya weaver near Tikal. We designed it together."

"Of course, you made friends with the local Maya."

"You can say that."

"What language do they speak?" asked Jennifer.

"Well, Ch'ol, but the younger people speak Spanish."

"Are they hard to get to know?"

"I don't know, I just fell in with them."

Philippa wanted to know whether she'd stayed in a thatched hut the whole time she was there, and Jennifer wanted to ask whether Tim Brown had been in touch with her, helping to develop her research. But at that point, Tom showed up to take her home by way of dinner.

He approved of the flowered peasant top she was wearing from Brenda's discard bag and was looking forward to the evening. He had questions. "So how's it going since you're back?" They were settling in to the Evergreen Italian restaurant. Naomi looked forward to the big bowl of spaghetti and meatballs, even with the iceberg lettuce salad she remembered from the past. However, the menu now had fettuccine Alfredo and mixed green salad à la carte as its specialty. She picked lasagna and, Tom had veal Marsala, urging her to share a mixed green salad, saying that they were quite large. Tom was friendly, pleasantly noncommittal, and acting as if there had not been a five-year hiatus in their relationship. Maybe he was just a little bit grand in taking her back without a word and wanting admiration. Naomi thought of telling him her story as a gesture of her consideration and honesty, picking up where they had left off at lunch.

"Tom," she began, toying with a piece of bread dipped in olive oil, "I haven't really been in the field. I mean, I was in Tikal, but not now."

"You mean you were somewhere else?" he said bewildered.

"No, it was Tikal all right, but at a different time."

"Well, certainly a great deal has changed since you left. You should not have stayed away so long. It's not good for you. Or for me. Now Joyce—"

"That's not what I meant: I was in ancient Tikal. I got to know Sky Rain. He was a really unpleasant man. He wanted me to be the wife of the lord of Uaxactún."

The fork stuck in Tom's mouth for a moment. "There is such a thing as getting too deeply involved in your research," he said, looking at the attractive woman in the flowered blouse, and he reached out a hand to touch hers. "There, there, you must have been terribly lonely."

Naomi stifled a tear of frustration and pulled her hand away. "Yes,

Tom, I was lonely," she said cheerily. "Now, Professor Brown—"

"Had you been in touch with Professor Brown?" Tom asked, pretending to be neutral when he was jealous.

"No. But I had that dream he was dead."

"So you came back because you think someone killed him. One of us?" He was trying to make it sound as ridiculous as he could while balancing the dripping fettuccine in front of his mouth.

"Something like that. But now I see that no one had a motive to kill him."

"You sound like a silly detective novel." He paused, trying to be funny rather than judgmental. "Well, Miss Marple, like I said, I was in the library stacks when Professor Brown had his accident, and I was alone. No one saw me. The librarian at the desk was on the phone turned away from me, when I left. I have no alibi. Is that good enough?"

"Well, Tom, you know I didn't mean that— What book were you getting out of the Library, by the way?"

"Er, I didn't get anything. I was just looking for something that wasn't there." And to turn the tables on her, he added, "How's the dissertation coming?" He told himself he wasn't going to mention it, and he just had.

"It isn't."

"You mean you're stuck on something? Maybe I can help. Let me see what you have so far." "You remember the pre-Columbian novel I started to write?"

"Vaguely. Really, Naomi that's a waste of time."

"Anyway, I'm now in it."

"You mean you're sort of obsessed by it? Is that where the lord of Uaxactún comes in?"

He decided that Naomi needed help. She had been alone in the field too much, and with that novel of hers had embarked on some ridiculous and perhaps dangerous fantasies. She needed a dose of reality. "Come home with me, and we'll watch the news together tonight. Do you even know who's running for president?"

Naomi just laughed but, sensing that Tom had no other motive, assented. Tom was the nicest imaginable guy. She decided that she did in fact want to know who was running for president.

10.

Everything happened very quickly. Naomi acquired a small, used car, sublet an apartment, and bought herself jeans and t-shirts at Wal-Mart, and a smashing pair of black pants, a flirty white skirt, and a few interesting tops in the boutique Sophie had mentioned. At Wal-Mart she also got basic kitchen utensils and bed linen. She ordered a computer and cell phone and still had money left over. Mr. Turner oohed and aahed over the jades and probably underpaid her, but on short order that was the best she could do. It was clear that he had a buyer in mind for them. Naomi was too busy with all this to think about her mission or predicament. There was little time to move from Brenda's and by "mistake" she took her favorite Tikal t-shirt and "forgot" to return it.

The widowed professor returned on Saturday looking rested and happy and satisfied that Naomi was making her own arrangements so successfully. Kyle and Ixchel seemed happily taken care of. Naomi was a find, and Brenda thought that she could be useful on one more task, preparing Tim's—and now her—Milford vacation house for renters arriving in a week's time. So she asked Naomi to go with her on Sunday, for the day.

That would be as much an outing as work. Naomi hesitated only a moment or so and said yes. Revisiting Milford might be an interesting experience, even with Brenda.

She made herself an omelet in the new frying pan, and settled down to watch the news, as Tom had suggested. The economic news was bad, the stock market had gone down. Two economists from rival think tanks were discussing the situation from opposite points of view. Naomi's mind wandered back to the day she had spent with Professor Brown in Milford. What really stuck in her memory was the neighbor with the hawk.

They had gone—or at least she had—without prior notice or preparation. She went to Professor Brown's office, as usual, carefully dressed for the occasion. He had commented on her wearing red, so she wore a red top with the blue jeans. She seemed to have had a special relationship with Professor Brown from the beginning of the time she became his assistant. She was aware that he looked on her as a woman, and that was sort of nice. She saw his voluminous publications, his far-flung correspondence; she heard his ringing baritone in class and was sure that he was a great man. He was muscular like a blue-collar worker, and he had slightly graying curly brown hair framing those blue eyes. He made no improper advances, such as touching her accidentally at the desk. He merely looked.

In the beginning, when it hadn't yet affected her, Naomi thought to herself that he looked at her as if she were a nice, large serving of filet mignon with all the trimmings. She had a reasonably high opinion of her looks and didn't mind being desirable. Eventually, she hoped that their hands would meet across a letter or envelope at the same time, telling herself that she was a silly goose, and she should be happy not to have fallen into his clutches, the way it was said others did. But if he looked at her seeing filet mignon, she couldn't resist seeing him as a fudge ice-cream sundae. She didn't need him, she didn't want him, but he was sort of there and nothing much else was. He gave off sensual vibes like an atomic power plant, and she could not but respond secretly. Dressing every morning to please and attract him was her way of returning the attraction. Sometimes she changed two or three times before finding herself satisfactory. She understood that the game was "no touching," and those parameters were just fine.

But there was that time when one Friday morning Professor Brown said: "I left some notes in my house in Milford; we will drive out to take care of some things, and you can take the bus back."

Naomi was glad to be going on an adventure with Professor Brown and didn't expect anything. On the way, he chattered about his house, which he'd inherited from his father, a doctor. Evidently Brenda did not like to stay there, so he often went alone. He was very fond of the little town of Milford, which did not have ugly strip malls and McDonalds like Morristown. In fact, Milford had a castle named Gray Towers, which was once the home of Gifford Pinchot, secretary of the interior under Teddy Roosevelt. It was built imitating a French château, and you could still imagine the gorgeous landscaping it once had. "The Park Service takes care of it now for tourists," he added. Would Naomi like to see it?

"Sure," she assumed that this was all part of the day's activities.

So they went to see Gray Towers, and then Professor Brown suggested walking over to the waterfall on the grounds. At that hour on a Friday midday, they were all alone, and the woods and the rushing waters of springtime were romantic, but neither one of them made a move.

They went back to the village of Milford, which consisted of two blocks on one street, and Professor Brown pointed out the School of Forestry Building, established by Gifford Pinchot on Main Street—now a drugstore—and the lovely little colonnaded library that was the Pinchot residence before Gray Towers. Naomi admired all these landmarks, having had no idea that Milford was such a pretty and noteworthy place. It added immensely to Professor Brown's stature that he came from such a place. Naomi grew up in the suburbs with her adoptive parents without such history. Comfort reigned rather than beauty and antiquity.

The coup de grâce was lunch at Faucheres, a somewhat dilapidated big house run as a restaurant by two elderly sisters. They ate homemade sausages on a bed of lettuce with French bread. By then, the weather had turned and it became chilly, so after lunch they stopped in at Bloomgarden's Department Store, also on Main Street, where Professor Brown insisted on buying her a sweater, something very old-fashioned looking. He bought some envelopes in the five-and-dime across the street. Having done Milford village, except for the bakery which Naomi saw had delicious-looking cakes in the window, they drove to Professor Brown's house tucked away in the woods. It was a large, wooden house that had seen better days, but what made it exceptional was its setting in the woods on a hill above a pond. It was isolated on all sides except one, where a neighbor's house was somewhat visible. By the time they entered the house, Professor Brown and Naomi were a couple.

"My neighbor has a hawk. Have you ever seen a hawk close up?" he suddenly said.

Naomi shook her head. No hawks in the suburbs. So he made a phone call, and out they went to the neighbor, who came obligingly with his hawking glove and released the bird that had been chained to the ground. The hawk flew up and went around in a big circle, flapping its wings near their heads, eventually returning obediently to his handler. To Naomi it looked absolutely enormous and terrifying while it was flying free. On their return to the house, they did finally have passionate sex in the master bedroom and a companionable tea in front of the fireplace, before she had to catch the bus back. But what was unforgettable was the hawk.

Naomi returned from her recollection to the TV being no longer on the news but some old-timers belting out bebop music from the fifties and sixties. They suddenly looked ridiculous. Naomi thought back on her day with Professor Brown. What a seduction that had been! No woman on earth could have resisted it. In his way, he was an artist. After the incident in Milford, everything went back to the way it had been, except there was a warm friendship between them. Eventually she and Tom became friends, and Professor Brown had another assistant. Had she meant more to him than the others? Had he meant more to her than she was admitting? There was something cruel in someone revealing himself so much and then withdrawing. But had he revealed himself? Hadn't she been the romantic, with ye olde Milford, the Pinchots and the hawk? She hadn't been there since, and on the morrow she was to go with Brenda to revisit the house with the prosaic purpose of getting it ready for rental.

11.

Milford, Pennsylvania, was about an hour's drive from Morristown. When they were on the highway Brenda said, "I just put the ad in the paper and someone wanted to rent it right away. It's too good to pass up."

Naomi nodded. "How was your trip?" she asked.

"Good, good. It's, er, a trip I go on every year. Sort of research. And pleasure. Coral reefs, you know. Belize. Fish."

"Oh," said Naomi to say something.

"I know it looked awful for me to dash away from poor Tim's funeral. I agonized about it, but what could I do? Everything had been settled. You turned up at a convenient time."

Brenda passed a slow car with great speed.

"I always liked you best among Tim's girls," she said finally.

Naomi remained silent.

"Not as smarmy as most of them—more cool," she added.

That was a compliment, so Naomi accepted it with a little cough. "How did you do it?"

"Well, Tim and I had been going in separate ways for years but had no reason to break up the household, at least I didn't until—" At this point Brenda geared up to pass a cement mixer and oil truck. Naomi held onto her seat.

"I hated that whole quaint little Milford world of his with the pseudo French château and his ancestral seat always needing a roof or paint or something." She honked. "I come from a Queens housing development, and my father was a policeman. Kyle will get Milford, all of it. He can do what he likes with it."

"So it's yours but you won't sell it?"

"No, I won't have Kyle hate me. It's his father's world."

With that they arrived in Milford and drove straight to the supermarket to buy jumbo plastic garbage bags and rolls and cold cuts for sandwiches. They ate the sandwiches in the screened porch overlooking the pond, which Brenda admitted was very nice. Then she jumped up and gave Naomi a garbage bag and told her to put all the contents of closets and the stuff in the bathroom into them to store in the basement, while she went off to make beds and sort towels. In a couple of hours, closets and drawers were empty, beds were made, the kitchen was neatened and ready for the cleaning woman and then the renter in the next week. Evidently Brenda planned to sort through her husband's things at a later time.

It was strange for Naomi to be undoing the place of her longtime romantic tryst with the man's widow, but there was also a completeness in it. It always was over, but now it was over even in her imagination. She asked Brenda about a hawk, but she said she never heard anything about it.

On the way back, they stopped in on Milford's Main Street to have coffee at Starbucks, which had taken the place of the old five-and-dime. Naomi noted that Bloomgarden's Department Store was also gone, replaced by a quilt emporium. She wanted to have a closer look at the gorgeous crazy quilt in the window. For a few minutes she toyed with the idea of buying it, knowing that she had the money, but decided that she might need the money for other purposes.

"You want to look at the other shops?" Brenda said indulgently, and she added with a sneer, "Milford has turned into the antiques capital of the USA."

Naomi could see that the bakery and drugstore were gone, and every window was now full of antique dolls, butter churns, rusting agricultural implements, cobalt glass, and heavy Victorian furniture. Even the vast second-floor space of the former Pinchot forestry building was filled to the brim with rugs, tables, gilded-edged tea sets, and racks of sequined flapper dresses. She stood in the midst of all this outpouring of old things and felt nausea. The little town that had seemed to her to be the perfectly beautiful and practical community she remembered in such a rosy light was gone. She wondered if this had made a difference to Professor Brown or not, but it made a difference to her. Even more than putting stuff in garbage bags, the visit to Milford finished off an episode in her life.

On the way home Naomi asked Brenda, "Do you have someone else?"

"I think men are disgusting," she answered with emphasis.

That could mean several things, thought Naomi, and she didn't want to probe it any further. But Brenda added a clarification: "If you want to know the truth, I feel liberated."

"Kyle, how is Kyle?" asked Naomi.

"Kyle is a sensible boy, he'll be fine. He and his father didn't always hit it off. He has taken up painting. His room is full of paper and brushes. Pretty weird stuff."

"Teens try all kinds of things." She wanted to ask about the staircase rug but didn't know how to bring it into the conversation. She let it go.

It had been a long, full day.

12.

Naomi was exhausted and depressed back in her new little place. She was pretty sure that somehow Brenda nudged, coaxed, or surprised Professor Brown into falling down the steps. There was no way that it could be proved, but Brenda benefited most from his death and had the most grudges against him. She could always sell that fifty-acre Milford property, and it would bring in a lot with or without Kyle. Brenda was a cool customer capable of plotting as well as taking opportunities if they presented themselves.

Naomi was not sure about Evelyn, but a change in lifestyle was a possibility. Most certainly she wouldn't go driving with Brenda again; she was glad to be home in one piece after that ride. Did she always drive like that, or was she under great emotional strain despite the attempt to be in control? Even if she was right that Brenda had something to do with Professor Brown's death, she could not call the police. She had no evidence.

She was tempted not to go in to work, but Sophie liked her to be there, so she showed up determined to suspend her "investigation" for a while and not try to get people in conversation. She would just work quietly. Sophie had her doing a poster for a lecture the following week on the Egyptian *Book of the Dead*, and that kept her busy in the morning. Later on, she was checking Sophie's PowerPoint for a lecture course, fussing with it at the computer in the corner of the classroom. The door was ajar, and she became aware of the voices of Philippa and Jennifer in the corridor.

"It wasn't an argument, it was a—" that was Jennifer's soprano.

"It was an argument. I told you to avoid it," Said Philippa's mezzo.

"You always think you know best just because . . . you and . . . he—"

"I know what I'm talking about," Philippa insisted.

"Well, you don't. *He* knew what I was talking about. That bitch had a girlfriend, and she wanted out. She just needed a springboard."

"Ha!" Philippa shot back. "He told you to get lost—it was out of the question."

Naomi could imagine Jennifer's eyes blazing right through the wall. "Anyway, Philippa," said the soprano in a beguiling voice, "no need to tell anyone about the er argument, if you so wish to call it. I mean it's over. I may have been silly, that's all."

At that point, a third student joined them, and they talked about their exam preparations.

Philippa wondered, not for the first time, about the interview she was sure had taken place between Jennifer and Professor Brown. She was bitter about Professor Brown precisely because, like Jennifer, she once had hopes that she was special and that it would last. She could imagine Jennifer giving him a slight shove that unbalanced him so he fell down the stairs. *No wonder Jennifer was hysterical.* Was it mean to entertain such thoughts? Philippa wondered. Jennifer was selfish at heart but a good friend. An indifferent student, she had coasted along on Professor Brown's biased recommendations and would now have little to go on. Whereas, she, Philippa, was an excellent student, recognized by all the faculty, certain of fellowships and fieldwork. Jennifer needed her protection now, but Philippa decided there would have to be truth between them.

Naomi waited for the class to be half full before leaving, but Philippa saw her. *Why was that woman everywhere?* Philippa thought, and Naomi felt she knew what Philippa was thinking. She rushed out, planning to tack up the posters in the main lobbies of various other departments and get out of the way of the Anthropology Department.

On her return she heard Bill's voice from Sophie's room, "I wish I knew where it was."

"Don't ask me," she replied. I don't want to have anything to do with it. Having anything to do with illegal antiquities in my field is the kiss of death. Besides, I don't believe in looting and collectors. As you know."

"I know."

"The Cairo Museum sells its third-rate pieces, and I think that is a good idea. Guatemala should do the same. Otherwise there's a thriving black market."

"I know all that," Bill replied flatly, "but it's water over the dam. You know as well as I do that Professor Brown had something very rare and unusual, and something needs to be done about it. If we can find it."

"You don't suppose it's here in the office?"

"It could be."

"Well I won't be party to any search," said Sophie.

"You could have some ideas."

"And if you find it, what do you propose to do?"

Bill hemmed and hawed. "We could sell it, and the party could give it to a museum."

"Who is 'we'? Is it Professor Brown's private property and it belongs to his heirs, or does it, God forbid, belong to the department?"

"Technically it's his private property, I guess, but really it belongs to those of us in archaeology," Bill asserted.

"It's messy, and I don't want anything to do with it. I won't stop you, and I won't rat on you, but leave me out of it!"

"We have to find it first," said Bill, and he left the room as Naomi was nonchalantly walking in.

Not investigating actively seemed to have brought dividends. Naomi immediately thought of the keys she and Kyle had pocketed from the desk. So professor Brown had acquired some kind of an artistic treasure that was hidden somewhere. She had no idea how big it was, but it couldn't be very small. The ancient Maya did not have gold and silver; their most precious possessions were jades and feathers. Obviously it couldn't be feathers, since they would not have lasted hundreds of years, and in any case Westerners did not value feathers. It could be jades. But recently the appetite of collectors went for stone sculptures or painted ceramics. There was a law against importing stone monuments, and somehow Naomi did not think that Professor Brown was crazy enough to go against it. No such law existed in Europe and Japan, and collectors there acquired great Maya carved stones, cut in pieces for illegal transport, and later reconstituted. But no American museum would buy or accept as a gift such a stone sculpture. So most likely what Professor Brown had was a painted ceramic piece, of which there are many. Such ceramics had scenes with gods and rulers associated with inscriptions. A great deal of excitement was created by new inscriptions for epigraphers to decipher. The paintings on some of the pots were as beautiful as Greek vase paintings. Maya vessels were very special.

Naomi decided that Professor Brown's treasure must be an extraordinary jade or pottery piece and need not be very large, but if ceramic, it will be fragile. Why would Professor Brown, who had spoken out and written so much about the illegal antiquities trade, have such a treasure hidden somewhere? Where and why did he acquire it? *And what does Bill have to do with it?* So far she has been following up the personal angles with Brenda and Jennifer, and here was a huge issue that could very well have led to his death. Thieves falling out and all that. She also knew that illegal antiquities were a multimillion-dollar business, and people who blundered into it sometimes ended up dead.

When she got home, she got a call from Brenda, who continued to be in the mood for clearing out the effects of Professor Brown. The department had called her saying that she should empty Professor Brown's office; due to a shortage of space, it had to be assigned to someone else quite soon. Brenda was asking Naomi to go over the materials, decide what should be kept and what should be thrown out, and she would somehow make room for his stuff in the house—but she didn't want to go through it herself. She seemed to think that since Naomi had returned with no real job, she was available for such tasks. Naomi didn't think that the "treasure" was necessarily in Professor Brown's office, but this was a great opportunity to find out where it might be, and it gave her legitimacy to poke around in his things. She made Brenda beg her to do this job for a while and then agreed graciously, but without enthusiasm.

Not bad for a day of depression and exhaustion. She still had Tom to look forward to in the evening. She had promised to make him chicken with chili-and-chocolate sauce. She set to in the kitchen.

Tom arrived while the chicken was still cooking, and they had a beer near the stove. He had just given his exam and was complaining about the students who wanted only easy questions. Naomi told him about Brenda and how they had gone to Milford and how it had turned into an antiques capital.

"What do you expect, Naomi, don't be naïve. Milford had a choice—they could either go the way of Burger King and fast food or take the high road via antiques. Morristown took the low road with Wal-Mart, The Home Depot, McDonalds. Did you know that they are building an even huger Wal-Mart on the outskirts of town? The bulldozers are just now digging up the ground. I'm not surprised Brenda escapes to Milford."

"Brenda doesn't escape to Milford; she hates it. She put it up for rental. I was along to help. Now she wants me to clear out Professor Brown's office at the university."

"Now, really, I should have been the one asked to do it," said Tom huffily. "I was his star student."

"She probably thought you were busy teaching and that I had nothing to do. Someone needs the office right away."

"Well, don't throw out any important papers without showing me."

The chicken was done and turned out to be pretty spicy. Tom was eating many tortillas with it and drinking a lot of water. Naomi had gotten used to spicy food in ancient America and just smiled. She passed him the avocado dip to cool him down.

"Tom," she asked, searching for the words, "do you know anything about some antiquities that Professor Brown or Bill had stashed away?"

"How can you ask that Naomi? You know that Professor Brown

was not a collector and was against the trade in illegal antiquities. He spoke about it many times. He was even interviewed on television on *60 Minutes*."

"Nevertheless, I heard a rumor that he had something very precious."

"Where did you hear it?"

"Around. I did not recognize the voice. Perhaps I misunderstood and the talk was about something else."

Naomi had bought tapioca pudding for dessert, and they settled down to watching television.

13.

Naomi added to her duties as Professor Sophie Parker's assistant the new task of clearing out Professor Brown's office. She hadn't been there more than an hour when Jennifer walked in.

"What are you doing here?" she asked with anger in her voice.

"I am going through Professor Brown's things. Brenda asked me."

"I should be the one doing that; I was his assistant. I know where everything is."

"If you know where everything is, would you know where the keys are to the bottom cabinets?"

"I don't feel like telling you. You're an—an interloper." 'Interloper' was a big word for Jennifer, and she said it with emphasis.

"Jennifer, don't be childish. You're taking exams, and I have the time to do this. If you know where the keys are, let me know. Otherwise Annie will have to call a locksmith."

"Oh, all right. The keys are not here. He took them home with him. And I don't know what's in those cabinets." She said as she stalked out.

Naomi closed the door and fished the set of keys she'd got from Professor Brown's desk from her purse. One key fitted perfectly, and she eagerly opened the doors. Professor Brown had been a neat and organized man, and his office had been well cared for. On the shelves of the locked cabinets were neatly piled, old student blue-book exams, going back five years. These were to be kept in case questions arose about a particular student. Evidently Professor Brown considered them confidential papers and locked them up. There was nothing next to them or behind them, although Naomi made a careful search. The exams did not cover up anything else. There was a pile of papers that turned out to be old exam questions, since Professor Brown seemed to ask the same ones every year. If the precious object was in the office, it was in the open, because no other part was locked. Naomi was disappointed, but had figured the search would not be easy.

So she reopened the office door and settled down to going over papers and books in a systematic manner. In the afternoon a shadow appeared in the doorway.

"Is it to be your office?" asked Naomi of Michael Corbett standing sheepishly at the door.

"Yes."

"It will take a little time to go over all this," she said, waving to the four walls covered in books and papers.

"What about the couch?"

"I don't know, I suppose that belongs to Brenda, if she wants it."

"I like to be comfortable," he said, hoping that he hadn't given her any other ideas.

"Ask Brenda."

Michael shuffled out as inconspicuously as he'd arrived.

Naomi worked quietly until five o'clock, when the administrative office closed, and beyond into the early evening. She went through piles of class notes and photocopied articles. The most interesting item was on his desk. It was the typescript of a lecture he had recently given at Colgate University. The date, a month before he died, and the word "Colgate" were written at the top in pencil. Naomi began to read it.

> The ancient Maya site of Tikal is located in the tropical forest area of northern Guatemala. Tikal has been settled since about 1000 BC, when it was a modest village. Major buildings were erected by 1 AD, but stone monuments with dated inscriptions are known only from about 300 AD to about 900 AD. At that time, the city was abandoned and fell into ruins.

She knew all that, but read on.

> Tikal had two periods of greatness, one in the Early Classic Period under the rule of Stormy Sky and one in the Late Classic Period, under the rule of Ruler A, also known as Sky Rain, and his sons, rulers B and C. Between the Early and Late Classic Periods, Tikal underwent a period of instability and was even, for a time, conquered by Calakmul.

She knew all that first-hand, but the lecture didn't say more about it. She read on.

> Tikal has some of the most distinguished architecture and the tallest pyramids of any Maya site. In the Early Classic Period, the pyramids, which were the burial temples of the rulers, were small and crowded together on a platform known as the North Acropolis. The greatest builder of the Late Classic Period was Sky Rain, who built the spectacular Temples I and II and impressive causeways throughout the site. These temples were well over 125 feet high and towered over the tropical forest, which is about 100 feet high. The Palace, known as the Central Acropolis, is a huge structure near a cenote reservoir and was mainly built in the Late Classic Period over Early Classic portions.
>
> Ruler B's burial temple, Temple IV, was even larger than Temples I and II.

Naomi stopped reading. There was not a word about Night Sky and Tikal village in this account, which glorified Sky Rain. Westerners seemed to be obsessed by huge masonry buildings, rather than the quality of life. They couldn't imagine that anything good could happen at a time when no pyramids were erected. She leafed through a couple more pages of introduction to the portion where Professor Brown described his own work.

> We have inherited from the past the idea that Maya cities were empty centers and had small populations. That's because no one has really done the right sort of work in the tropical forest. Scholars talk about the central Mexican city of Teotihuacán

> with its population of two hundred thousand, because they built masonry multifamily houses, and scholars disparage Maya cities. The Maya built more perishable houses, which were more practical in tropical areas, over platforms of stones. My students and I pioneered the count of these house mounds, which was no easy task, given the tropical vegetation that covers them. They were thought not to exist, because no one looked for them in the undergrowth. Our mapping shows that there were thousands of house mounds and that Tikal was a true city with a population of about 40,000 or more. All this shows that armchair theorizing does not get us anywhere, and archaeologists must go into the field.

That was vintage Professor Brown. Presumably Night Sky's thatched village houses got counted as some of the anonymous Tikal house mounds. Anonymity was hard for the Classic Maya, whose rulers wrote their names, birth dates and famous exploits on stone reliefs, often next to their portraits. And anonymity was not valued in twentieth century America, although the medium was celluloid rather than stone. In a perverse way, Night Sky had relished his future anonymity perhaps, because it made him live more fully in the present. She had admired him for it. Still, a mention in Professor Brown's talk would have been something special.

Reading about Tikal made her think of the world she had left behind and she wondered again how things were with Sky Rain and his court and Green Parrot, Night Sky's daughter, and how the bedridden Marigold, her Maya self, were getting on. Although on a few occasions she had been able to travel in time, she didn't want to abuse the privilege. She never knew whether the skill or perhaps the power would last to another time. She knew nothing of the power itself, where it came from and how long she would have it. It was not like a telephone where she could just make a quick call. Marigold had been left sick, sort of alive but sort of in a coma, and for this time, which was less than two weeks, that was probably all right. After accomplishing her mission, Naomi now intended to go back.

She liked the simplicity yet sophistication of Maya life. By comparison, her academic world was learned in some ways but simpleminded in others. Here was Michael Corbett, an authority on anthropological theory and "big" concepts, unable to get through a simple conversation with her. Or Tom, for whom everything had a simple explanation. Or Jennifer, who was living in her emotions without using her brains.

The Maya she had come to know had a sense of themselves and of other people and could control their emotions without becoming hard. Green Parrot lost three children in childbirth and has kept her optimism and charm, to say nothing of her figure. She doesn't rail at the gods or at her husband. Yet Naomi knew that she mourned deeply.

Maybe, Naomi wondered, the difference is that the Maya lived in a universe they believed would come to an end—that nothing is eternal. She was sure Americans in her present world still believed in progress—that computers will create a better world, and she imagined them retooling with great enthusiasm to keep up, using the latest science. But science has indicated possible cataclysmic ends to the earth, such as disastrous meteor strikes or troubles with the sun, or more immediately global warming, but she figured these dire predictions had not permeated the mindset of most people. *Apart from fringe cultists finding the end of the world in the Bible or in the Maya calendar, most people think in terms of technical advances over the past continuing on for the imaginable future.*

The Maya were so un-technological—they had corbel vaults for roofing, which changed form only slightly over hundreds of years. They had a clever and beautiful hieroglyphic writing system, and after a time it went out of fashion. Looking around the Morristown strip with its malls and fast-food places, it was hard for Naomi to see that twentieth-century America had advanced all that much over the Maya, if at all. *No wonder so many tourists visit Tikal in search of a time that was beautiful.* Then with a start she caught herself thinking of herself as living in the past.

It was getting late and she was sleepy. There was a lot more to be done in Professor Brown's office—it would have to wait for tomorrow. She got into her car, *a pretty neat invention of Western culture, after all*, and put the key in the ignition.

14.

Next day Sophie Parker reminded her about the lecture on the Egyptian *Book of the Dead* and looked at her strangely. "You know," she said with a sideways glance from her eyes, "I once had a strange experience with that book. I was sitting in my easy chair reading it, or more likely staring at it, when all of a sudden the room seemed to dissolve, and a big tunnel opened up scaring me out of my wits. At the far end of the tunnel, I could make out little figures that looked like ancient Egyptians and maybe even the goddess Isis. She seemed to be beckoning me to come to her. I clanged the book shut, and the vision disappeared. For a long time I thought I had fallen asleep and dreamt this. What do you think?"

Naomi couldn't tell if Sophie had guessed that something like it accounted for her strangeness and was testing her, or if it was a simple question. She couldn't decide whether to confide in Sophie or feign ignorance. "Did you ever dream this again?"

"No. I've been avoiding the Egyptian *Book of the Dead.* Perhaps I had a nervous spell."

"Are you concerned about the talk?"

"Not really, it's bound to be academic and nitpicking and not very inspiring."

"In that case why did you want me to come?"

"Well, to you it would all be new, and perhaps you could tell if the book had mystic powers."

So Sophie only but suspected, Naomi concluded. "What makes you think that the mystic powers are in the book and not in the reader? Perhaps you have special powers."

"Well, if I do, I shall make sure to keep away from them."

Naomi wasn't sure that was the case, as the professor seemed interested. Nevertheless, she didn't want to be classified in Sophie's eyes as a "mystic nut." It was something to think about, certainly; perhaps her experiences were not unique but were available to others.

Until now, Naomi thought of them as a personal quirk she could not share with anyone without being considered ridiculous. Here was Sophie, maybe suggesting that she come out of the closet.

Naomi went back to the safety of Professor Brown's office and shuffled papers. And then, in the bottom of a drawer in the desk under a pile of university stationary, she came upon a photograph. A large color photograph of a Maya vase of a type she had never seen before. It had an unusual black background, and on it was painted a single, reclining figure brushed in lightly with elegant outlines. The astonishing thing was that the image was that of a naked woman. Women of any kind were infrequent on Maya vases and naked women could be counted on one hand. This particular woman lay there openly like Goya's *Naked Maja*, challenging the gaze of anyone who looked at her. She was lying on a masklike, craggy shape that Naomi knew represented the earth with its caves and water sources. Evidently the woman was the moon goddess, Ixchel, the most important Maya goddess, not just of the moon, but of water, weaving and anything having to do with women.

Naomi was mesmerized by the beauty and rarity of the vessel and was quite sure that the original was somewhere, if only she could find it. Clifford Turner could sell a vessel like this for six figures or more. How on earth did it come into Professor Brown's possession?

She was so absorbed in contemplating the photograph that she didn't hear Bill's quiet footsteps approaching her. It was too late to try to hide it. Bill arrived with his briefcase and rummaged around in it until he found a piece of paper. Silently he put it on the desk next to the photograph. It was a bad photocopy of the same vessel. Naomi caught her breath.

"Have you found it?" he asked.

"No, I just found the photo. What is it?"

"Well, obviously, it's the greatest Maya vase of them all. A pair, with one now in a private collection.

"You mean there is another one like it?"

"Not exactly. It has the same black background, but the figure is a naked male. A beautiful young man." He looked through Professor Brown's bookshelf and found a picture of it in a journal. "There, that is it." The two vases were almost identical except one had a male and the other a female figure on it. They looked like they could have been painted by the same hand.

"Where does this come from?" she asked, pointing to the photo.

Bill shrugged. "Who knows. It was looted, and I assume it went through the hands of dealers and private collectors."

"Clifford Turner?"

"Perhaps, I don't know."

"I've seen nothing like it from Tikal."

"It's probably not from Tikal. I don't know where exactly it's from."

"That is so sad," said Naomi slowly, "because now we'll never know its history."

"On the other hand, we have the vases, and they are beautiful, no matter where they are from."

"Where did you get the Xerox of the photo?" she enquired suspiciously.

"Professor Brown gave it to me. He asked me to try to identify it."

"Did he tell you that he had it?"

"No, he merely asked me if I could identify it. From my vast experience with Maya things. But I suspected that he had it. Normally he wasn't interested in visual artifacts. His illustrations were graphs, not naked women."

"You suspected him?"

"I didn't suspect him of looting it himself, if that's what you mean. But I suspected him of having it for some other reason. There is something mysterious about that vase, and he hadn't taken me into his confidence. It's worth a lot of money."

"Had you found it, what were you going to do with it? Return in to Guatemala?"

"Probably not. Most Guatemalan officials are corrupt. It might just reappear on the Western art market."

"Would you sell it to a collector?" she persisted.

"Maybe, if it found its way into a reputable museum, eventually."

"But the museum could not exhibit stolen art, could it?"

"Not just now, but maybe in the future, when its history has cooled, so to speak. That has happened before."

"How long would it take to cool?"

"Fifty years. Maybe a hundred. Could be less."

"You weren't thinking of keeping it and enjoying it for yourself?"

Billy blushed and said, "That would be dangerous. I could be robbed and even killed for it. If you find it, I advise you not to hold on to it. The secret is out. After all, I know—probably the dealer knows, and have you asked Tom? He knows something he isn't telling."

"Tom doesn't know anything," said Naomi flatly, recalling their conversation.

Bill merely shook his head.

All this about the Maya vase was interesting, but did it have anything to do with the death of Professor Brown? It was clear from the conversation with Bill that the lure of something so beautiful and worth so much money was great, and murder could have been committed on account of it. But did anyone have the vase as a result of Professor Brown's death? Evidently Bill was still trying to find its whereabouts. *And the vase could very well be a side issue.* On the other hand, until she knew everything there was to be known about the vase, murder for its possession could not be ruled out. Professor Brown did have Clifford Turner's card in his drawer, and Turner was well acquainted with Maya jades and had paid her a pretty penny for them. She figured he was involved in this somehow. Bill had mentioned Tom, but that was out of the question. Tom was a straight arrow. But how well did she even know Tom?

15.

Tom was out of town visiting a sick aunt in Cincinnati. Naomi occupied herself in getting a used-book dealer to buy Professor Brown's books and Professor Parker, as temporary chair, negotiated with the university library to archive the most interesting parts of his far-flung correspondence. Professor Brenda Brown was willing to take the notes and class preparations, but did not want the photocopied articles. Those were made available for whoever wanted them in the department. The blue-book exams were moved to an office storage cabinet. His field journals made it to the archaeology lab. Slowly but surely, his office was dismantled and, after painting and cleaning, would be ready for the new occupant.

There were no surprises. Professor Brown hadn't kept a private journal, photographs, lists of names. Except for the Maya vase, everything had been simple, professional, as expected. His romantic affairs were a matter of oral history, and there was no Leporello to catalogue them. Also missing from the office materials was how likable he had been. It wasn't only women who'd liked him; men did too. He'd got on well with his colleagues and with Guatemalans, including Bill. You had to be somewhat genial to survive archaeological expeditions with people you were in close contact with for weeks and months. It's not that he hadn't an enemy in the world; there was plenty of envious and critical commentary about him in reviews, but nothing that would suggest murder.

Naomi was sorting piles of books, when she heard a commotion from the lounge. The voice was that of Jennifer, and the timbre of what she was saying overshadowed the content. She was hysterical.

"It's me, me, ME! I'm the one who did it. I'm the one who killed Professor Brown!"

"Don't be absurd," said Philippa, shushing her. "Here, have a glass of water."

"You know I did! I pushed him down the stairs. I know you think so."

This brought in everyone from the offices to watch.

"Don't be absurd child," said Sophie. "You couldn't have. You just gave him a slide tray. He fell afterwards."

"But I'm sure I nudged him, and after that he fell—" and she burst into new tears. "Take me to the police! I want to make a full confession."

It was unclear whether Jennifer wanted to vent her feelings in public or whether she did think that she might be guilty. Nor was she stupid enough not to realize that the best way to clear herself was to admit guilt as loudly as she could. This scene played for a while, and then everyone went back to what they were doing, and Philippa led Jennifer away. Naomi wondered what role Philippa had in all this. It seemed to be her purpose to discredit Jennifer at every step, while appearing to protect her. Philippa was ostensibly cynical about her affair with Professor Brown, but was that her true feeling? Was she really a good friend to Jennifer? Was she another one with a jealous motive? Naomi wondered.

Tom called in the evening with the news that his aunt had died and that he would remain for the funeral in Cincinnati. He asked Naomi what was new with her, but she said "nothing special"; she was still clearing out Professor Brown's office. What she had to ask him she could do only in person. Time was passing. Something would have to be done about Marigold in Tikal; Naomi could not stay away indefinitely, and this affair did not seem to wind up all that quickly.

She called Brenda to say that she had several boxes of papers to deliver to her house and did she want to see them. Brenda did not want to see them—she said the papers were Professor Brown's legacy for Kyle, for whenever he got interested in his father and his father's professional life. She did not want to see his bibliographies. Naomi should just put it all in the new metal filing cabinets, bought for the purpose, in the basement of Brenda's house.

Naomi had the papers arranged by year and spent some time in the basement putting them in the drawers. While there, she looked around at the tools and summer lawn furniture to see if there might be a hiding place for a Maya vase, but it was unimaginable. The basement was disorderly in an organized fashion but had no secure hiding places. Wondering what took her so long, Brenda eventually found her there. As always, the professor was in a hurry; she had to go to a conference in Boston the next day. Something about fish as dinosaurs, or dinosaurs as fish; it wasn't clear. Naomi took the opportunity to ask for keys, saying that she had more things to bring over. That was not true, but she wanted to get into the house while Kyle was in school, to look for the keys he had taken from his father's desk.

The next day it was pouring rain, and Naomi was worried about leaving stains on the floors and carpets, telltale signs that she had been snooping around the house. She took a good look at the living room but saw no place except the bottom drawers of the china cabinet, which were locked. *Probably full of teapots and crockery.* The glass shelves on top, whose doors were open, contained expensive earthenware cups and plates, the kind craft shops with names like Blue Heron sell. She gave a cursory look in the bedrooms, but she had done Brenda's closets quite thoroughly. She looked in Professor Brown's study, which hadn't changed since she was there last. She looked in the guestroom. Everywhere she went, she was leaving big wet footprints. The last room where she wanted to go was Kyle's, at the end of the house. It smelled of tobacco, as of someone who had recently taken up the habit. It was not yet the acrid odor of a room that had been smoked in for a long time. Kyle needed a talking to.

The door was ajar and revealed a mess, of course. But the mess was structured. One area of the room had clothes on the floor and on furniture, where he had literally stepped out of the pants and pulled off the shirts. There was a desk with schoolbooks, a microscope, DVDs, CDs in disarray. A television set. A computer. An easel with a painting of some kind of monster face. Similar monster faces were tacked up all along the walls. Did Kyle dream these? Were these in his subconscious? Somewhat besmirched in front of the easel was a book on Maya art with monstrous faces he was perhaps inspired by. Professor Brown might have been proud of him as a chip off the ol' block. The set of drums were in an alcove next to the unmade bed.

Naomi tried to figure out where he might have the keys, if they were in the room, and she went through all parts of the room in great detail. When she came to the table with the book and the paints, she nearly let out a scream. The Maya vase was there, right in the open, with a set of paint brushes sticking out of it next to coffee cans and jam jars holding other brushes and turpentine. In front of the vase was an ashtray with cigarette butts, ashes, and a set of keys. Evidently Kyle had found the vase and, knowing or not knowing its value, appropriated it. It must have something to do with the relationship of father and son to which she was not privy, she hypothesized, when someone yelled, "I've got you!" and put a plastic—hopefully toy plastic—gun into her ribs.

"Kyle, it's me—" stammered Naomi. "Put that thing away!"

"What are you doing in my room? Didn't my mother tell you to stay out of it?"

"Kyle, you must stop smoking—it's a dangerous habit."

"And you must stop snooping, which is even more dangerous."

"Why do you have a toy gun with you?"

"What are you doing in my room? What are you looking for? I saw your footprints all through the house."

"What are you doing home from school at this hour?"

Useless accusations went on for a while until Naomi cleared space on the bed and sat down. "If you calm down, Kyle, I will tell you." She needed to calm down first.

Kyle remembered this was the lady who fixed sandwiches in his mother's absence, and pulled up a chair. "It better be good."

"It is."

Saying nothing about her dream and suspecting that Professor Brown had been murdered, Naomi began with the clearing of the office and finding the photograph of the Maya vase, its illegal status, and concern for Professor Brown's family, if they happened to have it.

"You were going to steal it!—is that it? and sell it!" he interrupted.

"No, I was just going to put it in a place of safety. Various people know about the vase, and of course you and Brenda have inherited it and can decide what to do. But it isn't simple. I don't know the full story of how your father happened to have it. He was not the grave-robbing kind. Right now, it's best to keep quiet about it. Do your friends know anything?"

It was hard for Kyle to imagine that having a Maya vase could cause him trouble. "I saw him put it in the bottom of the china cabinet with the teapots and casseroles, when he thought no one was looking. I knew what it was, and I wanted to have it. It was after my father was dead—I wanted something of his that I thought he wouldn't want me to have. I didn't know it was such a big deal. The picture of the woman was funky, that's all."

"Your friends? Do they know?"

"I, I don't think so—someone may have been up here, I'm not sure."

"Did you talk about the vase, did you point it out?"

"I don't think so. We talked about music mostly."

Nothing much more would come out of Kyle with regard to his friends, at least not for now. Not knowing quite what to do, Naomi suggested putting the vase back in the china cabinet among the teapots and casseroles and locking the doors. With the design of the naked lady facing in, the vase was not conspicuous among the earthenware pots. She decided not to mention it to Bill and wait for Tom to come back from Cincinnati. She swore Kyle to secrecy, not even to tell Brenda, which he was glad not to do. She told him to lock the house doors when he wasn't there and not to let any strangers in. She put the china cabinet keys back in Kyle's ash tray, which seemed to be the best cover. Then she told him one more time that he should quit smoking because it would ruin his health. Kyle said to himself that she was crazy but sort of fun in a crazy way and did everything she asked. Except about the smoking.

Naomi couldn't believe that she had found the vase. She was so busy with Kyle, she didn't get a long hard look at it. But the vase seemed miraculously undamaged, with not a single chip or scratch. The black background was solid black, and the figure was painted in red lines with a cream background for the body. The lady had a serious expression on her face and a headdress with water lilies tucked into the band. Her hand gestures were gentle and elegant. *Move over Mona Lisa!* This lady from American antiquity was an ultimate depiction of feminine beauty and probably dated somewhere between 650 and 750 AD. She had the budding breasts of a young woman, but her private parts were partly hidden by scrolls from the monster image she was lying on. The whole effect was erotic with the innocent sexuality of a young woman, rather than the robustness of the matron or the wanton. To Marigold and the Maya, she was the young moon goddess, Ixchel.

In the evenings, TV news quelled the excitement of her days, so she turned it on to a necessary but boring discussion of the American educational system, which was chronically underfunded. She agreed silently, while munching her tortellini. She wondered why she cared so much about the Maya vase. Bill's teasing question came to mind from a week ago, before the vase had turned up at all: "Why is a nice girl like you so involved with American antiquity?"

She couldn't answer it then and had brushed it off by saying one lecture with Professor Brown was enough to convince her of its beauty and importance. It wasn't exactly untrue; she had taken a course with Professor Brown and liked it. But Bill didn't know the half of it, about her writing a novel about a pre-Columbian girl, Marigold, traveling to pre-Columbian times, and marrying Night Sky.

Tonight she wondered, not for the first time, whether it had to do with having been adopted. Naomi always felt different from others, even though she knew that there were many adopted children who lived happy and normal lives. Having been through therapy, she also knew that it was normal for her to feel estranged.

Naomi had spent much of her teenage years wondering who her real parents were and making up fantasies about them. She was very fond of her adopted parents, her father a civil engineer and her mother a housewife, who did their best to love her and give her anything a middleclass child could want. It was not their fault that a drunken driver had driven into their car and killed them both in her high school years.

Since the family finances had been based on her father's monthly salary, by the time Naomi went to college, her means were extremely limited. Had they been able to, they would have given her college as well. Even so, she'd had a good education with enough aid not just for college but graduate school as well.

She had been close to her mother, a woman who liked to cook and watched Julia Child whip up French meals on television. Despite her nice adoptive parents, or perhaps even because of them, Naomi yearned to know who her real mother was and even more remotely who her father was. She was blonde, while her adoptive parents had brown hair. They looked different. Perhaps out there, there was a gorgeous blonde woman yearning about a child she once gave up.

When she was old enough to understand about these things, with the help of her adoptive mother, Naomi put in an application to find her birth mother with the agency that had handled the adoption originally. There was no answer immediately, but by her sixteenth birthday there was news that the birth mother had been found and would be willing to see her daughter. Naomi was ecstatic. Now all her dreams would come true, and all her questions would be answered. She would finally know who she was and where she came from. She tried to reassure her adoptive mother that she loved and appreciated her, but her excitement was clearly for the coming reunion with a woman named Alyssa.

Alyssa was tall and muscular and into sports. She was a professional golfer. She arrived in elegant clothes and a new car and, oh yes, she had plenty of lovely blonde hair. Her story was the usual one of a teenage pregnancy. She had come from the wrong side of the tracks, and Naomi's father was a young man from a good family, expected to go to law school. Marriage was out of the question. Money changed hands, and Alyssa decided to bring the child to term but was in no financial position to keep her. She felt guilty about giving up the baby and grateful to the adoptive parents.

She fussed over Naomi and took her out to lunch. They seemed to have a lot in common. Alyssa lived in Tallahassee, Florida, and there was talk of Naomi going to visit her. Alyssa was now married and comfortably off. And had no other children. She was not particularly interested in Naomi's school, where her daughter excelled, but liked her wholesome, healthy looks. She got along well with Naomi's adoptive parents, and it looked like there would be visits between Florida and New Jersey for some time to come.

After the excitement of the reunion, there were phone calls back and forth planning a trip for Naomi, who felt that she had now found a new and more real life. In time, however, the phone calls became less frequent, the trip was put off further and further into the future, as Alyssa went back to her golfing life in Tallahassee, and Naomi was stuck in New Jersey.

It was hard for her not to think that her mother had given her up for the second time. She wondered if there was anything wrong with her self. It was obvious that she would never find her father and that the subject was now closed forever. She had seen her birth mother, but she wasn't her "real" mother. Her adoptive mother continued to be loving and kind, but neither was she her real mother, no matter how hard she tried. Naomi had to accept the disappointment and make do with her life as it was, a rather difficult thing to do in your teens. And two years after that, her adoptive parents were killed suddenly, leaving her all alone. She realized, belatedly, how much they had meant to her. The only structure she had left in life was college, and she felt lucky to have that.

Naomi went through the first few years of college in a state of numbness. She functioned academically and performed all the practical necessities of life but had an emptiness inside that friends and teachers could not fill. She was thought of as a self-possessed and yet mysterious person. When she encountered the pre-Columbian world in Professor Brown's lectures, she was immediately drawn to it, as if she had lived there in a previous existence.

16.

Tom arrived back the next day and came over for sandwiches of leftover ham. On the TV news, they were discussing yesterday's mass murder at a shopping center in Alabama. Was it due to the violence of Americans or to the ubiquity of guns? Naomi put the TV on mute to be able to talk. She came immediately to the point.

"You lied to me about Professor Brown. I found the Maya vase with the beautiful woman on it in his house. The looted vase. Bill said to ask you about it. I said you wouldn't know anything about looted objects, because I believed you. So what is the truth?"

Tom concentrated on his sandwich and on the TV screen where they were taking bodies out on a stretcher. Finally he said, almost mumbling, "I'm sorry I misled you. It was out of loyalty to Professor Brown."

"You mean he was involved in the illicit business?"

"No. But I do know something about the vase. In a way I'm responsible for it. I am sorry for not mentioning it before. I thought Professor Brown had somehow taken care of it, and there was nothing further to say. The subject is distasteful to me."

"What then do you know?"

"I was there when the vase turned up. It was towards the end of our season in Tikal. We were surveying and clearing the area and had only about a week left, when we happened upon a mound that was astronomically aligned. We wondered if it was like Group E from Uaxactún and tried to clear as much as possible to get a better idea. An astronomically aligned building has great importance in that it shows the scientific sophistication of the Maya."

"I know. But it wasn't like Group E, or I would have heard about it."

"Yes, it wasn't, but we didn't know that then. So when two men emerged from the forest asking for a job for a few days of shoveling, we thought it was Providence and didn't ask too many questions. They had their own gear and set up next to ours. We had enough rice and beans. They seemed hungry. We put them to clearing more of the newly found mound. Just the surface dirt."

Tom took a sip of water. "Finally, we were busy packing up for the trip to Flores, because we had planes to catch back. The two men said that they were on their way to an expedition to Seibal, and we paid little attention to them. They were paid, and we all bunked down for the night before the truck trip to Flores. I was first to wake in the morning at dawn and went into the forest for a call of nature. That's when I saw them. They were both dead, bleeding from knife wounds, one man sprawled on top of the other. One of them was Guatemalan or at any rate Hispanic, while the other was a small European. I tried to find out who the European was and looked in his knapsack—he had carried that knapsack with him everywhere. And there in the knapsack, wrapped in an old torn shirt, was the vase."

"What about the men, did you notify the authorities?"

"Authorities! In Guatemala? I would have been in jail immediately and forever. Besides, we were leaving that morning. I broke off some tree branches, and I covered the bodies. I was undecided as to what to do about the vase. I couldn't just leave it there—I took the vase in its wrappings and brought it back to Professor Brown. He didn't want to take it, but what could we do? He packed it in with the archaeological collections of potsherds and projectile points, tipped the customs official a hundred dollars, and it came back with us to Morristown."

"That's quite a story. How did the men die?"

"I'm no expert, but it looked like they'd been fighting with knives and both got killed in the process. I didn't examine them. I had never seen dead bodies before. I didn't go through all their things and don't know if they had other loot. It looked sort of as if they were waiting for someone, for a contact, and that's why they hung around with us. Or they needed a meal. Believe me, all I wanted was to get out of there."

"Was the European an American?"

"I don't know. He seemed Hispanic and spoke excellent Spanish. But he could have been French or American or anything. I never got his papers. My theory is that they fell out over the vase or what to do with the vase."

"So what do we do with the vase?"

"I wish I had never taken it—it's just trouble. Professor Brown said he'd take care of it, and I thought he had. But he died, and you found the vase as much trouble as ever."

"Pretty soon you'll say it has the curse of the ancient Maya on it."

"Don't be funny!—maybe it does. Those two men died in the forest because of it."

"One hears of looting leading to murder."

"It's one thing for you to say that based on some article you read, and another to find two dead men in the jungle."

"You kept your head pretty well under the circumstances," she said with obvious admiration. "I can understand that you didn't want to talk about it. Who else knows about this?"

"No one knows how I found the vase now, except you and me—and it better stay that way."

"Bill doesn't know?"

"He knows about the existence of the vase, but not how Professor Brown got it."

"So tell me about your aunt and Cincinnati—"

Tom was obviously exhausted and didn't stay long. He enjoyed Naomi's pleasant behavior and suggested going out for a soft ice cream, which they did. They parted with a light hug and kiss.

Naomi was shaken and excited by Tom's story. Of course, there was only Tom to vouch for its truth. Questions flew through her imagination. Did he really not go through the belongings of the dead men and find anything else? How long did it take him to decide whether the vase was worth taking? Were the men really dead, or could one or both have been saved by medics? Didn't Tom make an awful lot of decisions by himself, and then he passed on the vase to Professor Brown. And what was he going to do with it? Sell it and share the profits? Didn't the vase belong to Tom who found it? What had they discussed about it in private?

Bill had been a frequent visitor to Professor Brown's house; was he looking for the vase? *Bill's a patriotic Guatemalan, who is anxious to leave Guatemala behind. The money from the vase could be very welcome. He might wanted it for himself or even as a gift to the department, where he hopes to be taken on permanently.* He seemed to be ingratiating himself with Sophie. He knew enough not to be left out of the discussion about the vase. *Nevertheless, even if he had been in the house the day of the murder, and there is no proof either way, he didn't know where the vase was, which lets him off as a major murder suspect. Unless, of course, he murdered Professor Brown to make way for himself, but that seems farfetched.*

But Bill must have wondered about Tim when he asked Bill to identify the vase. Bill must see façades of righteousness and pretentiousness in the department, when he tries to fit in. He certainly doubts Tom. Bill could be in a position to blackmail, but he's not a criminal. As a Central American, he believes in the general corruptibility of people, except perhaps some Americans. Still, he would not be surprised if Americans turn out to be just like everyone else. Disappointed, perhaps, but not surprised.

Meanwhile, Bill was also mulling questions of the mysterious vase. *Take Naomi, for instance, there is obviously something fishy in all those years of "field work" at Tikal. What was she really doing? And how come everyone received her back with open arms? Not only that, Naomi is nosy and interested in matters that don't concern her.* Bill knew that he hadn't killed Professor Brown, but the idea that someone might have did not shock him anymore. There were all the jealous women in the professor's life, plus Tom, whose dealings with Professor Brown were mysterious. Was he like a son to him? And what about the real son? Lastly, Bill pondered the relationship between Tom and Naomi. They were apparently not exactly lovers, but somehow they were a team, and he didn't know why. The outwardly normal and placid department seemed to be seething with mysterious passions and motivations he could sense but not understand. Americans were said to be superficial, he opined, but they turned out to be as complicated as the Guatemalans underneath. He suspected he had been taken in by their good-natured manner. Maybe he should try to befriend that aloof young man, Michael Corbett, and see what he's like. *Will he walk around with a swelled head from his new office? He seems to be a man full of theories and little reality. He wouldn't last a day in Guatemala City.*

17.

Naomi woke up the next morning and saw a flickering green light in her closet. She rubbed her eyes and the light disappeared. She must have been dreaming, or it was a flash of sunlight on the Venetian blinds. She decided to spend a day without thinking about the vase. The obvious question was what to do with the vase, but the vase wasn't hers to do anything with, and it was not up to her to decide. Perhaps they all owned it together; Tom who found it, Professor Brown who brought it into the country, and his heirs Brenda and Kyle, and she herself who rediscovered it. Perhaps Bill who identified it. *That's five people. Who is to organize them?* Her head swam. Perhaps it was up to her—but not today. Today she was taking a vacation from Professor Brown's affairs, but first—

She went into the department, greeting Annie, and asking for the office keys for the last time. She looked through all the shelves and drawers, making sure they were empty. She had taken the yellowing maps and posters off the walls. The room looked very big and lacked character. One box on the floor already belonged to Michael Corbett and consisted of books of theory, without illustrations. Naomi looked through them. Would he have maps and posters on the walls?

Michael arrived carrying two heavy satchels of more books on his shoulders, Foucault, Barthes, Althusser, Kristeva, Derrida, Lacan, etc. Naomi knew the names, but had only a vague idea of what they stood for. Something about things being different from what they seem. Hidden texts under the apparently simple surface texts. A process called deconstruction to reveal the hidden texts. Deconstruction, which destroyed the simplicity and coherence of the original texts. As an archaeologist, she was involved in the reconstruction of ancient life mostly on the basis of things, because there were no texts to deconstruct. She was making up plausible stories.

"Hi," he said. "Thanks for clearing the room so neatly."

"I guess you kept the couch."

"It looked comfortable. Here, why don't you sit down on it. I'll pull up a chair."

Naomi accepted the offer. "How is it to do research without being localized somewhere on the globe?" she asked, to try to turn the conversation into a meaningful channel.

"You mean like Tikal is for you?"

"Yes. It could have been someplace else. Nigeria or ancient China, but it ended up being the Maya. It wouldn't have been nowhere."

"So you think theory is nowhere, and you wanted to be anchored somewhere real?"

"Yes."

"You have a need to be anchored?"

"Doesn't everybody? We're all anchored here at the university."

"That's different—that is our physical reality, which is anchored by nature, unless we're schizophrenic, and there are those who say that schizophrenia is actually good. Félix Guattari."

"Well, some of us need to be anchored in our mental universe, too. Maybe some of us are less well anchored in the here and now."

"Perhaps it's the modern condition," he said, trying to talk at her level.

"I don't know, but many of us share the same anchor, and that makes it sane," said Naomi, trying to get out of the mental mess she was getting into. She didn't want to say that her anchor was deeper down than others, although she was tempted. "You mean, if it's a mutual madness, it is not a madness?" she added, to get off her individual case.

"I don't know about that. Christianity and Islam are mutual anchors for a lot of people."

"I don't know what you're trying to get at," she said with a belligerent note creeping into her voice.

"You started this by asking me how come I'm not 'localized'."

"I wondered if your place was Paris."

"I've never been to Paris."

"Well, I was just curious." She must make sure never to get into a conversations with Michael again. She almost told him about Tikal and Night Sky and the tunnel. "You must be anxious to organize your office," she said, getting up.

"When I have it all done, you must come and see a short film, when you need relaxation. I will have a TV set!"

"Yeah."

Naomi escaped only to be caught by Sophie, who wanted her to work. The Egyptian *Book of the Dead* talk had been a disaster; the speaker mumbled on for an hour and a half and had to be stopped—graciously. In her excitement at seeing Tom again and the vase, Naomi had forgotten to attend. She apologized.

"You are very distracted these days," said Sophie. "What is happening?" Exams are over, and we all have time to do our own work; I need your services. You aren't by chance thinking of going back into your—field," and she emphasized the word "field" as if it had been a lie in the first place.

"Nooo," said Naomi, suddenly wondering if she were. As usual, Sophie seemed like she might read her thoughts before she thought them. Why should she go at all? To see Green Parrot and ask her about the vase? To see her household and revive Marigold out of her slumber? To see how that Tikal world seemed after Morristown and even Milford? To see what she thought of her academic world here? And of course Tom—was there was anything to decide about Tom?

Regardless of Michael—who apparently needed no place—having two places meant that one could make comparisons. How was Sky Rain getting on with the pyramids? She saw how Morristown was getting on with the new Home Depot. There was a lot to be said for having two places, and maybe someday she'd decide in which to settle for good. But until then, why not go back, if she could? Which brought her back, in spite of herself, to the vase. Something needed to be done about the vase. So she told Brenda as much of the story as she needed to know. The professor's reaction was annoyance that her husband had landed her with a mess from beyond the grave. She was all for selling it, for inviting the dealer to give an appraisal. Money was money, after all. They agreed to get together the next day, first without the dealer and then with. Brenda made it understood that the vase belonged to her—to do with as she liked. She didn't want Bill to come, but Naomi insisted that he was needed as a specialist to counter the dealer. She and Tom were not really needed, but Brenda wanted Naomi there and Naomi wanted Tom there.

Brenda's cupidity depressed Naomi, who now saw the vase full of dollar signs. She called Clifford Turner and arranged for him to come for something very special the next day. And then she planned to wash her hands of the whole affair. *The trip seems to have been a failure.* She didn't feel like cooking and had a Chinese take-out, from which enough was left for the next day's lunch. She turned on the TV news, where they were showing the remains of terrorist bombings in a city whose name she didn't catch. Maybe it was the Paris Michael had not visited.

18.

On waking, Naomi saw the green light in her closet and got up to turn off the bulb she must have left on the evening before. But it was not on. She shrugged. She dreaded the meeting in the afternoon and decided to visit the Purple Heart boutique beforehand for some impulse shopping. She could go directly from there to Brenda's. She didn't want to spend much, but she wanted something extravagant that would make her feel good. Something white and iridescent for summer evenings. The Purple Heart was empty in the late morning hours, and the owner was busy taking down merchandise for sale, including a white blouse that was just as she imagined, something cool and lovely. It now cost half of what it was marked up for. Naomi grabbed it, but then her eye was caught by the new merchandise the owner was putting on the counter, still in their plastic bags. Of course it was only June, but the fall things were already coming in. She unveiled one item onto a hanger in front of the mirror. It was a plush, black jacket with silver threads of unimaginable softness. She could not resist trying it on, and it enfolded her like second skin. It cost almost triple the white blouse. *For those evening lectures in the fall*, she told herself, and she bought it, carrying it like a trophy in its purple plastic bag.

* * *

Brenda was putting out iced-tea things and cookies. Two o'clock was early for tea, but tea might help with the discussion. She had put the vase well in the center of the coffee table so it wouldn't break accidentally. She locked the cat in her bedroom. Kyle arrived in a clean shirt and helped himself to ice tea. Tom and Bill arrived together, deep in specialist conversation. Brenda settled herself in Professor Brown's wing chair and was ready to control the get-together.

"This need not take long," she said amiably. "I mean to sell the vase and look forward to the arrival of Mr. Turner. There isn't much need for discussion."

"I, I disagree," stammered Kyle. "I think we should keep the vase, er, Mom."

"What on earth for?" Brenda was brisk.

"Because it's beautiful, and I like to have it around," he said stubbornly.

"That's ridiculous. In this house with that cat, the vase could be knocked down any minute. It would then be utterly worthless. Legally the vase is mine, and I can think of many ways to use the money. I've always wanted a sailboat, for instance."

"I should inherit the vase," insisted Kyle.

"Well, you won't. You can come sailing with me," she added oil to the fire.

"Really, the vase belongs to Tom, who found it," said Bill.

"No, it doesn't, and I did not. I was merely instrumental in giving it to Professor Brown," said Tom. "But I think that out of the proceeds of the vase, it would be nice if the department could benefit. A summer fellowship, maybe. Professor Brown would have wanted that."

"Yes!" said Bill enthusiastically, "a summer fellowship in the name of Professor Brown."

Brenda frowned. The yacht was turning into a rowboat. "Lets find out what it's worth first," she said pragmatically.

Naomi hadn't said anything so far and didn't think it was up to her to decide. But she spoke up for the vase. "What would be best for the vase?"

"Clearly a museum where it would be cared for and where people could see it," said Bill.

"But that's out of the question," said Naomi. "The best we can do is sell it to a private collector who leaves it to a museum, eventually. Which does mean selling it."

"That's just what I plan to do!" said Brenda triumphantly.

"With a summer fellowship," said Bill, and Tom nodded enphatically.

With that impasse, they munched on cookies. No one observed the vase, which looked forlornly abandoned on the coffee table.

Suddenly Tom broke the silence. "This is all ludicrous. No one of us here is seeing the bigger picture. This vase, even in the museum, is encouragement to further looting and the destruction of archaeological sites. We will never know where this comes from, whose burial it was in, man or woman. Nothing! There will be more beautiful and useless pieces in museums." He took a breath. "To say nothing of the lives lost in the process. Guards killed, and others . . ." He trailed off. "Is the vase worth a life? I think it should be hidden where no one can see it. Publish it, photograph it! I think Professor Brown already did too much. And I regret ever having saved it in the first place." With that Tom got up, stumbled over Bill's feet, and left the room.

"All that is fine," said Brenda, "but the fact is, the vase is here, thanks to Tom and Tim, and we might as well make the best of it." She was thinking of a small summer travel grant and a less extravagant yacht.

Clifford Turner arrived and tried not to show his enthusiasm, his excitement at seeing the vase. The owner of the vase with the male figure would likely buy this one for a handsome sum. He puckered his lips to whistle but controlled himself. The vessel was dynamite. He established that the owner of the vase was Brenda and sized her up shrewdly as someone who did not know the art market. He was a reasonably honest art dealer and planned to take advantage of this fact only a little. Brenda would still have her sailboat and the department the summer grant. He insisted that there be no publicity in the matter for the sake of the collector interested in the piece, and yes, indeed, the collector plans to leave his collection to a major museum after his death. In his collection, the vase will get museum quality care. He did not have the proper container, but his assistant would return in a few days with a crate and take the vase.

It seemed that this was not only the wisest path but the path with the least resistance. Kyle understood that the vase was too valuable to have it around the house. Brenda wanted to turn it into cash as soon as possible, and the summer travel grant satisfied Bill and presumably would do for Tom when he calmed down. Professor Brown could not have asked for anything better. Naomi had been supportive of the process and presumably was satisfied with the result.

Brenda put the vase back in the china cabinet; Kyle went to his room; Bill returned to the university, and Naomi went off to the bathroom, noting that the china-cabinet doors remained unlocked, as the key was still on the coffee table. She heard Brenda on the phone upstairs and slinked out of the bathroom, took the keys, grabbed the vase, and locked the china cabinet, as if Brenda had locked it, wiping it clear of prints with the hem of her white skirt. She then wrapped the vase in the black jacket, placed it into the purple plastic bag of her Purple Heart purchase and quietly left the room. Brenda waved goodbye to her from the kitchen.

Naomi's heart beat fast as she drove back home. She knew exactly what to do. She would take the vase back to the Maya. There was nothing much to pack for this journey. She left several emails.

Dear Professor Parker,
Urgent family matters have called me to Tallahassee and I will be gone one or two weeks. Perhaps you can find someone else to fill in, in the meantime.
Sincerely,
Naomi

Dear Tom,
Urgent family matters have called me to Tallahassee and I will be gone one or two weeks. Please eat the perishables that look good to you in the refrigerator and throw out the rest. The vase is on its way home.
Naomi

Dear Brenda,
Urgent family matters have called me to Tallahassee and I will be gone one or two weeks. Tom will be taking care of my apartment.
All my best,
Naomi

Then Naomi made herself comfortable on the sofa, held in her hand the purple plastic bag with the vase, and tried to concentrate on grey, swirling smoke in front of her mind's eye.

19.

Green Parrot held a herbal infusion for Marigold, who had been lying as if asleep on the bed. Green Parrot had her back to her. When she turned with the cup, the sick woman opened her eyes slightly and gave the smallest of a wan smile. Green Parrot almost dropped the cup but then hastened to her and had her drink the potion immediately. That moment signaled Naomi's full return to Tikal, as she made a face at the bitterness of the herbs. Green Parrot smiled with delight at the sudden recovery, which she attributed to her brew. She hugged and kissed Marigold, who was just as happy to see her, knowing that her trip had been successful. And she noted out of the corner of her eye that the precious vase was by her side. She surreptitiously moved it out of view behind the bed.

"Thank the gods you are back! We all thought your spirit had been stolen, and we were at our wits' end to figure out how to get it back. We have been planning a singing ritual, recalling all your ancestors, which was difficult because they were all at Teotihuacán. Also, we were waiting for an auspicious day. Since you were ill, there have been a spate of unlucky days. There was even a cave-in at Sky Rain's temple construction, burying thirteen workmen—in itself a terrible omen. Green Parrot babbled on. She decided not to tell her just now that her illness was one of the things that was thought to have caused the bad luck and that there was talk of— But that was beside the point, now that she was demonstrably well.

It was strange that Marigold was lying there in her finest dress, when she had been wearing an old shift a little while ago, but Green Parrot thought she may not have observed correctly in her emotional upset over the illness and in her concentration on the potion. The maids had no doubt dressed Marigold up for her visit. A silly detail to worry about now that she had recovered.

"So where have you been all this time?" Green Parrot asked.

"I've been lost. I have been wandering around in the future."

"How far in the future?"

"Oh, about several baktuns ahead, maybe more than a thousand years in the future."

"And, how is the future? How is Tikal?"

"Tikal is no more, it is in ruins. People visit it and admire the ruins."

"Do they remember Sky Rain?"

"Yes, they think he was a great man."

"Ugh, that pompous idiot!"

"I'm afraid that's how it is. It is his buildings."

"So, if it was all in ruins, where did you stay?"

"In a city of the future."

"Did that have splendid pyramids?"

"No, it had none at all. It was quite shabby." How to explain a city of strip malls and McDonalds?

"Was it a new creation of the world after ours ended?"

"Well, it was sort of a continuation and sort of new." She couldn't very well explain the Spanish conquest and the history of the United States.

This made no sense to Green Parrot, who wanted to know everything but realized that her patient might be tired. She said, "We will speak of all this later. Now, why don't you rest, and later on your maid will bring you food. There will be plenty of time for you to tell me all about it. Thank the gods you are back among normal people!"

The news that Marigold was well, after this long illness, spread quickly from maid to maid to cook to lady. A distinguished elderly woman came from the court the next day, both to wish her well and to testify to the rumor that she was indeed well. Generally, it was seen as a good omen. Sky Rain's personal diviner was sent to cast her horoscope—which was lucky for the foreseeable future. Marigold sat up in bed to receive all these notables and was talkative and animated. She took her time to recover fully. Everyone concurred that after such a long illness, she needed time to herself to regain her strength.

She was left alone with her maid, Pebbles, who was a girl from the village outside Tikal. Pebbles wanted to know if Marigold met up with any goddesses in her dream state and if she needed to make any sacrifices to them in thanks. Marigold pondered the question and decided that something of that sort might be needed. She and Pebbles sacrificed some quail-like little birds to Ixchel, and Pebbles made a delicious stew out of the meat.

Pebbles said there was disgruntlement about Sky Rain's building project, since he was taking men away from work in the fields. They were supposed to be constructing only in the dry season, but the rainy season was early. The men wished to be home working on their own products. But Sky Rain was concerned about the unfinished corbel vaulting on top of the temples and wanted the men to finish them in a hurry. The cave-in had something to do with that. And then came a series of unlucky days, when no building could be done at all. But since Marigold got well, there was an improvement in the weather and the men's morale.

Marigold hadn't quite figured out what to do with the vase when she got to Tikal, but it seemed obvious that she would have to give it to Sky Rain. Though he was an unpleasant man with despotic tendencies, he was the only one worthy of such a special object in his capacity as ruler. The vase was not from Tikal, and she didn't know where it was from exactly, but he would understand that it was a very special gift. She would ponder the question a little more.

Marigold spent some pleasant lazy weeks enjoying the tropical weather, the greenery practically at her door, with Pebbles grinding maize in the background. When she had left, she had a textile half finished and picked it up again. What had she been thinking while weaving it? It seemed remarkably dull, with a zigzag pattern. She wished she could put a metallic thread in it here or there, but of course such things were not available here in this world. She discussed with Pebbles the idea of dying some yarn with the bright red cochineal insects to vary the off-white of the natural cotton. Even this did not please her completely. While in the modern world, she had been in the habit of seeing everything at Tikal as just right; this time she was finding fault with little things. Maybe only little things. But there they were. It was strange.

And there were the green lights waking her up at night, which was unnerving. They did not come every night, and she did not know why she even woke up long enough to see them in the middle of the night. Mostly around midnight. She would have a strange sensation of being watched and open her eyes long enough to see a flicker of neon green. In Morristown, the green lights made some sense, in that there were police cars and fire trucks on the street emitting flashing lights. She could have been mistaken about the green color. But at Tikal, flashing lights were inexplicable. The tropical night was dense, dark, and quiet. Fires and torches were out by midnight, and they would have a reddish glow in any case. For a while, she wondered if they were the notorious extraterrestrial aliens talked about in the modern world, but she didn't believe in UFOs. She decided that whatever it was, it seemed not to bother or threaten her and decided to put up with it. Maybe she was imagining things, and it was all in her mind. She would wake up, note the flickering green light near the thatch, smile, and go back to sleep. One night she stayed up until dawn and saw nothing.

The thing was, Marigold did not have anything to do other than the vase and the puzzle of Professor Brown's murder. So she decided to get on with it. She needed to give the vase to Sky Rain in some significant fashion. She could pretend that it had belonged to Night Sky. But why give it now? Should she want to get something in return? She must appear as a petitioner. What would the vase be worth to Sky Rain? She had no idea. Or it could be a goodwill gift, to be repaid later? An occasion was coming up, the celebration of the finishing of the corbelled vaults. Perhaps she might give it to him then.

The celebration, however, was a bad time to do anything private. There were going to be sacrifices, dances, feasts and speeches, and Sky Rain would be prominent in all of them. He would have to draw blood in the publicity of his court, and that always put him in a bad humor. He had been criticized for not doing it with enough spirit and enough blood. Those nobles who could not criticize him for his policies, without seeming to be disloyal, could criticize him on religious grounds. Sky Rain complained that the priests were out to get him, because he had abandoned the ancestral North Acropolis and built huge temples taking up space on the sacred plaza. The nobles let that issue go, planning to have their burial temples in more grandiose places as well. Sky Rain seemed not to respect tradition, and he could be criticized obliquely. He insisted that the new temples were being built for the gods and for everyone, and the gods' images were going to be on the roof combs. But the roof combs had not yet been built, and everyone knew that the space for his future burial was already in the interior of the pyramid.

Definitely, going on the day of the festival was not a good idea. Marigold decided that two days before would be adequate to associate herself with the festival and yet be assured of a private audience. Certainly, some nobles and neighboring rulers would be about, but he wouldn't be scheduled in. She sent Pebbles to tell Sky Rain's palace chief that Marigold would like to come on a certain day to pay her respects. The news that she was no longer at death's door and a liability had reached the palace with the new rumor that she was cured thanks to the intervention of the goddess Ixchel herself. That was a good omen, and therefore her wish to have an audience before the festival was granted.

When the day came, Marigold dressed carefully in her best off-the-shoulder huipil, woven of the finest cotton gauze, and wore a yellow orchid in her hair. By ancient Maya standards, she was an over-the-hill matron, but in the modern world, she would still look like a beautiful twenty-year-old. It had been remarked that she had no children, but that made her look all the younger. She suspected that some women at the court would suggest that she had been dabbling in witchcraft to look so good. But, hey, it was wonderful to look good and show herself off at the palace.

Pebbles was to carry the vase. Pebbles thought the vase was ugly, and that its black background looked like it was accidentally misfired. She thought the naked woman on it was weird; she had never seen anything like that. But then, of course, Pebbles was no expert on vases.

"What are we going to put in it?" she asked her mistress.

"Nothing, we take it as is."

"How can you take a gift that has nothing in it? At least some honey wine, balché? Or grains? Or even flowers? It will look strange empty."

"Will it seem like bad luck?" Marigold asked.

"It will seem like you are offering nothing—at least it would where I come from," she added, authoritatively naming her village.

"All right, let it be flowers then. Fill it up with orchids!"

Marigold wasn't sure of this move, because she felt that the vase was enough of a gift in itself, but flowers seemed like a harmless addition. The Maya liked flowers on all occasions, and she didn't want to mess around with honey wine.

20.

When Marigold found Sky Rain, he was in his throne room, seated on a mat with a high back. He was plainly dressed without his ceremonial regalia, and a fat servant was painting his face and arms.

"So you've recovered, Marigold," he said indifferently. "They say your illness had something to do with the unlucky days. I don't believe that myself. A single person, perhaps a widow, is too unimportant for fate to take notice—"

"Night Sky was a great man," she interjected, knowing that she should have kept her mouth shut but could not resist.

Sky Rain waved dismissively with the free hand that wasn't being painted.

Marigold rushed in with words before she might be dismissed altogether: "In honor of your building project, I brought you a present, something that Night Sky had been keeping for a special occasion." She held out the vase with the orchids.

Sky Rain turned to have a look at it and saw that it was a vase full of orchids. The vase had a lot of black on it and a figure. He was not particularly interested in vases. Had it been a jade, his eye would have lit up. Still, it was a gift.

"Put it over by the throne, next to the others," he instructed her.

Marigold went over to the double-headed stone throne and put the vase next to the other vases. She noted that most were of local, Tikal manufacture, of lesser quality. She put her vase close to the throne, thinking that Sky Rain might take a closer look at it later.

"Now that you are well, Marigold, you must remarry." Sky Rain had a new thought, looking at the comely young matron before him. "Night Sky's widow has great prestige, and there are any number of lords who would find a relationship with my lineage an advantageous one. It is an opportunity for me to build alliances. You've been mourning, you've been sick, but now it is time to move. I want a wedding in twenty days."

"Yes, my lord," said Marigold quietly, knowing that she could not contradict him in general, only perhaps in specifics. "May I know whom you have in mind?"

"You know perfectly well whom I have in mind: the lord of Uaxactún."

"But the lord of Uaxactún is still very young," she protested.

"What difference does that make!" snapped Sky Rain. "He may be friendlier to us than his father was. He can always take a younger second wife. But prestige is prestige, and that is what you have. Now run along and let me make all the arrangements."

Sky Rain waved Marigold towards the entrance. The servant had finished painting him during this discussion and left by the back opening. Marigold went outside the entrance wall, but didn't leave entirely. She was curious to find out whether Sky Rain would now examine the vessel more closely and how he might react. She delayed, ostensibly appreciating an inscription on the lintel. She was listening for sounds. You couldn't exactly hear footsteps in leather sandals on the limestone floor, but she surmised that someone must have entered through the back way, because she heard the murmur of voices. Men's voices. One clearly Sky Rain, the other younger. The tones were increasingly loud, and Marigold could gather from the intonation that Sky Rain was telling the other man what to do. She couldn't hear the young man distinctly, who she thought was trying to remain deferential. All of a sudden a loud and angry voice rang out: "I will not!—" It was clearly the young lord of Uaxactún.

Marigold slid closer to the entrance. What were they talking about?

"I have in mind to marry a princess of Xpuhil!" came the challenge.

"You must be kidding," Sky Rain replied with a sneer. "Xpuhil is in the back provinces. They have imitation pyramids instead of real ones. What good would that do you?"

"It's an up-and-coming area. Unlike Tikal, which is a has-been." This was patently untrue but worth flinging out in the heat of an argument. "Besides, I am told that she is delicious."

"Who are you calling a has-been!" yelled Sky Rain, and he cackled derisively. There was a moment of silence and a loud "Ha!—" followed by a crash that sounded to Marigold like pottery breaking against a limestone wall.

She heard pieces scattering everywhere including near the entrance where she was loitering. She sneaked close to see what had happened and picked up a black sherd. Was that part of the precious black background of the vase? Could it be that Sky Rain had picked up the nearest vessel to him and thrown it at the young man?—and of course missed. The crash was followed by the rapid exit of the lord of Uaxactún, covering his head with his hand, expecting more missiles to be thrown. Marigold held her breath. He rushed past her, never noticing that someone was there.

She didn't know whether to laugh or cry. She had gone to so much trouble over the vase; she had thought she had done well by it, and it had come to naught. She had thought it was up to the Maya to do with it as they wished, and the Maya—in the form of Sky Rain—had destroyed it in a moment of royal rage. And wasn't she now Maya? What was there to complain about? The expensive masterpiece in the modern world may have been ordinary in the ancient Maya world.

She thought of Brenda, Kyle and the others and felt that she had stolen their property as much as any looter of ruins. She thought of Professor Brown who had carried the vase and had respected its importance. She felt she had betrayed him. What would have been the right course of action? Should she have given it to someone other than Sky Rain? Perhaps the lord of Uaxactún, who had the reputation of liking works of art. At the thought of him, she chuckled to herself, having witnessed him make his escape in the shower of sherds.

He would never know that a masterpiece had been thrown at him. And to think that Sky Rain threw the vase on her account!—because of the insolence of a young man. It was not exactly flattering to think of herself as "old" and "unattractive," but in this instance she did not mind. Whether or not the vase was in pieces, it may have been a factor in Professor Brown's death, and that was something she knew she must not forget while busy with affairs at Tikal.

The immediate question became, What was she still doing at Tikal, now that Night Sky was dead, and even her gift of the vase was smashed? Did she have any place there, any future? She suspected, that if Sky Rain insisted enough, the lord of Uaxactún would comply. And would that be so bad? With his slim figure and long unbound hair he was a handsome youth, about twenty years of age. He had shown spirit.

But having known the love of a gentle, older man, could she ever care for this one? Especially if he had a gaggle of young wives? She would end up having to play mother, and that would be no fun.

Mulling these thoughts, Marigold entered her house and asked Pebbles to make her a cooling chocolate drink. Actually, what she most wanted was an iced tea, but in the world of ancient Tikal, of course, there was no ice. The modern world wasn't all bad, she mused; it was certainly comfortable, if you had a bit of money. It was something of a paradox that there was smog, pesticides and global warming, while she could buy tomatoes and strawberries year round in the stores. At Tikal, fruits and vegetables were scarce in some seasons. In the dry season, acrid smoke hung in the air from the burning of the fields. But when water was plentiful, it was fresh and tasty. Well, of course, you could appreciate the joys of subsistence living in many places round the world and in many times past.

What was special at Tikal was the sophistication of Maya culture: The huge pyramids and palaces gleaming white in their plaster coating; the exotic dresses of the lords and ladies in finely woven textiles, animal skins, and feathers; and the exquisite arts in carving, mural painting, jades and of course pottery. There was also wood and bone carving, which would not lasted into modern times, but which she could see all about her. Except for Sky Rain, who was insensitive to art, everyone was interested in beauty and was something of a connoisseur. Compared to the McDonalds and Home Depots of Morristown, there was nothing ugly or shabby at Tikal.

There were the Mesoamerican sacrifices—the heart sacrifice of god impersonators at festivals and the killing of war captives. Marigold averted her eyes and thought of the thousands of victims sacrificed for speed by cars on the American highways every year. Modern culture had its sacrifices, but in different forms. At least the Maya died for a cause—to sustain the cosmos and its gods, not in meaningless and grotesque accidents. Nor did the modern era lack for wars and weapons of mass destruction, by which millions had perished with no end in sight. The Maya with their obsidian and flint knives were beginners in violence.

It was not for the first time that Marigold went through this litany of comparisons. Every time, when she calculated the horrors of Maya versus modern lifeways, she concluded that the Maya were not only not so bad, but because of their love of beauty were, in fact, superior to the moderns. Calculations such as these had brought her to Tikal in the first place and to a short but glorious marriage and partnership with Night Sky.

Politically, Night Sky had been a utopian dreamer, and that appealed to her. He had criticized his own "monument-mad"—as he would say—Maya culture and wanted to introduce something simpler in its stead. He actually got to put it into practice during the indifferent overlord-ship of Calakmul. It was not for long, but while it lasted, for Marigold it was heady stuff. She did not for a minute think of going back to the modern world. Tikal with Night Sky was the most exciting place to be on the planet.

Since the return of Sky Rain, she had felt less and less at home. He was exceptionally "monument-mad," and the madness had become widespread at Tikal. To be sure, his monuments were spectacular, elegant in outline, soaring in height, subtle in articulation, as his brilliant master mason had designed them. But they were built at the cost of the social fabric. Laborers continued to be pushed to the limit. Tikal lords and ladies vied with one another in building their own structures and exaggerated their own glamorous appearances. This had once attracted Naomi to the Maya in books, but after Night Sky, she found it excessively vain. She had acquired a taste for simplicity. She got tired of all the pompous inscriptions that declared the august genealogy and bravery of the ruler and elite. Night Sky had not bragged so. Moreover, unlike the present bunch, Night Sky had not aggrandized the truth. Did the gods even know what self-promotion was going to be on the roof combs of Sky Rain's temples when finished? What will they think when Sky Rain claims to be descended from one or another of them—a god himself!

She went back in her mind and thought of the vase. It had been a Maya vase, masterpiece or not, and she was sorry it was gone. She had kept the broken sherd of the black background; she knew not quite why. She put it in her change purse, next to the quarters and dimes for safekeeping—a private souvenir of her attempt at archaeology. Had it been a mistake to meddle in history? she wondered and tried to sleep, leaving big decisions for the morrow.

21.

She was awakened in the middle of the night by a light scratching noise in the roof, and when she opened her eyes, she saw the faint green light. For a minute she didn't know where she was, whether in Morristown or Tikal, but then she became aware of the mat-bed she was lying on. She looked around in panic because she had the feeling she was not alone. Someone was in the room with her and might be dangerous. She pulled up her knees to her chin and covered herself with sheets. The feeling that someone was there began to come from very near, and Marigold hunched herself up even smaller. Suddenly, she felt as if a light hand had touched her thigh, and she nearly screamed. Nearly, because another light hand was placed on her mouth and stifled the cry. Nevertheless, Marigold could see no one, only a pale green light in the space next to her on the sleeping mat. The hands, strong but light as moths, let her go. Evidently, whoever or whatever it was, was not planning to kill her, and she relaxed a little.

"Who are you?" she said quietly.

There was no answer. She darted a quick look at the green light next to her and thought she saw the figure of a man. He was not moving. "Can you hear me?" she asked, but there was no answer.

There was something about the way that he lay next to her that reminded her of Night Sky. She reached out a hand to touch him, but she felt only the bed. "Is that you, Night Sky?" she asked, touching the pillow where she imagined his head.

She did not need an answer. This shape next to her could only be Night Sky. She had spent so much time thinking about Night Sky that his ghost had come to visit her. She was glad of it suddenly and unafraid. She reached out a hand again and stroked him lightly where she felt him to be. "My dear," she murmured, "how I missed you."

She felt being caressed in turn, and a sense of joy and well-being enveloped her. They lay in a gentle embrace for a long time. Eventually,

Marigold's right arm got tired and she shifted over. The mood was broken.

"Is there something you want?" she asked. She was getting used to the idea that he would be silent, and she would have to speak for him. "Do you want me to do something?" She strained to receive some message.

"I sense you speaking to me in my mind, but I don't always understand it." There was a pause. "Tell me."

"Why should you want me to marry the young lord of Uaxactún? I am still keeping your memory. That's a bizarre request. And anyway, he doesn't want me."

Marigold turned the other way, where there was only the bed and told herself that she was imagining things and there was no one with her. But she did not turn back for fear of seeing the green light. The room was silent. There was a pale white light of the beginning of dawn. She finally turned back—and saw nothing. "There are no ghosts in either the modern or ancient Maya world. I must stop going back and forth between worlds. It is affecting my mental balance," she whispered to herself. Thereupon Marigold resolved to decide which world she belonged to, as soon as possible—and stay there.

She slept deeply and awoke refreshed. Pebbles brought a maize gruel with fruit and the news that one of the temple corbel vaults had collapsed during the night, despite the new struts, and killed a guard. The conversation with Night Sky, if it could be called that, seemed totally irrelevant to the events of the day.

Sky Rain was certain to order ceremonies and sacrifices, and the first on the list would be the master mason. The peasant workers had disappeared to their villages and fields, and no one was going to get them together until the agricultural work was done. Sky Rain was stuck with a pile of finely cut limestone in a heap.

While this news was of great interest, Marigold could not help but think of the incident with Night Sky. Was that his ghost, or did she dream it? Would he come again? Did she want him to come? Would he let her know why he wanted her to marry that specific person? She was distracted all day and ate and drank barely aware of whatever Pebbles brought to her. "Pebbles, do the dead come back after death to talk to you?"

For safety, Pebbles touched the earth with her forefinger when speaking of the dead. "Sometimes, when they have left unfinished something in life. The lord of Xibalba lets them out for a while."

"Are they dangerous?"

"Sometimes. They don't like to get contradicted. But if you plant two lily bulbs where they appeared, that can be counteracted. The scent of the lilies confuses them."

"Oh, lily bulbs."

"Have you had a visitation by someone?"

"No, I just forgot exactly how it is among you," said Marigold, remembering that she was from Teotihuacán, where they might have different lore. Pebbles looked at her suspiciously, looking for signs that her illness was returning, but Marigold looked well and waved her out.

The time to midnight went slowly, because she could not sleep. She was nervous about seeing Night Sky again and just as nervous about not seeing him. She tossed and turned for a while, staring at the thatch of the roof. She thought about the vase and what she would say in the modern world about it. Whatever she decided to do with her life later, she had to finish off the matter of Professor Brown's death and do something about the vase. She had taken on the responsibility when she'd bought it back. At the moment, she did not feel up to coping with these issues. The thoughts were soporific, and she fell into a light doze, from which she woke with a start. The green light was there, and she sensed that Night Sky was sitting on the edge of her bed, a hand on her arm. She jerked awake. "I didn't know that you were there!" she said in confusion but familiarly.

"I keep coming back because of my love for you," he seemed to say, leaning closer.

"I know, we had a wonderful love, and it's good to see you again, even like this. But it is a little strange why all of a sudden—"

"I've been looking for you for a while; I even had to go to another world to find you, but you did not see me."

Marigold remembered waking up that morning to the green light in her apartment and a day of uncertainty. She acknowledged the fact that he had been looking for her. "So, what do you want from me?"

Night Sky replied through his silences.

"You want me to marry the lord of Uaxactún. But why?"

"He is a good-looking young man, but couldn't I have someone more mature? Or, do you like the fact that he stands up to Sky Rain?"

There was more silence as Night Sky sat with his hand on her arm.

"You think that I, as a more mature woman, can lead him to follow in your footsteps and lead the Maya away from the destructive and foolish waste of resources?" After this thought, she looked meditatively into the distance, not realizing at what point her sensation of Night Sky disappeared.

After that, she really could not get to sleep. Somehow, it did not matter whether Night Sky was real or not. She could not help but think about his legacy and helping him to make it real. Never mind, that the lord of Uaxactún was not interested. That could always change or even be made to change. The big point in the whole visitation was that Night Sky wanted her to stay in the world of the Maya. If she was to work for his legacy, she would have to stay. That would immediately decide her next steps. At least for a long while. She owed something to Night Sky; he had picked her up after a foolish adventure and given her a worthwhile life. And she loved him.

22.

Marigold hoped that Night Sky would not visit her every night. She needed to catch up on sleep. To be sure, it was good to sense his presence, but was it really him or some impersonating spirit? And, although he was friendly, there was menace in his very seduction. He was not letting her go. His control extended to her own mind that seemed to channel his thoughts while he was there.

And, no, she was not going to marry anyone else in Maya-land, but she thought she might try to further Night Sky's cause in some other way. She would have to stay a while longer in Tikal. Certainly, she didn't want to be visited by ghosts in Morristown.

At the prospect of staying, Morristown began to look more attractive. She wondered how Tom was getting on without her—going back to Joyce?—and most irrelevantly, she thought of Michael watching *The Three Stooges* on Professor Brown's couch in his new office. It was not so much that it was a better world there—it was not— It was simply the world she had been a part of, she reflected. They probably thought that she was back in the field.

What exactly could she do at Tikal? She could seduce and poison Sky Rain—if nothing else, for breaking the vase. But Sky Rain was entirely impervious to her charms—and there was no way of getting close to him. On the other hand, she could agree to the marriage he wanted and thereby get further inside the court. She could always think of something to get out of the marriage at the last moment. That might also be a way of influencing the lord of Uaxactún. What was his name, anyway? Maybe Green Parrot would know.

Green Parrot was mixing a potion for one of her children who was sick. Naomi told her that Sky Rain wanted her to marry the lord of Uaxactún.

"No!" said Green Parrot with finality.

"Why not?" asked Marigold, surprised at this reaction.

"We are friendly with Uaxactún now, but that may not last. When we become enemies I will never see you."

"Maybe we won't be enemies again."

"Hah! That Shining Arrow is a hothead. I wouldn't trust him."

"What a name, Shining Arrow!" Marigold said.

"His mother was very eager to have a son after four girls, and the prognostications were good. But he was spoiled. I am told he wants everything his way."

"So what else is new? So does Sky Rain."

"That's just it, two such stubborn men are bound to get into conflict."

"But Sky Rain thinks he can control him."

"For a while, maybe, but watch out—"

Marigold was silent for a while and then said, "I don't see what choice I have."

Green Parrot cautioned, "Watch out, Marigold. Remember how sick you were recently. Shining Arrow can only cause you trouble. But then if Sky Rain wants it, there is nothing much that you can do. See that you have a favorable day for the wedding. Now I must go to my little one."

Marigold's next task was to talk to Shining Arrow, which was not easy, in that men and women did not mingle freely among the Maya. Shining Arrow was usually surrounded by boisterous young men. She was going to try to carry out Night Sky's legacy, both out of love and because she did not want to be haunted by him in the future. She was anxious to get back to the world of Professor Brown, but she still felt that her stay at Tikal was incomplete. After exploring various scenarios, such as waylaying him on a hunting expedition, she decided that the best approach was to summon him directly to talk with the "widow of Night Sky" in her own home. She suspected that his immediate reaction would be negative but that he might come out of curiosity.

* * *

"What does the widow of Night Sky want with me?" said Shining Arrow archly upon entering.

Marigold offered him the seat of honor next to her on the veranda. She was fanning herself with quetzal feathers. "I have been visited recently by my dear departed husband, Night Sky," she said importantly.

Shining Arrow moved to the edge of his seat. He expected a lot of openings concerning marriage, but nothing like this. He examined Marigold as a woman and found her reasonably attractive, even sexually alluring, despite her age. *If I did not have to wed her, an affair with such a good-looking and intelligent woman might not be bad,*" he thought.

"Night Sky said that he knew of you and thought that you had the potential to be a great leader," Marigold continued.

Shining Arrow was trying to focus on what she was saying, mystified by all this talk about Night Sky. He remembered stories of Night Sky as a worthy leader during Tikal's dark days, though perhaps ineffectual in comparison to the kings of his own time. As far as he could recall, Night Sky left no image of himself, no splendid buildings, and no inscriptions. Except in stories, he hardly existed at all. It was natural that his widow should think highly of him. Marigold kept talking, and Shining Arrow gathered that the ghost of Night Sky wanted something of him. He was at a loss as to what.

She tried to make it clear. "Night Sky created some changes in Maya life. To be sure, they originated at a time of hardship, and at the time their austerity made sense. He was against the wasting of resources in building and display. He wanted, honesty, simplicity, justice—"

"Yes, I have heard. Those were the dark years," he interrupted impatiently.

"They were dark, but in a way they were better than the present showiness," she countered.

"But the present is dynamic and exciting. Why are you harping on the past?"

"Night Sky thought that if you think about it, you might be the kind of leader who would value the ideas of his past—"

"I never thought about it. I always thought that we at Uaxactún should reach out to other Maya kingdoms and build greatness through alliances. We are not yet as great as Tikal, but—who knows, fortunes change. We too could build." His eyes began to glow. If he married her, would this woman continue to babble about Night Sky? Or would she help him forge a powerful kingdom that could take on Tikal itself? She was evidently interfering in political matters.

Marigold saw that the direct approach was not getting anywhere. Shining Arrow did not understand what she was talking about. But she knew that he was appraising her coolly and seemed to like what he saw. He didn't relate to all the stuff about Night Sky, but he liked the widow Marigold. Seduction seemed to be the only alternative.

"I am told that you come from the great city in the north," he said, changing the subject.

"Yes, Teotihuacán."

"Tell me what it's like," he asked, with the genuine eagerness of a young man. "I heard that it is impressive, but ugly."

This opening allowed Naomi to continue her politics. She gave a brief account of how at Teotihuacán more people are a part of the decision-making, process because they live in communal apartment compounds. All this put Shining Arrow into a daze, from which he woke up only when she started talking about her dancing-girl days. It would take some time to educate Shining Arrow into being an enlightened ruler, Marigold thought with a sigh.

Shining Arrow got up to leave, feeling that this bizarre interview was over. He leaned over Marigold. "Well? shall we join forces?"

She was too stunned to answer. Was this a proposal?

Shining Arrow took her stare as a yes and walked out with a cheerful smile. All that Marigold could make of it was that Shining Arrow had seen that she was not Sky Rain's creature and felt possibilities in an alliance with her. Her apparent and perhaps confused attachment to her dead husband did not particularly bother him. Would this satisfy Night Sky? she wondered.

She assessed Shining Arrow as a bright and brash young man, who might very well go places but who had no particular intellectual curiosity. He would not make much of a soul mate to herself. He needed a beautiful young woman, much like him. He could use an older woman as an advisor, but he was unlikely to listen to anything she said. Marigold was not above vanity. She thought self-indulgently that he might have thought her fascinating.

Night Sky did not appear that night nor the next several nights. Marigold wanted to contact him but did not know how to go about it. In the meantime, the twenty days stipulated by Sky Rain were passing, and preparations were made for the wedding. Green Parrot shook her head a lot. Pebbles was busy grinding corn. The household of Sky Rain was collecting cacao beans from everywhere. Sky Rain's wife summoned Marigold to the palace to chitchat with her in preparation for her role as queen of Uaxactún. Four women embroidered the fancy huipil. Marigold had to listen and admire all the women's children.

She asked herself what she was doing. She wasn't really going to go through with this? Couldn't she contact Night Sky from the modern world? She had done everything she could. Wasn't it time to go? But going was not easy. She had spent wonderful times in Tikal, and becoming queen of Uaxactún was an interesting prospect. There were still thirteen days left of the twenty to the wedding, and she was postponing the parting every day.

Shining Arrow came to visit her once and brought a vase full of honey-wine. Marigold noted the vase. It was in Tikal style, slightly misfired at the upper edges. Pebbles brought two cups, and they drank ceremoniously.

"I've thought a lot about what you said," he started, "and I think your deceased husband, Night Sky, had some good ideas. Of course, they're probably not ideas that can be put into practice in our times, in our imperfect world. But definitely something to think about. I hope that in the future we can discuss many such things," and he took a swig.

"I think it will be interesting to talk with you, since you seem to have such an open mind," she said with faint irony. "Perhaps Night Sky will talk with you directly."

At this Shining Arrow nearly dropped his cup. He didn't want to wed the ghost of Night Sky as well. But, on the whole, he was not afraid of ghosts, and his equanimity was soon restored. By the time the honey-wine was gone, they were on friendly terms.

That evening Night Sky finally appeared. The green light was pale, but the sense of a presence was definitely there. Marigold was eager to communicate. "I am trying very hard," she said immediately. "I've made friends with Shining Arrow, and the wedding is to be in a few days, as you wanted it. But he doesn't understand you and your ideas. I don't see how he can carry on your legacy."

She sensed a long silence. Then his thoughts emerged in her mind. "Well, maybe in time, with you at his side, the ideas will germinate."

She felt herself respond truthfully. "It might take many years. I can't always be at his side."

She was aware of a caressing hand on her shoulder, and responded, "I know you want me to stay, and a part of me wants to stay. But—"

She felt a light kiss on her lips and further talk stopped.

In the morning, Marigold heard from Pebbles that there had been some kind of a disaster during the night. Perhaps an ambush. The whole city was talking about it, and rumors flew with the swiftness of wings. One rumor said that something happened to Sky Rain; he was either dead or wounded. Another claimed that there was an attack on the palace or the unfinished temples. An unlikely third was that there had been an unexpected eclipse of the moon, due to the machinations of a well-known shaman.

"How did everyone know that there had been a disaster?" she asked.

"Some wounded warriors were brought into the city at dawn, and healers were sent to treat them," Pebbles explained.

By nightfall the stories coalesced, and it seemed that Shining Arrow was involved. He was on his way home, carried in a palanquin, when his group was attacked by warriors. Shining Arrow was thrown to the ground and suffered a head injury. He was carried back to Uaxactún by his men. Since then, he has been in a coma, and there was no knowing how long that would last.

The origin of the attackers were not clear. At first, they were said to be bandits. The subsequent rumor was that they were from Tikal itself. Sky Rain had internal enemies from a rival lineage. Perhaps they did not want the wedding alliance with Uaxactún to take place. Nothing exactly confirmed this, but it was the subject of many discussions. It was confirmed that Shining Arrow was in a bad way and could not attend any wedding.

After wandering around the city and listening to the stories of the night's happenings, Marigold realized that events had got ahead of her. She went home and distractedly sat down to some of Pebbles' venison stew. After a few spoonfuls, she felt she had no time to lose. She gave Pebbles some little jades from the family heirlooms and told her to go visit her own family in their village. Pebbles cried, wanting to know what she had done wrong. Marigold assured her that she had been a great help, but that now she was no longer needed. If ever she was needed again, she would contact her. On her way, she was to call on Green Parrot and give her a bundle that contained Marigold's clothes and textiles.

When Pebbles was gone, the more Marigold thought about the situation, the more she felt that being a woman with ideas at the center of an internal conflict at Tikal—over a wedding she didn't really want—was not worth fighting for, or dying for, at this time. Who knew at what moment a deluded conspirator would come looking for her and take her off as a victim for sacrifice or cut her down on the spot? She imagined she heard the leaves rustle.

Marigold made a great effort to concentrate and summoned forth the tunnel. She stepped in so hurriedly, she almost tripped.

23.

Naomi found herself on the sofa in her apartment, and her first thought was that she had left the beautiful jacket with the silver threads in the purple plastic bag at Tikal. What would Pebbles and Green Parrot make of that when they found it? Nothing could be done about it. She'd escaped by the skin of her teeth She should have known better than to get involved with political intrigue. Night Sky had been ridiculously naïve—which is why she had loved him so, Naomi sighed.

The room came into clearer focus. She saw her computer almost beckoning. She must have a thousand emails! There were eggs and sliced bread in the refrigerator, and Naomi made herself an omelet. One tomato was still salvageable. The seltzer was cold. Maybe not as good as venison stew—

She sat down with her meal in front of the TV and watched the news. There had been a major oil spill in Alaska. People wanted more charter schools. The economy was not doing well, and there were layoffs.

After that, she booted up the computer to look at her emails.

Brenda: "Where are you, something happened, the vase is gone. Do you know anything about it? Is it the dealer?"

Tom: "Where are you? Are you back in the field? Do you know that the vase is missing? Call me right away."

Bill: "Call on your return, we all worry about you and the vase."

Brenda: "I'm told you are back in the field. We need you here to deal with the vase problem. Respond."

Clifford Turner: "Where are you? What exactly is going on with the vase? I have a buyer for it."

Tom: If you get this at Tikal, respond right away. Things are in a pickle. We need you to find out what happened to the vase. I'm sure you know nothing about it, but every bit of information might help in the investigation."

Michael: "Would you like to go out for pizza some night?"

Naomi answered the last one affirmatively and did not have to wait long for a reply. They were to lunch the next day at the Pizza Hut near the university. As far as the questions about the vase and her absence were concerned, that required some thinking. To be sure, she had been back in Guatemala researching a difficult bit of her dissertation. Perhaps the best approach to the vase was to know nothing about it. As far as she knew, she had not been seen, and no one connected the disappearance of the vase with her absence.

She left a message to Brenda, Tom, Billy and Clifford that she was back in town after a brief trip to Guatemala. She knew nothing about the vase and was shocked to hear that it was missing. She needed a day or two to get over the jetlag and the fatigue of travel, but she would be back at the university shortly. She thanked everybody for their concern on her behalf.

She met Michael at the Pizza Hut, wearing no exotic Tikal clothing of any sort. She thought that a relative stranger might somehow shed light on her dilemma of how to deal with the vase and maybe even the case of Professor Brown. Michael sat down and smiled in a friendly way.

"I've been pondering what Nietzsche meant by saying that we stare into the void and the void stares back at us," he said by way of greeting.

"Hm—" said Naomi, as she ordered a large mushroom pie. She actually thought she knew what it meant but couldn't quite put it into words. "There are many more worlds out there than one would think," she said at last, trying to corral the conversation into her channels. "Michael, do you think it is wrong to return a work of art to the time and space where it was made?" she finally asked.

Michael picked up a mushroom that had fallen off his slice. "A work of art is a lie that tells the truth. Nietzsche also said that, and I believe it."

"What about a work of art that gets broken in the process?"

"Nietzsche doesn't say anything about that, but I presume that by then the work of art has told its truth and may now rest in peace—or pieces, if you like. Some things have to break," he continued without skipping a beat. "The world cannot support endless numbers of works of art."

Naomi smiled and sighed. "I'm afraid I agree with that." Then she tried another track. "What do people say about the death of Professor Brown?"

"They say that it was a terrible accident."

"Do you believe it was an accident, or do you think someone pushed him?" she replied, putting it into the open, hoping he wasn't going to quote Nietzsche.

"It was a terrible accident, either way."

"But if someone pushed him, don't you think he or she needs to be brought to justice?" Her voice rose shrilly.

"Justice is complicated and depends on one's point of view. For all you know, there may already have been justice; you just can't see it."

"Wouldn't Professor Brown like to see justice done?"

"Your good Professor Brown was a simple man at heart. Are you searching for his justice?"

Naomi hadn't thought of it that way. She felt that Professor Brown had reached out to her in death, and she had responded with her amateur investigation. She was searching for the truth, but she realized that Michael would tear her idea of truth into little pieces. And, was it Professor Brown's truth or her truth? Then she shook herself and said, "There are all those truths, as you say, but there is also a simple truth for us ordinary mortals."

"My dear Naomi, you are far from ordinary. Where have you left your exotic Mayan clothes? I like them."

And with that Naomi steered the conversation to the department and found out that Sophie Parker was in Egypt, Bill was gone, and

Tom had a hangdog look. They agreed that the pizza had a soggy quality. Michael invited her to watch some avant-garde short films in his office, but Naomi escaped as soon as she could.

When she got home, she heard a message being spoken into her phone. She leaped over and picked up in midstream. "This is Naomi; who is it?"

Clifford Turner's voice said, "Finally, I got you. What d'you say we go fifty-fifty on the vase? I know buyers in Japan and Brazil and a particularly eager one in the Netherlands."

"What are you talking about? I don't have the vase," she answered without hesitation.

"You must have the vase! You are the only one who could have taken it. Don't be coy—I know you have it. But you can't sell it without me."

"Please, understand, Clifford—I do not have the vase." For a few seconds she thought of offering that she did once have it, but she thought better of it. She kept repeating that she did not have the vase. In the present. And that was the simple truth.

Clifford did not give up. "Are you by chance trying to hide the vase for a good cause? Don't be a silly fool. Someone will take it from you. It is worth a million. Here, you know my number. Call me when you've thought it over."

Clifford was so shaken by Naomi's insistence; he was sure she had the vase. Unless he had been wrong? She was the one who understood its value, and she could have taken it. Maybe it had been that cool customer Brenda, all along. He fished out her number and called. Brenda picked up the phone. Clifford tried the line that he knew she had the vase, and they should go fifty-fifty—

Brenda said, "Go to hell!" and slammed down the phone.

"Stupid bitches," murmured Clifford to himself, and dialed the number of a private investigator.

Naomi called Brenda and found her fuming at home. "Where the hell have you been!" she barked.

Naomi gave her the tried and true fieldwork story, accompanied by complaints of the unusually severe rains in the rainy season in Guatemala. Many years of marriage to Tim Brown had accustomed her to such recitals. In a bored but mollified tone, she got right on the subject of the vase. "The Maya vase has disappeared, and I am out of a sailboat—I mean a million dollars. And on top of that, that idiot dealer thinks that I hid the vase! The vase just disappeared, but it couldn't have, could it? You were there; do you know what happened to it? I remember locking it up, and the next day it was gone. So that leaves you, Tom and Billy. Or Clifford. He doth protest too much." She took a breath. "He came the next day with a crate and bags of fillers like Styrofoam peanuts and oohed and aahed that the vase was gone. But he—or someone he sent—could have burgled the place at night. I sleep like a log. All that fifty-fifty talk could be a sham."

Naomi did her best to look sympathetic. "Have you thought of another explanation."

"What do you mean?"

"Something that isn't natural?"

"You mean the 'curse of the mummy' or some such superstition? Don't be silly, Naomi, the vase was not taken by a poltergeist. I am sure that sooner or later it will turn up, and I am its legal owner. So, how come you had to rush off to the field just as the vase disappeared? Did you by chance take it to your precious Maya?" she added, at least somewhat suspiciously.

Naomi laughed with her. It was unfair to Brenda to lie to her like this, but nothing suggested that Professor Brown intended the vase for her. Moreover, in Naomi's mind, Brenda was the prime suspect in Professor Brown's untimely death. It wasn't fair, exactly, but Naomi thought that it wasn't exactly unfair, either. Brenda could go on her cruises without a sailboat of her own. Not that Naomi thought herself one to judge and mete out justice of this sort, and she didn't do it to harm Brenda. *I did it for the sake of the vase.*

That in turn seemed to her a little absurd, even—or especially—if she looked at it through Michael's criteria. Taking the vase to Tikal had been a generous impulse, even though it turned out otherwise. The more Naomi thought about it, taking in the point of view of the interested persons in the case, the more confused she got. She decided to call Tom—talk to someone down-to-earth. Tom was delighted to hear from her and accepted the invitation to take-out Chinese at her place.

Naomi decided to tell Tom the truth and dressed in the Maya garb for the occasion. There was nothing in the refrigerator except cold seltzer, since she'd had pizza for lunch and no chance to shop. After the delicious, fresh diet of Tikal, the fast foods she had been eating in Morristown were unappealing. She decided that after this Chinese meal, she would start cooking healthy meals and salads herself. In fact, she was thinking of staying put somewhere, giving up this investigation, and especially the time travel. It was turning her life into chaos.

Tom arrived on time and said right away staring at her: "Where on earth have you been?"

Naomi sat him down on the sofa with a cold seltzer and asked him not to interrupt her story until she was entirely finished. She began with the meeting at Brenda's house and taking the vase in the purple plastic shopping bag. She mentioned briefly her time travel to Tikal and the decision to give the vase to Sky Rain. She described Sky Rain's fit of temper and his throwing it against the wall. She thought not to complicate things by mentioning Shining Arrow, Night Sky, and the wedding. She focused on how the vase broke into smithereens. In several places in the narrative Tom opened up his mouth to say something, but Naomi shushed him.

"Are you finished?" he finally said.

Naomi nodded. It felt good to tell someone about it, and she trusted Tom.

He tut-tutted. "This must be the novel you are writing instead of working on your dissertation. You don't really expect me to believe that you went back to ancient Tikal and gave the vase to a Maya king? Come, on now."

"That is exactly what I did."

"And I don't believe that you took the vase at all. It isn't like you. Are you on some new medication?"

"What do you think happened to the vase?"

"I don't know. I think it is suspicious that soon after it's disappearance Bill went back to Guatemala, saying that his aunt died. Maybe it's in the basement of the Guatemala National Museum."

"But Bill was so American—"

"So what. He was also just as Guatemalan."

Naomi didn't like the idea that Bill might be blamed for the disappearance of the vase. "Bill couldn't have done it. I was the last person to see the vase," she said, as the doorbell rang.

The Chinese delivery arrived, and they started into *lo mein* with vegetable tofu. Naomi was flattered that Tom didn't think her capable of stealing the vase, but the truth was the truth. She wanted to impress upon him that she didn't take it for profit. "I had this idea that the vase belonged to the Maya and not to us. The ancient Maya. But I was nonplussed that Sky Rain broke it so casually."

"My dear girl," said Tom just a little bit patronizingly, "what proof is there that the vase was broken?"

"There is proof," answered Naomi. "I picked up a sherd from it, and I have it." With that, she got her wallet from her purse and fished out the sherd from among the coins. Tom examined it eagerly.

"It is seventh or eighth century Maya. But you could have gotten it in lots of places. Still, let me take it and do a chemical analysis. The black in the black-background vase was very distinct."

Elated at the chance to do something pragmatic, Tom was chatting happily. At the end of his visit he cautioned Naomi not to run back to the field again, with or without time travel. On parting, he kissed her on the cheek.

When he left, Naomi collapsed in frustration: Tom had listened, but he did not believe her.

24.

The next day Naomi went to the university to collect her paycheck, and Annie gave her a postcard sent by Sophie from Cairo. On it was a picture of the gold coffin of Tutankhamen. The note was as follows.

> Dear Naomi,
> Having an interesting time in Cairo. I had a strange encounter with the *Book of the Dead.* I saw a tunnel and some little people, and this time I went in to explore. I want to talk to you about it when I return.
> Sophie
> P.S. Where did you disappear to? I left a pile of research queries and Xerox instructions on the right-hand corner of my desk. Please take care of them as soon as you can.

Naomi looked at the two-foot-high pile of papers and instructions with joy and relief. They would keep her in money for months to come. As far as Sophie's encounter with the *Book of the Dead* and the tunnel—that would indeed be interesting to discuss. Maybe Sophie would believe her.

She was standing by the photocopy machine when Michael came by. "At work, already," he said sheepishly.

"Well, you're still here," she said flippantly.

"Have you found out the truths yet?"

"I'm working on them. All of them."

"Will you tell me when you do?" His voice was casual.

"It doesn't matter to you! None of those people involved were your friends. They might as well have been the Three Stooges, as far as you care!"

"So, I am totally objective. I am just curious."

"Ha!" said Naomi, noting that Michael was human after all.

"Well, I guess it will have to wait until I return."

"Where are you going?" she asked with surprise and more interest than she cared to show.

"Paris."

"Oh, Paris."

"Yes, Paris. I am following your example. I am localizing myself in real space." Michael grinned.

"What are you going to do there?"

"You should ask! What do you do at Tikal? I will go to the top of the Eiffel Tower and pig out on French food."

"Hm, have a good time. When do you go?"

"In a few days."

With that, someone came by wanting to use the copy machine, and the conversation came to an end.

Naomi went home feeling let down. It was still early afternoon. Everyone was away or going away. Professor Brown's case was still in limbo. What was there for her to do? Maybe she should never have left Tikal in such a hurry. Maybe there was no real danger. Maybe Shining Arrow would have recovered. There was always something to see and do there.

She checked her mail absentmindedly and opened a note from the owner of the apartment she was subletting. The owner was coming back and wanted to reoccupy the apartment. Shortly, she would have to move. Naomi felt rejected, even though she remembered clearly that this was the original agreement between them. But the timing was not great.

She looked in the refrigerator and found the congealed remains of last night's Chinese food looking disgusting. The idea of going out to the gigantic supermarket to shop was enough to make her dizzy. She had fled back to Morristown from the "primitive" Maya, but the US, in the form of Morristown, again struck her as unbearably ugly and unfriendly. As she was going back and forth in her mind, she began to laugh. She wasn't going to spend her life shuttling back and forth between the ancient Maya and America!—or was she?

Then she thought of one American invention she had looked on positively and got her car keys. She would take a little ride into the country, away from the commercial strip of the city. As soon as the highway was bordered by trees, she felt better. When she was past Sparta, New Jersey, she had a sudden desire to drive all the way across the Delaware River to Milford, Pennsylvania, and have something homemade at the bakery. Milford was still the antiques capital of the USA, but this time it didn't bother her. The Quilt Shop was still there, and on impulse she bought the beautiful crazy quilt she had admired—all robust reds and browns. Then she had tea and a pastry at the bakery, and she did not worry whether this bakery was from the old or the new Milford. It overlooked a babbling brook, and that was all that mattered. She drove back in a happier frame of mind, stopping at the supermarket for eggs, ham, bread and salad.

"I must call Brenda tomorrow," she said to herself decisively. She went to bed thinking that she now knew the story of Professor Brown, but needed to sleep on it. She had trouble going to sleep, her mind on Brenda and their coming conversation. She tossed and turned. It must have been past eleven when she got to sleep. She was not pleased when at midnight she woke to see a green light in her room. "No, not you!" she said in all exasperation. "I thought I had left you behind in Tikal. Please don't start visiting me here!"

Of course, there was silence, but the sense that someone was in the room with her was very strong. Luckily, the vague sensation was near the closet and did not get on the bed.

"Look, I tried with Shining Arrow, but you could see he was not the right sort of person. Now, maybe, I did not give him enough time, not as you wished—or did you really want me to marry him? I was beginning to think that you really just wanted me to stay at Tikal, close to you. Is that the truth? Did you want me to stay close to you?"

Naomi felt a gentle hand caressing her temple and her hair, and she was a mixture of pleasure and frustration. "I did love you, and I do like Tikal—although just now the political situation is not advantageous to me. And I am not saying I will never go back. You are right, I did leave my jacket behind. It was not necessarily Freudian, but mere forgetfulness. It is a special jacket, but in this modern world, I can find another jacket just as nice. Green Parrot will have some use for the purple plastic bag; she is very inventive. Certainly I have no need for it. Now, go away and let me be in my world. It is not such a beautiful world, but it is my world."

With that, the green light faded, and Naomi shivered in bed. Eventually she closed one of the windows and got another blanket against the pending dampness of the cool dawn. It must have been three a.m. when she fell into a deep sleep. Sometime later, she woke with a start. The green light was back! "No, not you again! Am I to have no sleep tonight?"

"How can you sleep with an unsolved murder on your mind?" said a male baritone quite unlike Night Sky's voice, yet who could it be but Night Sky? Naomi was startled that he was speaking openly. She was also startled by the evil gleam in his eye. "I thought your precious Professor Brown was the great love of your life," he said sardonically.

Naomi could not speak; she just opened her mouth.

"You know perfectly well that it is Brenda who pushed him down the stairs. Well, nudged, nudged him over her deathly carpet. Why don't you do something about it?"

Naomi tried to get her mouth to say something, but nothing came out of it.

"Well, if you won't do it, I will."

Brenda suddenly appeared in his arms clad only in a nightgown, her hair all tousled. She was squirming to get free, but his grip was stronger. "We know what to do with women like these." He dragged her to a nearby Tikal pyramid and forced her to go up the stairs. Brenda went like a sleepwalker or someone on drugs. At the top threshold of the stairway, he pushed her onto a stone, and a waiting priest came by with a big, sharp, flint knife and cut off her head. Night Sky was laughing fiendishly all the while.

Naomi woke suddenly, still hearing the laugh, a scream stifled in her throat. Her heart was beating fast. But she was in her bed in Morristown; there were no green lights. It was just an extremely vivid nightmare. Night Sky had nothing to do with it. She was overwrought. She swore never again to get involved in other people's affairs and decided not to go back to sleep but got up to have some orange juice and cereal. This breakfast at dawn made her feel better. Maybe she felt guilty about leaving Night Sky and had imagined him as a vengeful monster, she wondered. It was just a dream, not reality. Maybe all the green lights were dreams too, and when she settles down, they will go away.

It was only after five a.m., and the milk and cereal were making her soporific. Her eyelids were getting heavy. She would get a few more hours of sleep. She crawled under the covers again. Her sleep was light this time, and she kept on dreaming, mostly without remembering. But one dream she recalled very clearly, as she tried to hold onto it as she awoke. This was the gist of it.

Professor Brown was at home in his armchair, smoking a pipe. "Thank you, Naomi," he said. "I knew I could count on you." His voice was warm and friendly.

"I haven't done anything, really."

"Yes, you have."

"What have I done?"

"You took the vase away from Brenda."

"You mean, Brenda—"

"It is not that important anymore—" and the dream came to an abrupt end. She returned to full consciousness, registered the dream so she could remember it, and fell back into peaceful sleep.

When she woke up around eight, Naomi had the sense of having slept well. The name Brenda stuck in her mind, and she had a hazy recollection that she'd had a nightmare about human sacrifice. Well, that was not surprising, given her interest in the Maya. But it was quite unpleasant as she came face to face with the memory. She decided to have a second breakfast of orange juice and cereal. *One should feed one's demons*, she thought happily in the clear daylight. Then she remembered that she planned to call on Brenda that day.

25.

Brenda welcomed Naomi at home after work, wearing an expensive dark pants outfit. She offered her tea or a drink. "Are you staying around a little longer, this time?" she asked somewhat acidly.

"I am planning to, although I have to leave my sublet and find somewhere else to stay."

"Don't talk to me about sublets! I am so frustrated. At the last minute, my renters in Milford pulled out of the agreement, and I can start all over again with the realtors. My affairs are not doing well. First I lose a million dollars in an expensive Maya vase, and then I can't find renters for Tim's cottage. I need to come up with the tax money."

"Poor Brenda."

"Well, it is not as bad as all that. In a few weeks, I go on a cruise in the Caribbean with Evelyn. You may be interested to know that one of the features of this cruise is a day spent at Tikal. We're flying in by helicopter."

"Will you climb the pyramids?"

"Certainly, although I've been having nightmares about the Maya coming back and offering me up for sacrifice. Ugh, nasty custom. Some of Tim's old friends, no doubt," she added as a bit of humor.

"Have you been reading up on it?"

"That's probably it. I should stop reading and just enjoy it."

"Too bad your husband won't be there to give you information."

"You know, Tim was dry as dust as a lecturer. I shall do fine without him."

Naomi wanted to ask whether Brenda thought that someone had something to do with Professor Brown's death but didn't quite know how to put it. "You passed him on the staircase just before he fell, didn't you?" she finally said rather bluntly.

"I might have. I don't remember very clearly."

Naomi looked at her with intense eyes. Brenda seemed shaken for a moment. "I guess I do remember it. It was awful. It will take a long time for me to forget. If only I had the Maya vase, at least Tim would have left me something useful."

"You didn't want the vase. You wanted a sailboat."

"What's wrong with that?"

Clearly, Brenda was not conscience stricken. She would be left in the care of her dreams. Suddenly, Naomi had an idea. "Brenda," she said, with excitement in her voice, "since you have no renters, may I rent Professor Brown's Milford cottage? It would be a good place to finish my dissertation."

EPILOGUE

Naomi settled into the Milford cottage and spent every afternoon on the porch overlooking the pond, rewriting her dissertation in earnest. There were no green lights, no nightmares. The rustling sounds in the woods were deer and black bear. She often had afternoon tea and a pastry from the bakery. Tom came by frequently, and they discussed the ins and outs of the archaeology of Tikal.

A couple of weeks after she moved in, Tom came bringing interesting news. "Remember the sherd you gave me to test? The results have come back." And he brought the sherd in an envelope out of his pocket.

"Don't keep me in suspense—"

"It is not from the black-background vase, or at least it is unlike the companion piece with the youth on it."

"But it looks so black—"

"Yes, it is a misfire. A very badly fired piece; the carbon recombined with the clay. And, the paste is typically Tikal, not the exotic vessel we saw. So your story does not hold water. Admit that you made it up!"

Naomi did not answer. She was plunged in thought. *So Sky Rain threw an ordinary Tikal pot at the lord of Uaxactún. The beautiful masterpiece of Maya vase painting was still whole in his throne room. Perhaps, even in one glace, he saw its value and reached for something else to throw.*

"Naomi!" said Tom several times, as she seemed far away.

"Yes, Tom, it is very interesting. I'm glad you had it tested. Now, would you like some tea? I have fresh scones to go with it."

ꙮ ꙮ

Author's Note

HIDDEN CONNECTIONS

The deciding fact of my life was coming to the United States as a refugee. Whatever my life task would have been back in Hungary, it now became getting to know the US. This was very difficult to do directly, because the US was ostensibly not all that different from Europe. Or was it. It took a lifetime to find out.

My first view of the States was from a bus window. We were driving from the airport to the military base lodgings across a bit of New Jersey suburbia. The flights out of Vienna had started a couple of weeks from the Hungarian Revolution in Budapest. Altogether less than two months had passed. I craned my neck to see out of the window of the bus. There were houses, sort of mid-size, with pitched roofs, porches, picture windows, dormer windows. Sort of a tan or white, with shutters in black or green. What struck me forcefully, even to my thirteen-year-old eyes, was that they looked old fashioned. Maybe even out of an old storybook. Was this the New World? What did I expect? A wigwam with Indians? I knew a little about Indians, so a wigwam might not have been out of the question.

More than likely, I expected something very modern and futuristic. After all, even my neighborhood in Budapest consisted of hard-edge concrete villas with little or flat roofs in thirties Bauhaus style. Surely American houses were more extremely modern than this. But as I looked out of the windows of the bus, American houses were made out of wood and paint and looked nearly as flimsy as my ideas of wigwams. I was disappointed. In the "Three Little Pigs" story, the wolf would have blown them down easily. And yet this was the richest and most advanced country in the world, and my homeland with the concrete terraces was a mess occupied by foreign, Russian armies.

The infrastructure of highways, overpasses, bridges, with cars whizzing by reassured me of America's modernity. This looked like an illustration out of a Jules Verne or H. G. Wells novel. That was what I expected; there was no mystery about it. (Even though I did not know that these parts of the interstate highway system had not been there from time immemorial but had been built recently in the 1950s; they were, in fact, new and fresh.) I admired them, and I took them for granted. But that first view of the New Jersey houses remained as an oddity in my memory. It required explanation.

From that first day on, everything normalized. The US was the US as it was. New York had the requisite skyscrapers. The streets were multiracial and multiethnic. I was going from one school to another, learning algebra, history, English composition, biology, geology, art, dance—boning up on musicals, rock 'n' roll, jazz. Television, *I love Lucy*, horror movies. I was stuffing in facts for exams and stuffing in facts to blend in. I became a citizen, and I am sure one time or another I read the Constitution.

I was successfully living in the US, but I had no idea what the US was like. What made them tick? And, anyway, where was the US? Massachusetts, South Carolina, Ohio, California? I knew enough to know that they were different, but similar. And anyway, if one lived in the metropolis of New York, who cared? They were bound to be provincial and uninteresting. Occasionally, when the US made a foreign relations blunder, we asked what the US was up to? Why, with all that talent, things happened as they did? The US was a mystery, and there were no courses on the subject. It was the elephant in the room, and one did one's best to manoeuvre between trunk and legs. Also, the US was forgiving—it didn't mind not being known, not being loved. It seemed to like confusion and giving shelter, anyway. It wasn't a place, it was a matrix.

My every bone, sinew and instinct knew Hungary and by extension Europe. Class, style, super education, subtle intelligence, talent, refinement, to say nothing of good cooking were all there. But then so were the wars and the ethnic hates. Which is why we weren't there anymore. So in America we recreated the good that was in Hungary—the intelligence, the elegance we deemed superior to America, and cooked chicken *paprikash*, and authentic goulash. We went to social events pretending that it was the "good old days" of Hungary—1900 or 1930. I did not particularly like Hungarians: they were abrasive and stabbed you in the back.

A number of refugees capitalized on their knowledge of Hungary and Europe; they became historians in universities, wrote papers, and gave talks about the Hungary they no longer lived in. They had one great advantage; they could speak Hungarian. Lots of people asked me whether I planned to teach Hungarian art or history, as a natural development of my immigration. I said no from the beginning. I did not come to America to be a "professional Hungarian." Perish the thought!

I couldn't exactly become a "professional American," either, since I did not know America all that well, but I could be anything else. America was global—an "Orientalist," an "Africanist," an "Ancient Americanist." And through a process of trial and error, I ended up studying ancient America, which anyone can study, since it came to an end a long time ago, and no one knows quite how it was. Moreover, though ancient and Indian, it was "American," at least geographically. Unlike Hungary and the US, it did not ask for my allegiance and patriotism, and I could belong to it in a spirit of wonder without emotional complications.

Ancient America was a mass of detail: buildings, dates, offerings, sculpture, sixteenth-century descriptions, techniques, and endless data to be digested. Who conquered whom, who preceded whom, how far back things went. Could glyphs and symbols be deciphered? But the overall evaluation of ancient America had not changed much from the sixteenth-century conquerors: There were some great ruins, but it was a poor civilization, using stone tools, minimal metals, with no cattle or horses, no wheel, and generally backward. But, with the repellent custom of human sacrifice. Easy prey to the higher civilization of Europe and the Old World—a predation too easily justified.

Away from the nitty-gritty, I looked back on ancient America from the distance of time. Wasn't there something good about it? What about those fantastic ruins? I stood the issue on its head. Was the Old World so great? Why did they rush from stone, to bronze, to iron age? The picture I then had of the Old World was that of a tough, competitive world of many civilizations and constant invasions in mortal combat, where the premium was on weapons invention and a mindset of conquest. Such a mindset may have gone back to the time of early man and conflict with Neanderthals. Not all that nice a place.

The lush nature of the Americas was settled by roving bands of Asian people cooperating in the hunt of Pleistocene mammals. Though poor in domesticable fauna, it was rich in plant foods, so much so that much of the modern world still lives off it. The only two major civilizations of the New World were barely in contact, let alone conflict, and there were no major conquests from land or sea. While there were local wars and human sacrifices, they were small scale compared to Old World destruction of peoples. Old World wars and inquisitions crescendoed into the millions. Stone tools were evidently fine for carving and masonry, if given enough time and patience, judging by the results. Workers were apparently incorporated into projects more or less willingly, and in time the ancient Americans built cities, pyramids, road systems of superhuman scale. Which world was really better?

It seemed to me that the Old World had developed a predatory mindset in its own place and had taken that across the sea to the New World. They had specialized into a "carnivore" style. The New World was used to large populations at peace, more-or-less, loosely comparable to the world of herbivores in the animal kingdom. They had "carnivores," but not on the scale of the Old World. The confrontation between them was entirely unequal. Even if, as modern research shows, disease took most of the toll in the conquest, it was shiploads of conquistadors who spread disease while lusting after gold.

It then occurred to me to ask whether there was any place in the world that had the same favorable circumstances that ancient Americans had enjoyed that allowed them to build a more relaxed civilization. As mentioned earlier in this book, there was one example, and I was living in it. Of course, the United States. The US was created in a land rich in resources, which they saw as a wilderness, after cruelly removing the North American Indian population. While in most areas of the South, it was settled by aristocratic plantation owners, in much of the US homesteaders and small business owners with democratic and participatory ideas dominated. The land was rich, the people spread out, the country became wealthy, and it was relatively easy to develop the values of kindness and egalitarianism. It apparently was not a problem that they had up-to-date metal tools.

Fast forward, the US became wealthy and acquired a veneer of

European "sophistication," which did not fool insightful American writers, like Henry James, who saw Europeans as clever and evil and Americans as more moral and innocent. He didn't use the words "carnivore" and "herbivore," but he could have. After all, in his century, European powers carved up the entire world and its peoples into colonies to be exploited. In the following century, Europeans, including the modernized Japanese, turned against each other in disastrous world wars that left them in a state of collapse. The US came both times to create world order. As a result, somewhat unexpectedly, the US became the greatest economic, political and military power in the world. Its core values had not changed, and it tried to do good on a world scale, first with the League of Nations and successfully with the United Nations.

As a superpower, the US tried to be an imperialistic carnivore, waging a series of limited wars, but never quite as ruthlessly as the Old World nations, and generally lost. At the same time, the US assumed that everyone shared it's herbivore values of tolerance and egalitarianism and tried to push democratic government on others, also unsuccessfully.

Of course, the overt humanistic values of the US were greatly tarnished by the treatment of African Americans and Indians, and it can be said that European countries tend now to be more civilized in this respect. Nevertheless, the US can be described as a great, imperfect, bumbling, mostly well-intentioned, "herbivore" culture.

Recently, a conflict has reappeared inside the US. A large minority wants to transform the it into an Old World-style carnivore country, reaping more advantages from the rest of the world, keeping "riffraff" out, and keeping wealth in the hands of the few.

Two-thirds of the US still live by the old herbivore values: tolerating all colors, all ethnicities, encouraging women, accepting homosexuals, supporting those with disabilities and of course the poor. Where these values appear in other countries, they are often inspired by the US. The amazing work on disabilities in the US is gradually imitated elsewhere but can't really be afforded to the same extent. These herbivore values can exist only in a rich country. The current political argument is whether the US is rich enough to continue to export them or whether, in the more intense competition of carnivore countries like Russia, China, and Iran, the US too must become carnivore. Decline and maybe fall is not hard to imagine.

So what about my glimpse of the New Jersey houses out of the bus window in 1956? A few million modest, wooden, single-family houses, not very impressive in themselves. Indicative of widespread wealth and standard of living, as well as participatory politics—and the availability of large forests and quantities of wood. They showed a lack of high education and high style and a shared democratic community. As far as I know, there are no such large tracts of single-family houses in other places.

I came to a view of modern America through ancient America. The similarities are not ones of obvious detail but of structure and context. Of course, with the exception of places like Teotihuacán, we do not see it in the houses of ordinary people in ancient times. We see it in the public structures that have survived as ruins, most likely built by the labor of ordinary people for collective purposes, like the interstate highways. In the absence of predatory outside cultures, ancient America lasted about five thousand years. Modern America has so far had about three hundred years, and struggles in an unfriendly world eager for its spoils. It has been a privilege to try to comprehend it by being a part of it.

ଓ ଛ

Esther Pasztory is Lisa and Bernard Selz Professor emerita of pre-Columbian Art History and Archaeology at Columbia University. She has published extensively in the field of pre-Columbian art, including the first art historical manuscripts on Teotihuacán and the Aztecs. Born in Hungary, she emigrated to the United States in 1956, after the anti-Communist revolution. She attended Vassar College and Barnard Collage where she received a BA in art history. With her dissertation at Columbia, entitled *The Murals of Tepantitla, Teotihuacán*, she received her PhD in 1971. Esther now lives in San Francisco, California.

www.ingramcontent.com/pod-product-compliance
Lightning Source LLC
LaVergne TN
LVHW041928090826
845145LV00017B/1710

* 9 7 8 1 8 8 2 1 9 0 8 2 9 *